THE THREAT OF IMPENDING DISASTER

Contributions to the Psychology of Stress

GEORGE H. GROSSER
HENRY WECHSLER
MILTON GREENBLATT
Editors

THE THREAT OF IMPENDING DISASTER
Contributions to the Psychology of Stress

THE M.I.T. PRESS
MASSACHUSETTS INSTITUTE OF TECHNOLOGY
CAMBRIDGE, MASSACHUSETTS

FIRST M.I.T. PRESS PAPERBACK EDITION, AUGUST 1971

ISBN 0 262 07013 8 (HARDCOVER)
ISBN 0 262 57027 0 (PAPERBACK)

LIBRARY OF CONGRESS CATALOG CARD NUMBER 64-8072
PRINTED IN THE UNITED STATES OF AMERICA

EDITORS AND CONTRIBUTORS

EDITORS

George H. Grosser, Ph.D.
Research Associate, Massachusetts Mental Health Center *
Department of Psychiatry, Harvard Medical School
Boston, Massachusetts

Henry Wechsler, Ph.D.
Research Associate, Massachusetts Mental Health Center
Department of Psychiatry, Harvard Medical School
Boston, Massachusetts

Milton Greenblatt, M.D.
Superintendent, Boston State Hospital
Professor of Psychiatry, Tufts University Medical School
Boston, Massachusetts

CONTRIBUTORS

Claus Bahne Bahnson, Ph.D.
Associate Professor of Psychiatry (Psychology)
Jefferson Medical College, Department of Psychiatry
Philadelphia, Pennsylvania

George W. Baker, Ph.D.
Program Director, Science Facilities Evaluation Group
Division of Institutional Programs
National Science Foundation, Washington, D. C.

Albert D. Biderman, Ph.D.
Senior Research Associate
Bureau of Social Science Research, Inc.,
Washington, D. C.

EDITORS AND CONTRIBUTORS

Lester Grinspoon, M.D.
Clinical Associate in Psychiatry, Harvard Medical School
Director of Psychiatry (Research)
Massachusetts Mental Health Center
Boston, Massachusetts

Thomas P. Hackett, M.D.
Instructor in Psychiatry, Harvard Medical School
Associate Psychiatrist, Massachusetts General Hospital
Boston, Massachusetts

Sheldon J. Korchin, Ph.D.
Professor of Psychology, Head of Psychology Clinic
University of California, Berkeley, California

Gladys Engel Lang, Ph.D.
Lecturer in Sociology
Queen's College, Flushing, New York

Kurt Lang, Ph.D.
Professor of Sociology
State University of New York Long Island Center
Stony Brook, New York

Richard S. Lazarus, Ph.D.
Professor of Psychology
University of California, Berkeley, California

Robert Jay Lifton, M.D.
Foundations' Fund for Research in Psychiatry Associate Professor
Member of Council on East Asian Studies
Yale University, New Haven, Connecticut

Roy W. Menninger, M.D.
Co-Director, Division of School Mental Health
The Menninger Foundation
Topeka, Kansas

James G. Miller, M.D., Ph.D.
Professor of Psychiatry and Psychology
Director, Mental Health Research Institute
The University of Michigan, Ann Arbor, Michigan

George E. Ruff, M.D.
Associate Professor of Psychiatry
University of Pennsylvania School of Medicine
Philadelphia, Pennsylvania

John P. Spiegel, M.D.
Lecturer
Department of Social Relations
Harvard University, Cambridge, Massachusetts

Avery D. Weisman, M.D.
Assistant Clinical Professor of Psychiatry, Harvard Medical School
Psychiatrist, Massachusetts General Hospital
Boston, Massachusetts

Harry B. Williams, Ph.D.
Assistant Director for Mental Health Training and Research
Southern Regional Education Board
Atlanta, Georgia

Stephen B. Withey, Ph.D.
Professor, University of Michigan
Research Program Director
Institute for Social Research
Ann Arbor, Michigan

CONTENTS

CONTENTS

PART ONE

INTRODUCTION

INTRODUCTION

FOR SOME TIME the world has been trying to grasp the significance of a nuclear holocaust, to imagine the resulting destruction, and to find possible ways to cope with the disaster. The magnitude of the threat was stark and terrifying indeed during the days of the "great confrontation" in the Cuban missile crisis when total annihilation hung over us all. It was in the aftermath of this shaking event that the symposium herein reported was held in Philadelphia, in December 1962, under the combined auspices of the American Association for the Advancement of Science and the American Psychiatric Association through its Committee on Research. Here we tried to understand what it meant to live through the atomic blast in Hiroshima, prisoner-of-war camps, enemy occupation, the uncertainties of space flights, and threats of death from mortal illness. A major portion of these proceedings has been preserved in the present volume, which ranges broadly and deeply over the spectrum of fears and terrors that beset modern man.

A highly select group of scientists from different disciplines — some with personal experience of disaster, all with basic data and observations — gathered together to share knowledge and to search for common scientific and conceptual themes that might apply to a great variety of situations of abnormal stress. The enrichment experienced by this scientific group encouraged the authors to organize and present the material of the conference within a single volume.

The contributors to this symposium volume have presented a broad variety of stress situations that share a common theme—the threat of impending disaster. The responses to these varied stress situations were characterized by considerable ambiguity, since the disasters, though imminent, had not as yet occurred. A further similarity lay in the fact that the individual could exercise little or no control over the situation and society could not provide adequate avenues of response to it. An attempt was made to select as contributors to the symposium individuals from different disciplines so that no single point of view would be forced upon the proceedings.

The symposium begins with a theoretical section. James G. Miller, employing general systems theory, conceptualizes an overloading of the system through sensory input as one method of producing overwhelming threat. His paper deals with an analysis of the general properties of systems and the manner in which they compensate for input overloading.

Different perceptions of concomitant emotional reactions to the same stimulus are explored by Richard S. Lazarus through the paradigm of the concept of perceptual set and the fit between set and attitudinal factors. In addition to the presentation of his own research, the author addresses himself to the problem of studying stress in the laboratory.

Kurt and Gladys Lang use a sociological approach, emphasizing collective reactions rather than the individual response to threatening situations. They point out the implications of the fact that adaptation of the individual and adaptation of the group are not necessarily compatible.

Stimulus properties and response patterns to the stress signal are discussed in the second section. The paper by Harry B. Williams employs traditional models of perception to account for differential impact of warning messages. His examples tend to demonstrate that the nature of the stimulus configuration may influence whether adaptive or maladaptive responses are made to a disaster situation.

Stephen B. Withey concentrates on the response patterns and successive adjustments made to threatening stimuli through the principle of feedback. His thesis is that an understanding of response patterns requires the study not only of the traditionally enumerated stages in disaster phenomena, but also of the way in which each preceding step alters the perception and thus the nature of the succeeding step.

The remaining sections of the symposium deal with specific types of threatening situations. The threat of nuclear disaster is discussed by three psychiatrists. Lester Grinspoon analyzes the role of defense mechanisms in the reaction to nuclear threat. He examines the attitudes toward the fallout shelter program and the general apathetic reaction to the contemplation of nuclear attack. The prominence of denial as a mechanism of defense is of particular interest here.

Roy Menninger reports on a pilot study of the reaction of psychiatric patients to the Cuban crisis. Although the attitudes of patients reflected stereotyped reactions of the population, he found that the patients responded in terms of their own personality dynamics when asked what solution they would advocate.

One of the few published accounts of the reactions of victims of the Hiroshima bombings appears in the contribution of Robert J. Lifton. This retrospective study illustrates not only the incomprehensible magnitude of the disaster, but also the confusion, guilt, and anxiety of the survivors.

Space flight presents new and potentially threatening situations for which society has no previous experience. Sheldon J. Korchin and George E. Ruff show that personality configurations and life experiences may be factors in the degree to which an individual adapts to highly threatening situations. How much of the adaptation is also due to training and preparation is a matter for further study.

The situation of helpless exposure to arbitrary or unpredictable exercise of power over life and death by an enemy is reported in two papers. The first deals with experiences of American soldiers in prisoner-of-war camps. The paper illustrates that the only model for response available to the soldiers was their stereotyped notion of the American prison system, and that expectations drawn from this model were inappropriate. Albert D. Biderman demonstrates that under such conditions the viability of the individual depends on the solidarity of the group.

Claus Bahne Bahnson discusses survival in a different type of situation by examining behavior under wartime occupation by enemy forces. Using a model which postulates the interchangeability of external and internal threat, he relates threat of such occupation as well as threat of death from somatic illness to early childhood learning experiences.

A different type of stress situation is covered in the last part of the symposium. Responses to the threat of physical illness and death, although the most universal of all situations, have perhaps not received as much systematic study as have other stress situations. These are discussed from two different points of view.

John P. Spiegel views the threat of death from the point of view of differences in cultural attitudes toward death and illness and points out the role that value systems play in determining behavior in such situations.

Thomas P. Hackett and Avery D. Weisman, who examined a number of patients with severe or terminal illness, discuss the problem of how the reality testing of these patients is influenced by environmental cues. Their paper examines the manner in which patients deal with anxiety, and the way in which the perception of their illness is mediated by the persons ministering to them.

Although the symposium does not contain any study of natural disasters, the final paper by George W. Baker contains a review of some disaster research studies, their methodological problems, and an appraisal of the current status of this field. Dr. Baker suggests guidelines for future research applicable not only to natural disaster but also to the type of threatening situation discussed in the symposium.

The editors of the symposium have brought together the works of these authors to serve two basic purposes. For students of psychology, psychiatry, and the allied social sciences, this volume is intended to provide basic information as well as theoretical perspectives about man's reactions to situations of impending disaster. The problems discussed within the papers are both substantive and methodological. It is hoped that certain common elements may be abstracted from the variety of situations analyzed here. A full coverage of disaster research has not been attempted here, nor do we offer a cross section of all types of disaster situations. For example, studies of natural catastrophes and of more biologically oriented research have been largely omitted. We hope that such omissions will not convey an erroneous impression of the state of the field, but will rather stimulate further thought and investigation by our readers.

Though none of the papers presents suggestions for direct action, the reader is invited to see as a second purpose of this volume a contribution to the formulation of programs for action. Each of the papers may offer implications for action to persons engaged in civil defense and preparedness activities, as well as to the citizen who is concerned about such problems. The possibilities for practical applications may range from ways of dealing with group solidarity in prisoner-of-war camps to a more thoughtful approach to working with terminally ill patients. It is for this reason that the editors have gone beyond the confines of the laboratory and methodological discourse and have included subjective and anecdotal material along with the more experimentally oriented articles.

The editors acknowledge appreciatively the interest in the topic of the symposium evinced by the American Association for the Advancement of Science. This interest, and the sponsorship of the Committee on Research of the American Psychiatric Association, greatly facilitated the task of organizing the symposium and contributed to the stimulating experience of these sessions.

The success of the meetings was in no small part due to the able leadership of Francis J. Braceland, M.D., and Kenneth Appel, M.D., who, in their capacity as chairmen and discussion leaders, gave freely of their time and interest. The impact of the contributions in this volume was further enhanced by the two able discussants, Jerome Frank, M.D., and Donald Michael, Ph.D., whose thought-provoking comments were appreciated by audience and speakers alike.

George H. Grosser
Henry Wechsler
Milton Greenblatt

PART TWO

THEORETICAL
PERSPECTIVES

JAMES G. MILLER

A THEORETICAL REVIEW OF INDIVIDUAL AND GROUP PSYCHOLOGICAL REACTIONS TO STRESS

ONE OF THE definitions of "stress" in the Oxford dictionary is: "the overpowering pressure of some adverse force or influence." Selye (1956), in describing the general adaptation syndrome, gave the word a specific medical meaning, referring to generalized physiological response to illness, trauma, or severe environmental fluctuations. The word comes down to us from Middle English, and it is interesting to note that there was neither an equivalent word nor even a convenient phrase in French. Consequently, after Selye's (1956) work had become current in France, the French Academy recently acted to add the word "le stress" to the French language.

The title of this paper assumes that there is a relationship between the responses to stresses by individuals and the responses by groups or larger social systems. This is also assumed in our common language. After a siege or a catastrophe like Hiroshima, one can refer to the "death of a city." If we can say "birth of a nation," then "death of a nation" follows.

The Levels, Types, and Characteristics of Systems

The approach of general systems-behavior theory finds similarities among all forms of life from cells to societies,

11

based upon analysis of all of them into "systems" composed of smaller subsystems and composing suprasystems. The cell is composed of small and large atoms, ions, and molecules; organs are built of cells; organisms are systems of organs; groups include more than one organism; organizations or institutions contain subsystems that are groups; societies are composed of organizations. And there are probably larger living, unliving, or mixed systems.

A concern with system aspects of phenomena is a common characteristic of a number of current theories. The theories differ, however, in their choices of units and relationships. The hierarchy of systems just described is composed of *concrete* systems. Each of these units is a "thing," a bounded region in space and time, many of whose relationships are directly observable. It is possible to build a systems theory around *abstracted* systems in which the units and relationships are conceptualized by a scientist to conform to his interests, frame of reference, philosophical point of view, or other considerations. The physical limits of abstracted systems may not coincide with concrete system boundaries, and their units are relationships rather than entities. Reference to abstracted systems is more common in social science, whereas biologists and physical scientists emphasize concrete systems. Parsons and Shils (1951) conceptualize society as a set of abstracted systems. The unit of the social system is not the individual but the "role," since an individual may behave quite differently in different social contexts. This system is a set of relationships in action. Persons fit into the relationships. The theoretical structure of classical economics is also based upon abstracted systems, in which the particular attributes of the society that are thought to be important and certain of their relationships are considered together, apart from all the non-economic variables.

General systems-behavior theory is concerned with concrete systems, their structure and process. By *structure* is meant the three-dimensional spatial organization of the subsystems of any system at a given time. The structure of an organ like the brain is the arrangement of its component cells. The structure of a society is the configuration of its component organizations, each with its characteristic activities. *Process* is either function, reversible action of systems; or history, irreversible action, like growth, trauma, or decay.

Living systems are open to their environments, having significant amounts of inputs and outputs. A living system requires inputs of energy to combat entropy, to make up for energy it has used up. It must also remove the waste products of its activities. It also requires inputs of information, patterns of organization, nonrandomness. Included are those patterns that activate the sense organs of an organism, as well as those that carry news to a society. And there are informational outputs — communications — as well.

Equilibrium and Stress

A living system, by regulating inputs and outputs of energy and information, maintains the rates of functioning of its subsystems in a condition of equilibrium. This is done by means of feedback processes appropriate to each kind of system. Bodily homeostasis is maintained in an organism by complicated regulating mechanisms which operate to keep the compositions of the blood, tissue fluids, and other substances within narrow limits. The organism orients itself in space by means of information coming to its organs of sight, balance, and proprioception. The society regulates its actions in the international situation by means of a flow of information about the results of its former actions and the behavior of other nations. Disturbance of feedback at any of these levels leads to abnormal function, and even to dissolution of the system.

It is in these terms that we can understand the concept of "stress." A stress is any force that pushes the functioning of important subsystems beyond their ability to restore equilibrium through ordinary, nonemergency adjustment processes. A stress may either consist of a *lack* of some essential input like food, air, or water, or of an *excess*, in which too much heat or cold or other input floods the system. We have used energy flows as examples, but it should be realized that stresses may be either of matter-energy or of information. Denying information input to a system results in stress as surely as does denying material inputs. Research on sensory deprivation (Kubzansky, 1961) has shown that cutting off the normal sensory input to a human individual may result rather rapidly in pathological behavior, which is reversed by the restoration of normal sensory experience. Glutting a person with more information than he can process may also lead to disturbance. This can be demonstrated, in fact, at several levels of living systems including cells, organs, organisms, groups, organizations, societies, and supranational systems.

When a stress is experienced, a system's emergency adjustment processes are called into play. It is possible, however, for stress to be anticipated. Information that a stress is imminent constitutes a *threat* to the system. Comprehension of such a threat must, of course, be based on previously stored (usually learned) information about such situations. A pattern of events has meaning for the system — the smell of the hunter on the wind, a change in the aridity of fluids around a cell, a whirling cloud approaching the city — when they are capable of calling forth adjustment behaviors specifically aimed at avoiding danger.

The Critical Subsystems

In order to examine more carefully the reactions of systems to stress, it is important to understand that certain functional subsystems are common to systems at all levels (see Table 1). Without these *critical subsystems* a system cannot survive unless it exists in a parasitic or symbiotic relationship with another system which supplies the missing function. A system that has all the requirements for living independently in its environment is *totipotential*. If some critical functions are supplied by another system, it is *partipotential*. Some critical subsystems process matter-energy and others process information. Some process both.

TABLE 1

The Critical Subsystems

Matter-Energy Processing Subsystems	Subsystems that Process Both Matter-Energy and Information	Information Processing Subsystems
	Boundary	
Ingestor		Input transducer (Internal transducer)
Distributor		Channel and net
Decomposer		Decoder
Producer		Learner
Energy storage		Memory
		Decider
Excretor		Encoder
Motor		Output transducer
Supporter		
	Reproducer	

The first of the critical subsystems is the *boundary*, which mediates both matter-energy and information. At the levels of cell, organ, and organism the boundary subsystems are cell membranes, organ capsules, and the skin or other outer covering. These subsystems are protective against unwanted inputs, yet permeable to specific sorts of energy, materials, and information. In organisms the skin has openings for admission and excretion of matter-energy. The sense organs provide boundary processing of information, each sensitive to pat-

terns in certain frequency bands, or to other special characteristics of stimuli. At the level of social groups of all
sizes, the geographical borders or limits of a system's territory and its boundary subsystem are different. The boundary
subsystem is to be found along the periphery of the territory. It is made up of individual organisms, groups, or organizations which maintain the integrity of this territory or
which control the passage of energy or materials, or of messages, into or out of it. Armies, customs and immigration
organizations, and news censors are examples of boundary
matter-energy and information processing subsystems of societies.

Inputs of energy are necessary for all living systems, so the
ingestor is a critical subsystem. Gaps in walls of cells perform
this function. At the level of society, inputs of food, raw
materials, energy, and manufactured items are processed by
a subsystem which is analogous to the subsystem that brings
food, water, air, and other needs into the body of
the organism.

Information inputs are processed by the *input transducer*.
In the nerve cells at the synapses, the patterns that are
conducted by acetylcholine may be transduced to neural
pulses. At the level of the organism, the sense organs
change information from the form in which it arrives at the
system to the nervous impulses which are propagated through
the nervous system. At other levels there are analogous subsystems. The *internal transducer* is an information-processing
subsystem which carries information that coordinates the subsystems into a unitary system. This information activates, at
all levels, feedback processes which adjust rates and quan-
tities of energy and material flows in the system. The information that the oxygen content of the blood is low, for example, is responded to by more rapid breathing, which increases the blood oxygen. An inspector general in an army
or public-opinion polltakers in nations are internal trans-
ducers in organizations and societies.

Other critical subsystems to process matter-energy and information are: the *distributor*, which transmits matter-energy to all parts of the system, and the *channel and net* which connect subsystems, permitting information to flow from one subsystem to another. The *decomposer* breaks down material and energy inputs into components usable in the system, and the *decoder* comparably changes information into a form understandable by the system. The *producer* synthesizes material units in the system into substances useful within it. This occurs in protein metabolism in the body and in the manufacture of new products in a factory. The *learner* carries out a similar informational process, associating bits of information into organized knowledge. Learning goes on in systems from cells to societies.

Matter-energy storage and memory are comparable subsystems. The first holds the necessary energy and useful materials until they are needed, and the second retains useful information. Cells store the former in adenosine triphosphate, glucose, and fats, and the latter perhaps in ribonucleic acid. Organisms store matter-energy in fat deposits and information in brain cells. Societies store matter-energy in supply dumps and information in libraries and archives. The *decider* is a central information-processing subsystem. This the central nervous system does for individual animals, the leader does for groups, management for organizations, and government for societies. The *excretor* outputs wastes, and all living systems have excretory organs or refuse disposers. The *encoder* prepares information for output. It must be put into the external language of the suprasystem in which it finds itself, or it will not be comprehensible. The *motor* puts out energy and provides motion in space for part or all of the system. This includes the pseudopodia of amoebas, the muscles of the heart, the legs and arms of the body, the front-line troops of a battalion, and the traders and armies of a nation. Analogously, the *output transducer* sends information over the boundary out of the system, perhaps using a part of the motor subsystem to do so. A neural cell outputs information by excreting a chemical mediator at the point where it ends in a synaptic junction. A person speaks to another with his muscles of speech. Groups and higher-level social systems send out representatives with messages for other groups, organizations, societies, or supranational systems. The *supporter* holds up the entire system and keeps the subsystems in stable spatial relationships to each other. The colloidal protoplasm and certain organelles do this in cells; organs have stromas which hold up their more active cells; skeletons do this for organisms; and groups, organizations, and societies depend on the support of the ground and of the buildings and other structures which are their dwellings, offices, factories, and meeting places.

The *reproducer* is not an essential subsystem for continuation of a particular system, but it is crucial if other members of the species are to be generated. It processes both matter-energy and the genetic information that guides the development of the new system. This process is understood in much detail for cells, organs, and organisms. The higher levels of human social systems are perpetuated by reproduction dispersed to mating sexual pairs.

Since cells, organs, organisms, groups, institutions, and societies all have these critical functional subsystems, inputs and outputs are being processed not only at the boundary of a system at any level, but at each subsystem boundary within it, each subsubsystem boundary, and so on. Decisions, for example, are made at the level of the retinal receptors, which either do or do not respond to the light rays that bombard it; at the level of the organ, when the optic pathways either do or do not transmit an image; at the level of the organism, when the sentry decides whether friend or foe is approaching; at the level of the group, when the sergeant decides whether or not to report an attack to headquarters; at the level of the organization, when the headquarters decides to inform the government of a provocation; at the level of society, when the cabinet acts to condemn the aggressor; and at the international level when the UN Security Council votes on the whole affair.

Adjustments That Maintain Equilibria

At each of these levels, many matter-energy and informational variables are being kept in equilibrium. If one variable is forced out of its equilibrium range, adjustments are made to restore it. Critical variables are protected, if need be, at the expense of less critical ones (Ashby, 1952).

One characteristic of these equilibrating processes can be illustrated by the example of an army cot. It is made of wires, each of which would break under a 300-pound weight, yet it can easily support a sleeper of that weight. The weight is applied to certain wires, and as it becomes greater, first nearby links and then those farther and farther away take up part of the load. Thus a heavy weight which would break any of the component wires alone can be sustained. In a living system, if one component cannot handle a stress, more and more others are recruited to help. Eventually the entire capacity of the system may be involved in coping with the situation. A bacterial invasion of an organism illustrates this point. There is, first, the boundary barrier against the infection — the skin and mucosa exclude most of the bacteria that move toward the boundary. If some bacteria enter the blood stream, immunity processes kill them or reticuloendothelial and white cells consume them or greatly limit their numbers. If these measures are not entirely successful, a final line of defense is invoked: a central process by which foreign protein raises body temperature and the entire body fights the invader.

Variables kept in equilibrium differ with the level of the system. Free-living cells maintain the composition of their internal fluids constant by selective alterations of the permeability of their membranes. They avoid noxious substances in the water around them or extreme changes in temperature by swimming away from danger. Organs exercise selectivity in what they admit from the surrounding tissue fluids. Changes in secretions commonly follow variations in input to preserve the homeostasis of the organ. Organisms have many similar

over-all homeostatic mechanisms that control matter-ener-
gic variables like blood oxygen, carbon dioxide, acidity, or
pressure, body temperature, and metabolic rate. Also, depending upon their complexity, they keep few or many informational variables within a given range — rate of speaking, proximity
to others, a preferential hierarchy of behaviors. Organizations
and societies maintain within limits both central and local political power, the authority of different agencies of management or government, the influence of any one man, rates of
monetary flow, balance between rates of input of raw materials
and output of manufactured products, and many other variables.

A set of adjustment processes to the overload of information
input can be demonstrated at several levels of living systems
(Miller, 1962). If more information is presented than the system can process, it may use *omission,* leaving out some of the
message in order to keep up. It may make an *error* and not
take time to correct it but speed on. It may make an attempt
at *queuing* part of the message, delaying some of it while the
rest is processed. *Filtering,* whereby some sorts of priority information are processed first, is another adjustment process.
Approximation, rather than complete, detailed transmission
can also be used. *Multiple channels,* the use of two or more
parallel transmitters, can get more information across in a
given time. *Chunking,* the use of single symbols for larger
units in the message, like common phrases, also speeds the
process; and *escape* from the input entirely can relieve the
stress. Systems show a characteristic performance curve, which
first rises as the information input rate increases, then reaches
a channel capacity at which it operates for a time, then begins
to fall as the adjustment mechanisms are unable any longer
to cope with the rising rate of information input. Finally
there is a sharp drop-off toward zero in the system performance. The larger systems, with their many channels and large
number of resources, may never completely break down, but
they may be able to handle only a small percentage of a message at a very rapid rate. The number of bits per minute

which a single channel can process varies with the level of the system it is in, being in general smaller the larger the system is, but the form of the curve is strikingly similar at all levels.

Feedbacks, whereby part of the output of the system or subsystem is led back to the input to regulate it, control equilibria at all levels of living systems. These feedbacks always operate with some lag. When the organism maintains its balance in space, this lag is caused by the slowness of transmissions in the nervous system, but is only of the order of hundredths of a second. A social institution such as a manufacturing firm may take hours to correct a breakdown in an assembly line, and days or weeks to correct a bad management decision. In a society the lag can sometimes be so great that, in effect, it comes too late. General staffs often plan for the last war rather than the next. Governments receive feedbacks from the society at elections or more quickly through the press, other mass media, pickets, or demonstrators. Public-opinion surveys can accelerate the social feedback process. The speed and accuracy of feedback have much to do with the effectiveness of the adjustment process it mobilizes.

A Person's Adjustment to Stress

Every person has many ways to adjust under stress. He may physically attack the source of stress — horsewhip the editor who libeled him, for example. Or he may use the matter-energy adjustment defense of a psychosomatic illness to avoid facing the stress, whether energic or informational. A soldier may suffer from neurocirculatory asthenia and so avoid battle, and a child may complain of a stomach ache and so delay taking an examination in school.

We have seen earlier that systems, including human individuals, have a similar set of adjustments to increasing *rate* of input. A decrease in the input of information *below* the rate necessary for normal functioning is met by a search for more input. Prisoners in solitary confinement may talk and sing to themselves, recite poetry from memory, do mathematics problems, and indulge in fantasy to avoid becoming psychotic.

A person may also meet information stresses of various kinds by the classically recognized psychoanalytic "defense mechanisms" such as sublimation, repression, rationalization, regression, and many others.

All adjustment processes have their costs. This may be a cost in human effort, in physical energy, in material resources, in convenience, or in taxing the good will of one's associates. In a chess game, pawns are usually expended first, and then the more powerful pieces; but the queen is protected as long as possible, for when she is lost checkmate is a desperate probability. Similarly every person works to keep in equilibrium his most vital variables, as ordered along a hierarchy of values which he may be quite unable to report. He tries to use the least expensive adjustments first, employing the more costly ones as the stress increases, until he handles the emergency or runs out of resources. The result may be psychosis or even death.

Under psychological stress a man may first use an inexpensive defense like sublimation, in which he redirects his energy, frequently in a healthy way. Then he may use repression, which is often held to be more expensive because of the consequences of keeping the offending material from consciousness. If that fails, he may turn to a much more pathological defense like psychotic regression, a dependent infantilism which costs him his normal way of life.

Adjustments of the body to physiological stresses are also mobilized in what is probably a rough ascending order of cost. One moment a man may be comfortably and quietly minding his own business, keeping his physiological, psychological, and social affairs under control by a set of adjustments whose cost he can easily afford. Suddenly there comes a threat, a warning that a stress is about to impinge on him. The warning may enable him to avert the oncoming danger. He may slow his car to within the speed limit, or hurry to pay his income tax before the deadline, or move from under the falling tree. If he neglects the warning or has no means at his disposal to avert the stress, then it is upon him. The fistfight takes place, the operation must be done. After the full force of the stress is spent, there is often a period of confusion followed by a slow recognition of just what did happen. There is a lag while the damage is assessed; then he can proceed to find a remedy that may lead to eventual recovery. He may never return to his original equilibrium state. He may become bankrupt; he may lose his gall bladder, his wife, or his job. But he achieves a new steady state, his future baseline.

Social Systems' Adjustment to Stress

Large social bodies such as organizations, communities, and societies have normal adjustment processes to control energy and information flow so that neither excess nor lack is experienced. Materials are stored in warehouses or reservoirs for later use; dikes are built to exclude flood waters; migrations are controlled; necessary materials are imported; armies, fire departments, and police are maintained. Records are kept. Censorship may be carried out. Economic changes are made by varying the amount of money in circulation, or by varying the tax structure. Thousands of adjustments to thousands of variables keep a society functioning properly. At any time chronic or temporary stresses are being exerted on any society, but usually it is well able to compensate. At times, however, society can also sustain stresses which force crucial variables out of their equilibrium ranges and even irreversibly destroy the existing structure. Revolutions and wars throughout the ages have done this to nations. Insurrections and riots, severe storms, flood, and explosions, financial panics, and bankruptcies have done it to smaller communities and social organizations.

Natural Disasters

Natural disasters which strike communities show with a clarity approaching that of controlled experiments how societies react to stress. Powell defines a disaster as "the impinging upon a structured community, or one of its sections, of an external force capable of destroying human life or its resources for survival, on a scale wide enough to excite public alarm, to disrupt normal patterns of behavior, and to impair or overload any of the central services necessary to the conduct of normal affairs or to the prevention or alleviation of suffering and loss. Usually, the term disaster refers to an episode with tragic consequences to a substantial portion of the population . . . it is . . . *stress* on people, and on their group and community patterns" (Powell, 1954, p. 1). Powell identifies several time stages in disasters which are quite similar to stages of a single person's reaction to stress. These are *warning, threat, impact, inventory, rescue, remedy,* and *recovery* (1954, pp. 5, 13).

Wallace (1956) uses a spatial diagram to depict the zones in the society which disaster produces when it strikes (see Figure 1). Most central is the area of total impact (not total

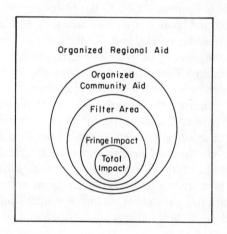

Figure 1. *Disaster regions.*

destruction, but the full fury of the disaster), then come the areas of fringe impact, the filter area, and those of organized community aid and organized regional aid. These regions are much like those mentioned above in which a stress imposed on one subsystem elicits adjustment processes in surrounding subsystems, the nearer one being more involved than those farther away, and more subsystems being involved when the stress is large. Let us now look at findings from disaster studies in the temporal and spatial frameworks of Powell and Wallace.

Disasters result from excess inputs of energy across a societal boundary, as in a tornado, or from lacks of such inputs, as in a famine. Wallace (1956, p. 7), using as his example the 1953 tornado disaster at Worcester, Massachusetts, points out that a system will probably be in equilibrium, or nearly so, at the time of any given disaster. The situations at the times of warning, threat, or impact are important determinants of what happens as the disaster proceeds.

Warning may be given by a natural event like the appearance of a tornado funnel, or there may be broadcast warning of the coming danger. In the 1955 Udall, Kansas, tornado which blew away the entire town, the weather bureau had several hours' notice of severe storms and tornadoes advancing toward the areas that were finally hit (Hamilton, Taylor, and Rice, 1955). Warnings were broadcast by local radio stations. Yet communication was so faulty that three-quarters of the victims later interviewed denied receiving any notice. Perhaps verbatim reading of technical weather reports over the radio was relatively meaningless to many, and something simpler would have been more effective.

Moore describes a similar situation in his book on the 1953 Waco-San Angelo tornadoes: "Early that morning weather bureaus had broadcast a warning that masses of warm, moisture-laden air moving up from the Gulf of Mexico would meet a front of cold air somewhere near a line extending from Waco to San Angelo and that tornadoes were a possibility in that general area. During the early afternoon heavy rain began to fall. It was welcomed, as rain always is in Texas, especially in the growing season.

"Storm warnings continued. They, and the rain, kept many

persons from going shopping, it may be assumed. But it is also likely that the storm warnings did not create as much apprehension in Waco as they would have in other cities: Waco was immune to tornadoes, according to an ancient Indian legend repeated in a 1951 Chamber of Commerce publication.

"Perhaps the immunization had run out; perhaps the Indian Spirit whose duty it was to protect the city nodded. Disaster dealt death and destruction that afternoon with a heavy hand. Waco and San Angelo bore the brunt of the blows" (Moore, 1958, p. 3).

These examples make it clear that the communication of a warning must not only cross the border into the affected area but be coded properly to be understood, be strong enough to be heard, and be impressive enough to overcome the natural reluctance of people to believe that the current tranquility will be upset.

Threat may be almost simultaneous with both warning and impact in a sudden disaster. Powell (1954) says threat begins with the perception of a change of conditions indicating specific local and personal danger, and continues beyond impact. It may be of varying duration, may occur at various times and in diverse ways for different individuals, may be cumulative or occur in a sort of wave pattern. At this point, whatever warning is given, persons in the society become aware of danger. They react individualistically. One may run to the basement or storm cellar; another may panic and run in circles; another may simply hide his head under the bedclothes and hold his breath.

In the period of *impact,* disaster strikes. Activities are reduced to withstanding the onslaught with whatever self-protection is possible. The boundary of the system has been invaded, communications within it are usually disrupted, and the subsubsystems and subsystems — individual persons and groups — are more-or-less isolated for a time. Members of a school classroom may stay together and retain their organization under the guidance of the teacher. A mother may gather

her children around her and seek cover. However, the usual structure of the community is fragmented. System-wide coordination and controls disappear. Wallace (1956) calls this the time of *isolation*.

Next comes the period of *inventory*. Moore says: "With no plans made, or with plans which often prove to be wholly inadequate, the first reaction (to a disaster) may be one of dazed bewilderment, sometimes one of disbelief, or at least of refusal to accept the fact. This, it seems to us, is the essential explanation of the behavior of persons and groups in Waco when it was devastated in 1953. It explains why citizens and officials alike had to have time for a minimum reorientation before going into action. On the personal level, it explains why a girl climbed into a music store through a broken display window, calmly purchased a record, and walked out again, even though the plate-glass front of the building had blown out and articles were flying through the air inside the building. This may explain, too, why institutions set up for relief of human suffering seemed to suffer a paralysis, their functionaries unable to assign tasks to others who were anxious to go into action" (1958, p. 311). Such devastating events narcotize a person ad prevent him from comprehending the extent to which his situation has changed. A Udall, Kansas, housewife said: "After it was over, my husband and I just got up and jumped out the window and ran. I don't know where we were running to but . . . I didn't care. I just wanted to run. We heard people hollering and everything" (Hamilton, Taylor, and Rice, 1955, p. 27).

Some persons trained for special functions, like doctors, ministers, and nurses, tend to begin functioning much more quickly than others. A machinist in Texas City said: "As soon as I had gotten out of the machine shop and realized that there had been a terrible explosion, I went right over to the first aid station here at the plant. You see, I'd had first aid training and I thought I could be of some use there" (Logan, Killian, and Mars, 1952, p. 95).

Wallace says: "It is difficult to comment on the patterns of leadership in the impact area during the isolation period at Worcester. The data given above suggest that during the first fifteen minutes after impact very few persons assumed roles of leadership responsibility (i.e. community oriented roles) who had not held roles of formal responsibility to the community before impact" (1956, p. 66).

In Udall, the only person to give a real report after the tornado was a boy who had been in four previous tornados. He hitchhiked to another town to inform police and ask for help. His behavior was adaptive also in that he first took care of his mother and the other children while many of the adults were completely unable to function (Hamilton, Taylor, and Rice, 1955, p. 28).

This period of confusion and isolation is similar to the lag seen in other feedback adjustment processes, before correction toward equilibrium occurs. In Hiroshima this lag lasted 36 hours (Siemes, 1945). Information must get out to the surrounding areas and help must come. The bigger the disaster, the harder this is, and the longer it takes.

The stage of *rescue* is when the people of the impact zone begin to help themselves and each other, and when the supra-system sends aid to the damaged system. In the Texas City explosion, people in the impact zone remained basically social creatures. "The rescue work that was done by the survivors . . . for each other did not consist merely of individual acts of heroism and altruism. It consisted of cooperation and organized group activity which started almost immediately. This organization was new and spontaneous; it was extremely informal; and it was on a small scale. But organization it was, for new group structures emerged here and there in the stricken area" (Logan, Killian, and Mars, 1952, pp. 30-31).

An example of such organization is given by Logan, Killian, and Mars: "Just as I got outside the building, Foster fell right in front of me. I was crawling. I said, 'Come on Foster, let's get out of here.' He said, 'I can't walk, I'm dying!' I said, 'Come on, you can crawl, I'll guide you.' Then Johnny and Clyde came along. I said, 'Johnny help us — we can't walk.' His arms were broken and he said, 'I can't help you, but I'll stay with you. If you can crawl, I'll guide you.' Talk about cheer — that helped me more than anything, just when he said, 'I'll stay with you.' Johnny guided us out. Clyde was blinded, but he held on to Johnny's arm. Foster and I crawled behind them. We didn't pay any attention to anybody that didn't look like he was alive. I just thought, 'He's dead' " (1952, p. 31).

The necessities for cooperation in the rescue period may alter typical patterns of community organization. For instance, when a derailed tank car released a huge cloud of chlorine gas in 1961 between New Roads and Morganza, Louisiana, men and animals alike were in danger of poisoning (Segaloff, 1961, p. 31). Racial distinctions between Negroes and whites which were strongly enforced in that area were completely disregarded during the emergency, only to reappear afterward.

The areas surrounding the impact zone usually provide earliest aid. The impact area itself lacks the necessary communication. Frequently its roads have been made impassable. Telephone lines may be down and the central exchange may be destroyed as well. In the great Holland floods of February 1953, in which more than 1700 people lost their lives and one-fifth of the country was under water, the rescue and relief work required helicopters and amphibious transport (Ludwig, 1954). Seaplanes could not land on the shallow water, and even most small boats had too much draft to get through. There were no operating telephone systems. From the city of Zierikzee only one ham radio operator was able to transmit a call for help. The victims who were not drowned in their beds sometimes waited as long as 36 hours before they could make their plight known. Rescue was hampered by the need to use very long, circuitous lines of communication, by conflict among Dutch agencies, and by too much control from top governmental officials who hampered effective field operations. In Udall, Kansas, the electrical disturbance from the storm was so great that radios were almost useless when ham operators arrived (Hamilton, Taylor, and Rice, 1955).

Bounding the disaster area is the *filter area,* which is permeable to some inputs and outputs but not to others. Fritz and Mathewson (1957) have found that disasters elicit "convergence behavior," a mass movement of people and supplies toward the stricken zone. This energy flow creates traffic-control problems and retards organized relief. Among the converging mass are needed supplies, experts, and helpers, but there often are also sightseers, thrill seekers, and potential vandals. Efficient filtering is required. Roadblocks are frequently set up to permit the inward flow of needed goods and services and keep out people who have no business in the area. An example of improper filtering occurred when the policeman at one roadblock refused to allow ambulances in until he was argued into understanding the need for them. He had been told to exclude vehicles and he did.

There is also a convergence of messages from the outside world, so that almost every disaster involves overloading of whatever channels may be operating. Requests for information, attempts to reach family and friends, offers of assistance, and so forth pour into the stricken area and require filtering.

The rescue process, once it is initiated by information of the disaster, involves a rapidly increasing input of supplies, helpers, and messages. They come first from nearby, and then from farther — sometimes, in our modern world of instantaneous communication and rapid transportation, from great distances. After the Worcester, Massachusetts, tornado, more than 100 nurses arrived in trailers, coming all the way from Oklahoma City (Wallace, 1956). By the time they arrived, all necessary nursing services had been arranged for. Wallace calls such "overshoot" of the rescue process "the cornucopia principle," and it has been common after modern disasters in the United States and some other parts of the world where rescue needs are usually met promptly and reasonably well.

Disruption of the communication network may allow rumors to spread. These may be false. In a study of tornado disasters Rosow (1954, pp. 396-397) reports a case in which the communication breakdown was heightened by total darkness. Nobody in authority undertook a real survey of the damage. Instead, officials acted upon word-of-mouth information which citizens brought them. Consequently, the most seriously damaged area was not identified immediately or reached rapidly by official assistance. Also, because of misinformation, important State Police equipment was dispatched in the wrong direction and wasted two hours trying to get back. In the absence of reliable communication, a rumor sprang up that a drive-in theater known to be crowded with people had been hit. Equipment was sent there because of this false report, only to become snarled in traffic and confusion outside the real center of the disaster.

After the rescue period comes the stage of *remedy*. An aspect of this phase in the Udall tornado was a release into almost cheerful behavior, which has been called "fiesta at the disaster" (Hamilton, Taylor, and Rice, 1955, pp. 56-57). Now the community begins to reorganize. Specialists take charge in their specific spheres of competence (Rosow, 1954, p. 449). Government officials reassume their authority. The suprasystem takes over functions the system cannot carry out for itself, using State Police, National Guard, or Red Cross. If possible, inhabitants usually return to their old groups, and organizations begin to function.

The final state of the system develops in the period of *recovery*. All that can be done is done, but the system does not return to its predisaster equilibrium, for some of the changes are irreversible. People are dead and old landmarks are gone. There may be permanent changes in community attitudes. In Flagler, Colorado, an airplane dived into a crowd, killing 20 persons — over 2 per cent of the population of the town — and injuring 30 others (National Opinion Research Center, 1953). The heroic behavior of the Catholic priest who happened to be there and the fact that some Catholic families suffered severely and became the focus of community sympathy, led to improvement in the status of Catholic families and a diminution of anti-Catholic feeling in this predominantly Protestant town. The houses of Udall, all of which

James G. Miller

were destroyed, were rebuilt as modern, ranch-style homes, with a view to becoming a commuter's suburb for Wichita workers instead of the sleepy village that had been there before (Hamilton, Taylor, and Rice, 1955). Instead of red brick false-front stores, the businesses reopened in modern buildings with new facades, new fixtures, and new goods. Since most of the people immediately after the restoration were those who had lived there before, it was in one way still the "same town." But there was an entirely new equilibrium. This is an extreme case of change, since Udall suffered the most complete disaster in the history of the American Red Cross. Warsaw, Poland, 85 per cent destroyed in World War II, became a new city except for the most ancient section of the city, which was restored exactly as it had been.

Conclusion

This paper has analyzed in some detail the way living systems at different levels — single individuals and social groups particularly — share interesting similarities in their subsystems and the way they adjust to stress. There are, of course, many differences, but the approach of general systems behavior theory throws some light on the common fight waged by all forms of life, large and small, to maintain their integrity and to continue effective existence in a constantly changing world plagued by threats, dangers, and possible destruction.

References

ASHBY, W. R. *Design for a Brain*. New York: John Wiley, 1952.
FRITZ, C. E., and MATHEWSON, J. H. "Convergence Behavior in Disasters; A Problem in Social Control." Report No. 9. Washington, D. C.: National Academy of Sciences — National Research Council, Committee on Disaster Studies, Publication No. 476, 1957.
HAMILTON, R. V., TAYLOR, R. M., and RICE, G. E., JR. "A Social Psychological Interpretation of the Udall, Kansas, Tornado." Washington, D. C.: National Academy of Sciences — National Research Council, Committee on Disaster Studies, 1955.
KUBZANSKY, P. E. The effects of reduced environmental stimulation on human behavior: A review. In A. Biderman and H. Zimmer, *The Manipulation of Human Behavior*. New York: John Wiley, 1961.

LOGAN, L., KILLIAN, L. M., and MARS, W. "A Study of the Effect of Catastrophe on Social Disorganization." Memorandum ORO-T-194, Operations Research Office, Chevy Chase, Maryland, 1952.

LUDWIG, H. Sanitary engineering in operation tulip. *U.S. Publ. Hlth Rep.,* 1954, 69, 533–537.

MILLER, J. G. Information input overload. In M. C. Yovits, G. T. Jacobi, and G. D. Goldstein (Eds.), *Self-Organizing Systems.* Washington, D. C.: Spartan, 1962.

MOORE, H. E. *Tornadoes over Texas.* Austin: University of Texas Press, 1958.

National Opinion Research Center. "Conference on Field Studies of Reactions to Disasters." Report No. 47, University of Chicago, 1953.

PARSONS, T., and SHILS, E. A. (Eds.). *Toward a General Theory of Action.* Cambridge, Mass.: Harvard University Press, 1951.

POWELL, J. W. In J. W. POWELL, J. E. FINESINGER, and M. H. GREENHILL, "An Introduction to the Natural History of Disaster." Vol. II. Final Contract Report, Disaster Research Project, Psychiatric Institute, University of Maryland, 1954.

ROSOW, I. L. "Public Authorities in Two Tornadoes." Washington, D. C.: National Academy of Sciences — National Research Council, Committee on Disaster Studies, 1954.

SEGALOFF, L. "Task Sirocco, Community Reaction to an Accidental Chlorine Exposure." Philadelphia: Institute for Cooperative Research, University of Pennsylvania, 1961.

SELYE, H. *The Stress of Life.* New York: McGraw-Hill, 1956.

SIEMES, FR. J. A. "Eyewitness Account, Hiroshima, August 6, 1945." Unpublished.

WALLACE, A. F. C. "Tornado in Worcester: An Exploratory Study of Individual and Community Behavior in an Extreme Situation." Washington, D. C.: National Academy of Sciences — National Research Council, Committee on Disaster Studies, Publication No. 178, 1956.

RICHARD S. LAZARUS

A LABORATORY APPROACH
TO THE DYNAMICS
OF PSYCHOLOGICAL STRESS*

THE IMPORTANCE of the topic of stress is reflected in the tremendous quantity of relevant multidisciplined experimentation in recent years. Whether the term used to describe this work is *emotion, stress, threat, defense, anxiety,* or *conflict,* to name a few of the more common terms designating the broad problem area, scarcely an issue of a psychological journal goes by without containing at least one experimental article on this subject. An attempt at a general review of this work would be beyond the scope of this paper. Some of the problems posed by such a review include the multitude of different issues addressed by the research, the variety of variables studied and methods used which makes comparison of the experiments difficult if not impossible, and the grossly different meanings given to the term *stress.*

This paper undertakes two somewhat limited tasks, first, an analysis of some of the key problems in experimentation, and second, the presentation of a brief account of some research from the author's own laboratory which was designed to throw light on some of the psychological mechanisms underlying stress reactions.

* Reprinted with permission from the *American Psychologist,* 1964, *19,* 400–411. Copyright© 1964 by the American Psychological Association, Inc.

A great portion of the experimentation in the field of stress does not add significantly to our knowledge of the psychological principles underlying the problem. If we are to understand the reasons for this, we need to recognize that, to be valuable, laboratory experiments must be effective analogues of postulated processes in the naturalistic phenomena of stress. These phenomena come to our attention through observations of people in real life. Our concern with stress phenomena arises from such observations as the behavior of people in disasters (Baker and Chapman, 1962), of mourning following bereavement (Lindemann, 1944), of various forms of psychopathology (Hambling, 1959), of the nature and effects of concentration camps (Bettelheim, 1943), and military combat (Grinker and Spiegel, 1945), and of patients anticipating surgery (Janis, 1958), to mention a few of the more prominent examples of field studies which have enriched the recent literature.

As a first step in understanding these phenomena, they are placed in a loose way under the rubric of stress. Thus, for example, various somatic symptoms such as ulcers and hypertension are conceived to be the result of stress processes, as are the symptoms of battle fatigue or schizophrenia, or the deterioration of skilled performance in battle, and the disorganization of social systems in disaster. Analytic statements are then evolved which identify the antecedent conditions of the so-called stress reactions and the processes involved. An examination of the field-study literature reveals abundant conceptualizations about the sources of threat, the mechanisms of threat production, the coping processes following threat, and the behavioral and physiological consequences. Some of the most significant of these conceptualizations may be found in the work of Janis (1958, 1962).

Now the laboratory makes it possible for us to test the adequacy of our conceptualizations by making the relevant processes happen under conditions of careful control and measurement. Although it is not always strictly the case, laboratory experimentation usually depends upon the definition of problems originating in our observations of nature and the development of theories about the processes that underlie what is observed.

What then is a laboratory analogue? First of all, it is an experiment performed under controlled conditions so that a variable, or several variables, can be unequivocally related to some effect being measured. But what about the term *analogue?* This refers to the manipulations in the experiment which parallel, or are similar to, the processes that are postulated to take place in nature. We are never really interested in the limited conditions of the experiment itself. Rather, we assume that these conditions represent those in real life, and that the findings can be generalized to conditions like them in nature. If an experimenter creates stress by exposing his experimental subjects to an experience of failure by doing or saying certain things to them, he expects to generalize his results to all those situations in life that involve such failure. The laboratory experiment on stress is but a miniature of these life experiences, and most importantly, one whose procedures, by analogy, are thought to correspond to or be isomorphic with the processes we postulate as taking place in nature.

All laboratory experiments are, in a sense, analogues, although they are not necessarily good analogues to postulated processes, nor are they necessarily well designed to identify the relationships between the variables which confirm or disconfirm the postulated process. Experiments that serve to advance our understanding depend upon a clear conceptual analysis of a problem. Very little of the recent experimental work on the problem of psychological stress falls into this category, sometimes because of the painful absence of a clear conception, sometimes because of the failure of adequate design.

These critical statements can be brought home by turning to substantive problems in the field, emphasizing the question of what psychological processes mediate stress reactions. We must ask, when will a stimulus produce stress reactions and what factors determine whether it will or will not?

In raising these questions, we must resist the temptation to digress into the equally important problem of what reactions define stress. An enormous variety of measures are employed to this end, ranging from biochemical studies of adrenal cortical or medulla secretions in the blood, to autonomic-nervous-system indicators of arousal such as skin conductance, heart rate, and respiration, as well as a large class of behavioral reactions including reports of affect, observations of behavioral and cognitive disorganization, and motor and postural manifestations. These indicators reflect, for one thing, different levels of analysis, physiological as well as psychological. Little is known about the relationships among them. In fact, what is known suggests that stress indicators are poorly correlated (Lazarus, Speisman, and Mordkoff, 1963), and it is difficult to identify the conditions under which stress should be indexed by one or the other. And yet, the many measures employed are all identified as stress reactions. However, the many problems inherent in the definition of stress and stress reactions must be excluded here as beyond the possibility of the present discussion.

Returning to the matter of what produces stress reactions, experimenters have employed a remarkable variety of procedures. Included are efforts to attack the self-esteem of subjects or other significant personal needs such as achievement or affiliation, frightening subjects by making them believe that they are in danger of electrocution from a malfunctioning electrical instrument, employing insulting remarks to induce anger, making ego-threatening interpretations in a psychiatric interview, presenting movies dealing with threatening experiences, blowing a loud horn behind the subject's head, requiring the performance of intellectual tasks such as mental arithmetic, producing sensory deprivation, and having subjects plunge their arm into a bucket of ice cold water. This list is by no means exhaustive, but it is fairly representative of the kinds of experimental conditions used in laboratory research. Often great ingenuity is employed by the experimenter in setting up the conditions producing stress, as in a recent study by Korchin and Herz (1960), in which by a clever ruse the subject is made to think he has autistically misperceived the contents of perceptual stimuli.

Now what about the mechanism by which the stimulus condition results in the measured stress reaction? By what reasoning does plunging the arm into ice cold water or doing mental arithmetic get placed in the same category of stressor stimuli as do conditions designed to threaten self-esteem? It is true that changes in heart rate, elevation of skin conductance, and other autonomic indices of stress reaction can be demonstrated to occur as a consequence of each of these procedures, and many more, including an experience of failure or watching a disturbing movie. It can also be demonstrated that increased hydrocortisone may be found in the blood following an experience of failure, attacks on the subject's ability to perceive correctly, living in a strange environment, or watching threatening movies. Experiments demonstrating merely that autonomic, behavioral and adrenal cortical responses follow the use of some specific, so-called stressor procedure, have proliferated.

What is missing from much of this work is a clear set of notions about why this diverse variety of stimulus conditions produces the reactions identified as stress. Without an analysis of the psychological or physically noxious nature of these stimulus conditions, and the processes that intervene between them and the measured stress reaction, the only link between them must remain the response measure, say, elevation of hydrocortisone or skin conductance, which is found to be a common response to all these stimuli.

But is the reason why plunging the arm into iced water produces such responses the same as is assumed to be the case for mental arithmetic or for assaults on the self-esteem? In assaults on self-esteem the intervening process is often assumed to be the production of threat in the psychological sense. Do we then assume also that plunging the arm into ice cold water is threatening, or is there a more direct, homeostatic mechanism of temperature regulation involved in that procedure that is not present in assaults on self-esteem? Similarly, does mental arithmetic produce stress responses because of potential psychological threats involved in performing such a task, or is it merely a matter of activation or mobilization of effort?

It is possible that both the state of being threatened, and physical demands upon the tissues, tend to activate the organism and produce similar autonomic and biochemical changes, and that even nonthreatening kinds of experiences such as watching a funny movie, or running up and down a hillside or golf course in sheer pleasure, have similar effects. The changes that are called stress reactions may not be at all specific to psychologically threatening conditions, and perhaps positive affective experiences might produce the same reactions although in lesser degree. If this is true, then on what grounds do we identify all such reactions as stress? Similarly with the adrenal cortical reactions emphasized by Selye (1956), serum hydrocortisone elevation may follow any biological demand, rather than be necessarily associated with the psychological state of being threatened. Have we not here begged the key question concerning the mechanisms by which these effects are produced?

There are many variables confounded in the data alluded to above, which leave indeterminate the bases, physiological and psychological, on which the so-called stress reactions depend. Perhaps the easiest one to recognize is confounding the physiological and psychological levels of explanation. The process of having a tooth pulled results in increased hydrocortisone in the blood. Shannon and his colleagues (1962) have shown, however, that merely anticipating such dental work leads to the same results. In the anticipation the mechanisms intervening between the threat of dental surgery and the stress reaction are psychological, since there is no direct assault on the tissue system at all — merely the recognition by the patients of a danger to come. To return to another stress situation, it is possible that plunging the arm into cold water has psychological implications that are connected with the stress reactions, but this is not the explanation that would normally be accepted. Rather, what is assumed is the direct disturbance of the tissue system; and the natural defensive

39

or homeostatic reactions of the body to such noxious conditions, referred to by Selye as "the adaptation syndrome" (1956), are called into play. But the levels of explanation are entirely different in instances of threat and direct tissue damage. Although it is true that the ultimate physiological mechanisms may be the same once the subject has been threatened psychologically or once a directly noxious stimulus has assaulted a tissue system, the key psychological questions are begged unless the researcher attempts to specify the psychological processes that determine whether these changes will indeed be activated.

Most of the experiments performed on stress simply ignore this question of psychological process and serve merely as demonstrations that such and such a condition results in some stress reaction, usually defined by a single measure. They are not analogues of psychological stress at all, in the sense that they permit evaluation of some postulated process of stress production. Strangely enough, most are not even psychological in character, since typically one cannot find a single psychological question that has been elucidated. And often even the physiological mechanism by which the hydrocortisone, skin conductance change, or whatever comes about is not clarified, so that such studies are not even physiological analogues of the kinds of processes Selye (1956), Lindsley (1957), or other physiologically oriented theorists are so concerned with.

The impression that all experimental studies ignore psychological questions should not be created, although those that tackle them are often woefully inadequate to the task. A good example is the recent paper by Alexander and his colleagues (1961), dealing with the psychological mechanism of stress production in patients suffering from hyperthyroidism. Alexander started with two assumptions. One, of less interest here, was that hyperthyroid disorder leads to specificity of reaction to stress, that for such patients the preferred organismic response is in the category of heightened thyroid activity. The other, dealing more with the psychodynamics of stress production, was that the hyperthyroid patient is especially vulnerable to threat in situations engendering fear for biological survival. This fear then is the postulated fundamental source of stress in the hyperthyroid patient.

Here is a postulate about the mechanism underlying stress in a particular group, a postulate which Alexander attempted to check by an experimental analogue. The analogue consisted of employing as a stimulus a movie called "The Wages of Fear" which was thought to deal with the theme of threat to biological survival. The film was presented to a group of untreated thyrotoxic patients, a treated group, and a group of normal controls. Thyroid functioning was found to be elevated in the untreated patients as a result of viewing the film.

Although the Alexander study did attempt to identify the psychological mechanism underlying stress in the hyperthyroid patient, it failed for design reasons. The trouble is that there is no way of knowing from this study whether the reactions of the patients were specific to this film, with its particular contents revolving around the theme of biological survival threats. Perhaps any disturbing film would have had the same effects, regardless of theme. To support the hypothesis about the specific kind of threat production in these patients, it was necessary to demonstrate that the stress reaction of heightened thyroid activity did not occur when another film was shown, a film which because of other kinds of threatening content could indeed produce stress reactions in another type of population.

Still, the study of Alexander goes in the right direction in its attempt to spell out and test psychodynamic factors in stress production. It failed, simply for methodological reasons, to demonstrate that fear for biological survival is the necessary and sufficient condition of stress production in a hyperthyroid group. It is an analogue of stress because it was designed to test, empirically, a postulate about the mechanism of stress production by creating conditions that could be considered appropriate for this mechanism. Such process-oriented studies exist but are disturbingly rare. Without them, and without systematic research programs based upon well-articulated theories of psychological stress, laboratory studies continue to proliferate without leading to significant advances in our generalizable knowledge.

Attention will now be shifted from general statements about the field of experimentation as a whole to a presentation of some work from the author's laboratory in which a research group has been seeking to test and elaborate certain theoretical principles of psychological stress production.* While this program is many-faceted and deals with a number of key theoretical issues in psychological stress, one particular concept which has led to some extremely interesting findings will be touched on in the remainder of this paper.

An important feature of stress in the psychological sense is seen in the literature on disaster. In that literature, it is often implied that stress depends on the *anticipation* of something harmful in the future, and that it requires an interpretation by the person about the personal significance of the stimulus situation. Janis (1962), for example, discusses this problem in the concept of "anticipatory fear." This anticipation of potential harm or motive thwarting is the key to the concept of *threat*. Threat can be regarded as the central intervening variable in psychological stress.

Just before the 1953 Worcester tornado, the spring storm with thunder and lightning and dark clouds that preceded the disaster did not communicate threat to the residents. There was no expectation of harm and hence no threat until the tragic event happened. Subsequently, however, after the experience of the tornado, ordinary storms carried an ominous quality. People were subsequently frightened by summer storms that had previously carried no threat. The crucial

* The research findings reported here are based on investigations supported by a Research Grant (MH-02136) from the National Institute of Mental Health of the Public Health Service.

issue here in the production of threat is the process of discrimination of dangerous or threatening conditions from benign ones.

It is this idea of the dependence of threat upon a discrimination, a judgment, or an interpretation that will be developed briefly now. For this process the term *appraisal* will be used. The process of appraising which circumstances are harmful and which are benign is crucial to the production of stress reactions, at least at the psychological level of analysis. In fact, as Arnold (1960) has recently argued most persuasively, any emotion implies an evaluation of a stimulus as either harmful or beneficial. But Arnold has not described the conditions that determine the appraisal, and without such analysis, experimental studies of the process are not possible. Among other things, beliefs or expectations about events, based upon both past experience and the present stimulus configuration, determine whether or not a stimulus will be reacted to as threatening.

Let us consider for a moment what the concept that we call appraisal means concerning the production of threat. For one thing, it means that the same stimulus can be threatening or not, depending upon the interpretation the person makes concerning its future personal significance. This is an important point. The threat is not simply out there as an attribute of the stimulus. Rather it depends for its threat value on this appraisal process, which in turn depends upon the person's beliefs about what the stimulus means for the thwarting of motives of importance to him.

In the research project which forms the basis of this discussion,* experimental analogues of cognitive appraisal have been created and the factors that determine this appraisal manipulated. A stimulus that is normally threatening to most

* The author's colleagues and students whose work is referred to here or who have participated in this project include: Dr. Joseph C. Speisman, Mr. Arnold M. Mordkoff, Mr. Leslie A. Davison, Mr. Cliff A. Jones, Jr., and Mrs. Elizabeth Alfert.

experimental subjects has been made relatively benign by influencing the way in which subjects interpret it.

The basic method of producing threat has been to show motion picture films, and to manipulate the orientation toward them by introductory statements and/or by sound tracks during the film which cast the events viewed in the way the experimenters choose (Speisman et al., 1964). One of these films shows a primitive ritual of an Australian stone-age tribe. It involves a series of crude operations on the genitals of the native boys when they have reached puberty. The operation is called "subincision." The film is generally quite disturbing to watch. This same film has previously been employed by Aas (1958) and Schwartz (1956) as a means of studying the Freudian concept of castration anxiety, although unpublished experimental studies in our laboratory suggest that there are other sources of threat in the film as well as the mutilative or castration-relevant content.

In the typical experiment using the subincision film, subjects watch the film individually. Continuous recordings are made of autonomic variables such as skin conductance, heart rate, respiration, and motor activity, depending upon our interests at the moment, and at the end of the film, reports of the subjects' affective state are solicited, usually by an interview or an adjectival check-list of mood. Merely watching the film produces marked stress reactions, some of which can be quite severe, with symptoms of disgust, nausea, and anxiety (Lazarus et al., 1962). To give some picture of the ebb and flow of the typical stress reaction to this film, Figure 1 portrays the pattern of skin conductance shown by fifty subjects over the entire seventeen minutes of the subincision film.

You will notice in Figure 1 the ups and downs — the high points in skin conductance signifying arousal or threat, the low points indicating more benign states. The peak periods occur when the surgical operations are taking place, especially the first three which seem to be the most disturbing to watch. In the second operation, for example, the native boy is obviously distressed and in pain, immediately following

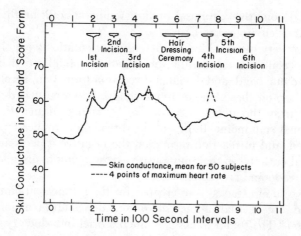

FIGURE 1. *Variation in the skin conductance of fifty subjects during the subincision film.*

which he sobs and appears to suffer considerably. The deep trough in skin conductance in the middle of the film occurs in relation to the relatively benign ceremonial activity of hair tying, in which one native binds the hair of another who has recently been operated upon. It may be noted also that this curve of autonomic reactivity is extremely stable in reflecting the stimulus impact, since in each new study with a sizable sample, the same basic pattern is generated. This shows how desirable continuous recording of skin conductance is in indicating the ups and downs of stress reaction.

It has been said that this same film stimulus, which is so disturbing, could be made relatively benign by altering the interpretation which the subject places upon the events which are portrayed, presumably by eliminating the threatening significance (Speisman et al., 1964.) How can threatening material be viewed so as to be nonthreatening? One kind of answer to this question can be found in the theory of ego defense, which postulates in a rather loose way certain mental operations that are conceived of as ways of reducing threat. Such mechanisms can be thought of as resulting in

Richard S. Lazarus

altered cognitive appraisal of threatening stimuli, be they internal or environmental.

Two very general kinds of defensive orientation were chosen as especially suitable for the subincision film, intellectualization on the one hand, and denial and reaction formation, employed together, on the other. In intellectualization, one gets detachment from threatening experiences by taking an analytic, impersonal standpoint. In denial the threatening implications are denied, and in reaction formation the negative aspects are reversed entirely, so that only positive, rosy qualities are allowed expression and are emphasized.

Two sound tracks were created for the subincision film, one called "intellectualization," the other, "denial and reaction formation." The sound tracks contained a brief introductory statement, followed by a narrative, like a travelogue that ran simultaneously with the film itself. In "intellectualization" the orientation of the anthropologist was taken, who, like the viewer, is observing an interesting specimen of human behavior and describing it analytically. In it no reference is made to feelings of any kind. In the "denial and reaction formation" statement, the idea that the operative procedures damaged the functioning of the natives, threatened their health, or resulted in significant pain was denied. It was further suggested that the native boys had looked forward all their lives to this happy experience which permitted them to join their brothers as emerging adults and full members of the society. Everything that happened, however gruesome, was given a rosy glow.

A third control sound track was also created for comparison with both the silent film and the two defensively oriented sound tracks. This was euphemistically called the trauma track, since it pointed up all the major sources of threat in the film, the filth, the pain, the danger of the operation, and the sadism of the procedure, although this presentation was made in the same calm tone of the narrator's voice as that used on the other two sound tracks.

Two groups of subjects were employed in this experiment with the defensive sound tracks, one a college student group, the other consisting of middle-level airline executives who graciously consented to participate in the study. The reasoning behind the choice of groups had to do with an interest in defensive dispositions, that is, the habitual way in which the subjects coped with threat. One might assume that a person who usually denies threat would be most responsive to the denial-and-reaction-formation sound track, whereas the person whose preferred mode of defense is intellectualization would get the greatest threat reduction from the intellectualized sound track which was more compatible with his "natural" way of coping.

The assumption was made that college students, aside from whatever dispositional qualities led them into the system of higher education in the first place, are continually exposed to intellectualized modes of thought. Every facet of the world, physical, biological, psychological, social, and artistic, is placed in the context of analysis and intellectual understanding. For example, in an anthropology class one is taught about how people in other cultures live. In physiology one gets accustomed to examining and even dissecting tissues and inspecting the anatomies of human and infrahuman species. The entire context of higher education poses a continual force toward intellectualized modes of thought.

With business executives the matter would appear to be quite different. The educational background of the group was, in the main, high-school level. The activities of life of the executive are more action-oriented. Decision is emphasized, rather than intellectual introspection. Managerial people are apt to be subjected far more to the social atmosphere that emphasizes such denial slogans as "the power of positive thinking" and the conviction that, if you believe in yourself, chances of success are good. Understanding and knowledge are favorably seen less for their own sake and more for their power to produce desired results. As it turns out, some personality-test data on both groups of subjects were available, and this appeared to support our assumption that students were more apt to be intellectualizers, and executives more disposed to the denial type of defense. Two scales of the Minnesota Multi-

Richard S. Lazarus

phasic Personality Inventory were most relevant. One, identified as Psychasthenia, could be regarded as a measure of
anxiety and obsessive-compulsive tendencies which are considered a consequence of intellectualized defenses. The other,
a derived scale of the MMPI called Hysteria Denial, is presumed to measure tendencies to deny threatening or unacceptable thoughts, impulses, and the threatening aspects of events.
The college student group was found to be significantly higher
than the executives on the Pt scale, whereas the executives
showed significantly higher scores than the students on the
Hy Denial scale.

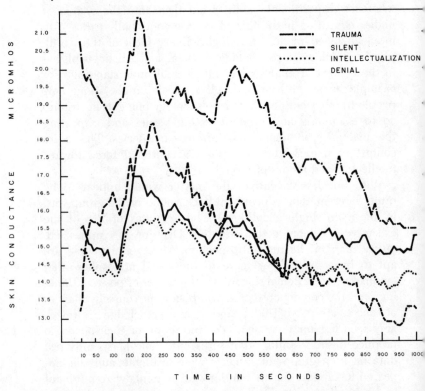

FIGURE 2. *Skin-conductance patterns during the subincision film as
determined by the various sound-track conditions.*

The results of the study showed that, in general, the defensive sound tracks significantly reduced the threatening impact of the subincision film, while the trauma track increased it (Speisman et al., 1964). This is shown in Figure 2, illustrated, as before, for the autonomic-nervous-system variable of skin conductance. In the figure are presented the skin conductance results for the subincision film without any sound track, the film accompanied by the trauma track, and the film accompanied by either the denial-and-reaction-formation track or the intellectualization track.

While both defensive sound tracks reduced threat, their effectiveness did appear to depend, as expected, on compatibility with the natural defensive dispositions of the subject populations. Intellectualization was most effective in reducing stress reaction in the student group and less effective with executives. In contrast, denial and reaction formation worked best with the executives but was far less successful with the students. It is as if the students simply did not accept as fully as the executives the orientation provided in the denial-and-reaction-formation sound track.

This interaction between the subject groups and the two defensive sound tracks is shown in Figure 3. Examination of the figure reveals that the students who heard the denial-and-reaction-formation sound track showed a stress reaction only slightly lower than the reaction to the silent version, as compared with the difference found when the students heard the intellectualization track, or when the executive group heard the denial-and-reaction-formation track.

Lest these findings on personality and the effectiveness of different modes of cognitive appraisal be taken as more pat than they really are, a perplexing sour note must be introduced into the discussion. Up to this point in the analysis, there seemed no reason to doubt that whatever was being measured by the Pt and Hy Denial scales of the MMPI accounted for the interesting and sensible differences between the students and the executives. If this were true, then the interaction between defensive disposition and sound-track effects could also be

Richard S. Lazarus

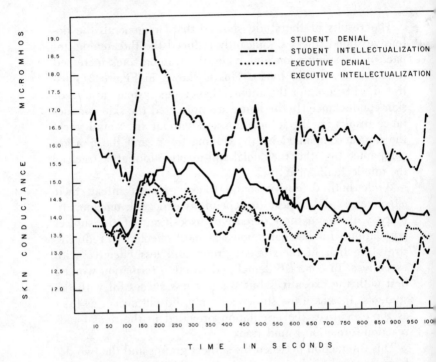

FIGURE 3. *Interaction effects on skin-conductance patterns of subject groups and defensive sound-track conditions.*

shown, and even strengthened, if we were to ignore the social group to which the subject belonged and array the data entirely on the basis of the MMPI scales. That is, the effectiveness of the sound tracks could be compared between those subjects who scored high in Hy Denial and those who scored low, and between those subjects who scored high in Pt and those who scored low. When this was done, the interaction found earlier simply disappeared.

This latter finding somewhat embarrasses the interpretation of the interplay between defensive disposition and the effects of the defensive sound tracks. At least it tells us that the differences between the students and executives are not accounted for on the basis of the Hy Denial and Pt personality scales. The original interpretation is still reasonable, however, that executives are more prone in their modes of thought to denial and reaction-formation, and students more oriented toward intellectualization, as part of the social pattern to which they are exposed. And additional data have been appearing which further support the original interpretation. In any event, the findings on the general success of the defensive sound tracks in reducing the threat normally conveyed by the sub-incision movie are not in doubt.

These findings have been replicated and extended in another study (Lazarus and Alfert, 1964) which is even more dramatic in showing the power of cognitive appraisal. This time the film was presented with no sound track at all, merely a prior orientation session, and still the subjects were able to view the silent film with equanimity once they had been led to interpret the events portrayed in a benign way. In this study, only the denial-and-reaction-formation statements were used, and they were presented to subjects as orienting instructions before the film began. Figure 4 shows that the lowest stress reactions occur in this condition, compared with either a sound track involving denial and reaction formation, or a silent film version with no effort to manipulate appraisal. Stress reaction, as we would expect, is greatest with the silent film. It should be added also that psychological assessments of the beliefs of the subjects about the film events, made at the end of the film, follow what might be expected from the levels of stress reaction found. The appraisal of threat is indeed lowest in the denial-and-reaction-formation conditions, with the most threatening interpretations found in the untreated group.

Finally, the study of Lazarus and Alfert (1964) tends to confirm the principle that the defense-oriented communication must be compatible with defensive dispositions in the subject in order to reduce stress reaction. As assessed by scales of the Minnesota Multiphasic Personality Inventory considered to tap the disposition toward denial as a defense, subjects high in denial tendency showed marked stress reduction as a result of the denial communications, whereas subjects low in denial

Richard S. Lazarus

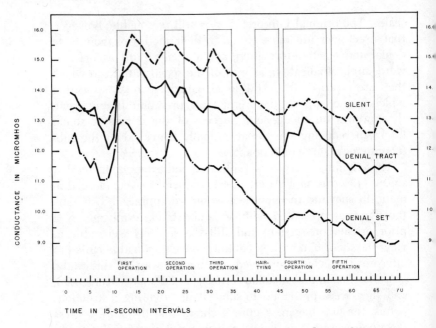

FIGURE 4. *Effects of experimental treatments on skin conductance during the subincision film.*

tendency were not so influenced. The personality dispositions determined whether or not the denial communications, presented either prior to or along with the threatening film as a sound track, would reduce the usual stress reaction to the film.

It has been shown here that threat, or at least stress reactions that are mediated psychologically, depend upon the appraisal of a stimulus. This is another way of talking about the interpretation of the personal significance of the stimulus. Moreover, two kinds of appraisal, intellectualized on the one hand, and based on denial and reaction formation on the other, result in the short-circuiting of the expected threat arousal. These modes of viewing a potentially threatening stimulus, based on the theory of ego defense, are not as readily accepted by all persons, but if they are, they make for a non-threatening appraisal.

52

The experimental analogue involves two steps. One is the assumption that the subject, in watching a motion picture film, identifies himself with the actors in the film as though he were one of them, and could thus be threatened by what is happening to them. The second stage in the analogue concerns the process of appraisal, in particular, that the orienting instructions and sound tracks produce varying appraisal processes of the sort involved in the concepts of denial and reaction formation or intellectualization, and that these, in turn, correspond to what occurs in the natural context.

It should be made absolutely clear that, although the discussion has referred to ego-defense theory and employs the terms intellectualization and denial and reaction formation in describing the sound tracks, the experiments are analogues of appraisal only and not of ego defense. We have merely borrowed from defense theory in constructing our appraisal statements. Defense is usually considered to involve, first, the arousal of threat, and then, by principles that are still not clear to us, the activation of certain self-induced modes of thought which reduce the threat that has once been aroused. In these experiments, the modes of thought that short-circuit threat are encouraged by manipulation of the situation; they do not follow the generation of threat in the subject, nor are they self-induced by the subject. We cannot consider our findings as resulting from defensive processes, although we can learn something about the threat-reducing effectiveness of various defensive modes of thought from systematic manipulation of the kinds of statements we give in orienting the subjects. Thus, indirectly, they contribute to the theory of ego defense.

Those familiar with the literature on ego defense will recognize the vagueness of these concepts, even though the general idea of defensive appraisal has wide acceptance. The specific mental operations involved are not clearly understood, their comparative effectiveness is not known, nor is their relationship with each other. From the point of view of the experimental analogue, some key questions can be phrased in this way: What are the necessary and sufficient mental operations for the successful defensive appraisal of various kinds of threatening events? And what are the conditions under which these coping processes will be activated and successful? By means of the experimental paradigm described above, it is possible to subject a variety of carefully defined modes of defensive appraisal to the test of effectiveness in reducing the physiological as well as the behavioral manifestations of threat. By the proper analysis of such maneuvers as intellectualization, for example, we can separate out of this global concept the precise elements of thought that are capable of making a threatening stimulus less threatening or even benign.

About the experiments themselves, I would say at the present time that, when the belief is created that the surgical procedures in the subincision film are neither painful nor harmful and are viewed by the natives with joy, then, assuming that the subject has placed himself in their shoes, there is no threat associated with vicariously undergoing the subincision experience. Similarly, from the vantage point of intellectualized detachment, events that would normally be threatening can be looked at without emotionalized, empathic involvement and can be placed in the context of a neutral conceptual framework.

In making this point about intellectualization, one may think of the experience of Hamlet in coming upon the grave digger unearthing a skull. Hamlet says poignantly, "Alas, poor Yorick, I knew him." This emotional statement is the dramatist's way of involving Hamlet and therefore the audience with the image of a friend, a fellow human being, dead, now nothing more than bones. In the context of the kind of arguments made about intellectualization, he might have said with far less emotional impact, "Isn't this an interesting specimen of primate bone?" In fact, is this not exactly what the anatomist or surgeon does when he dons his scientist's hat and observes pathology? Yorick as a dead friend is a threatening thought, but Yorick as a nameless primate bone short-circuits the threat by employing a nonthreatening framework within which to view the same event which could be most disturbing from another point of view.

At this point again, the temptation is strong and must be resisted to digress to the issues inherent in using the vicarious procedure of motion picture films to produce threat, and to issues concerned with advantages and disadvantages and the assumed processes by which marked stress reactions can be so easily produced by this laboratory method. But these questions themselves are complex and require extensive exposition. Moreover, the purpose of illustrating the laboratory analogue of stress processes has been fulfilled in the presentation of some studies dealing with processes of threat production and reduction.

It must be clear by now that, implicitly or explicitly, laboratory analogues of stress must start from some conceptualization of the very processes underlying the phenomena observed. In the film technique, the analogue involves assumptions about the process of identification with the actors in the film, to mention one example. With the sound tracks, there is available an analogue of the process of appraisal, with the different sound tracks representing different frames of reference within which the film events are viewed.

It is remarkable that, in the quarter of a century that has seen interest in stress phenomena grow so greatly, psychological stress theory has had so little influence on experimental research on the subject. Some researchers seem to believe that Selye's (1956) work on the adaptation syndrome has solved our problems concerning the psychology of stress, when, in reality, it leaves all the psychological questions untouched. Selye has added perhaps to the measures indexing stress, and to our sophistication about the physiological mechanisms underlying these measures, but not to the understanding of the psychological processes that determine when a stress reaction will or will not occur.

Richard S. Lazarus

The current work on the physiology of arousal tends to confuse psychological threat with activation, to confuse the jumping up and down in happy enthusiasm and the physiological mobilization involved in this activity with the state of being threatened by the sight of something, by the thought of something, by a small change in environment which betokens a potential harm. The theoretical and methodological problems inherent in the field of psychological stress will never be solved merely by repeated demonstrations that this or that condition results in a blood-chemistry effect, a change in affect, or an autonomic-nervous-system reaction — unless at the same time attention is given to the psychological processes involved, and to the empirical conditions which identify these processes. In the experimental laboratory, what we need are more carefully thought-out analogues of these psychological processes.

References

AAS, A. *Mutilation Fantasies and Automatic Response.* Oslo, Norway: Oslo University Press, 1958.

ALEXANDER, F., FLAGG, G. R., FOSTER, S., CLEMENS, T., and BLAHD, W. Experimental studies of emotional stress: 1. Hyperthyroidism. *Psychosom. Med.,* 1961, 22, 104–114.

ARNOLD, MAGDA B. *Emotions and Personality.* Vol. I. New York: Columbia University Press, 1960.

BAKER, G. W., and CHAPMAN, D. W. *Man and Society in Disaster.* New York: Basic Books, 1962.

BETTELHEIM, B. Individual and mass behavior in extreme situations. *J. Abnorm. Soc. Psychol.,* 1943, 33, 417–452.

GRINKER, R. R., and SPIEGEL, J. P. *Men under Stress.* New York: Blakiston, 1945.

HAMBLING, J. *The Nature of Stress Disorder, Conference of the Society for Psychosomatic Research Held at the Royal College of Physicians, May, 1958.* Springfield, Ill.: C. C. Thomas, 1959.

JANIS, I. L. *Psychological Stress.* New York: John Wiley, 1958.

JANIS, I. L. Psychological effects of warnings. In G. W. Baker and D. W. Chapman (Eds.), *Man and Society in Disaster.* New York: Basic Books, 1962.

KORCHIN, S. J., and HERZ, M. Differential effects of "shame" and "disintegrative" threats on emotional and adrenocortical functioning. *A.M.A. Arch. gen. Psychiat.,* 1960, 2, 640–651.

LAZARUS, R. S., and ALFERT, ELIZABETH. The short-circuiting of threat by experimentally altering cognitive appraisal. *J. Abnorm. Soc. Psychol.,* 1964, *69,* 195–205.

LAZARUS, R. S., SPEISMAN, J. C., and MORDKOFF, A. M. The relationship between autonomic indicators of psychological stress. Heart rate and skin conductance. *Psychosom. Med.,* 1963, *25,* 19-30.

LAZARUS, R. S., SPEISMAN, J. C., MORDKOFF, A. M., and DAVISON, L. A. A laboratory study of psychological stress produced by a motion picture film, *Psychol. Monogr.,* 1962, 76 (34), Whole No. 553.

LINDEMANN, E. Symptomatology and management of acute grief. *Amer. J. Psychiat.,* 1944, *101,* 141–148.

LINDSLEY, D. B. Psychophysiology and motivation. In M. R. JONES (Ed.), *Nebraska Symposium on Motivation, 1957.* Lincoln: University of Nebraska Press, 1957.

SCHWARTZ, B. J. An empirical test of two Freudian hypotheses concerning castration anxiety. *J. Personality,* 1956, *24,* 318–327.

SELYE, H. *The Stress of Life.* New York: McGraw-Hill, 1956.

SHANNON, I. L., ISBELL, G. M., and HESTER, W. R. "Stress in Dental Patients." Report, School of Aerospace Medicine, Brooks Air Force Base, Texas, April 1962.

SPEISMAN, J. C., LAZARUS, R. S., MORDKOFF, A. M., and DAVISON, L. A. Experimental reduction of stress based on ego-defense theory. *J. Abnorm. Soc. Psychol.,* 1964, *68,* 367–380.

KURT LANG AND GLADYS ENGEL LANG

COLLECTIVE RESPONSES
TO THE THREAT OF DISASTER

WHEN DISASTER THREATENS over a long period of time, the cohesive forces that hold a group together are subject to strain. Groups and individuals show signs of demoralization. Various forms of bizarre and schismatic behavior — e.g., mass hysteria and delinquency, rioting, extremist social movements — can be attributed to stresses produced by uncertainty and expectations of danger. This paper outlines a framework for the study of such collective responses to the threat of impending disaster, beginning with a consideration of the nature of morale.

Morale

The measure of morale is found in the exertion and effort that members of a collectivity reveal in pursuit of shared objectives when they encounter serious obstacles. The collectivity may refer to a small group based on face-to-face interaction or to an abstract grouping, like a nation, as long as it has some sense of its common identity. Morale also has an individual, an interpersonal, and a sociological dimension.

Morale, in its individual aspect, takes the form of *personal esprit*, seen as a state of optimism and sense of well-being. High personal esprit is often reflected in effective performance.

World War II studies of infantrymen, for example, have documented the association between personal esprit and performance. The higher an individual's esprit, the greater his willingness for combat, and so forth.

Personal esprit is partly a function of individual personality. Some individuals have greater psychological resources than do others for coping with stress produced in trying circumstances. But personal esprit also depends on interpersonal support. In one group, for example, the members exhibit significantly greater liking for each other, as well as greater satisfaction with their position in their group, than they do for other groups. Since not all groups are alike in this regard, both mutual attraction and satisfaction are group characteristics. For example, where soldiers in military units continue to hold favorable opinions of their buddies, their noncoms, and their officers, they behave more effectively on the average in the face of a common threat than do those in units where satisfaction and interpersonal attraction are more tenuous (Stouffer et al., 1949). Thus the ability of members of a group to stick together under stress is not solely a matter of individual esprit but also of the *cohesiveness* of the group. High interpersonal satisfactions enable persons in a group enterprise to cope collectively and in a cooperative manner with threatening situations from which they would withdraw as individuals.

Still, interpersonal attraction promotes performance in support of collective goals only if the face-to-face group effectively conveys the appropriate norms for behavior. Since this does not always happen, cohesiveness and group morale are not exactly one and the same thing. The ultimate criterion of morale is continued organizational effectiveness in situations of stress. Thus the American Marines planting the flag on Iwo Jima or the platoon accomplishing its mission under heavy enemy fire symbolize morale evidenced in successful performance: the group (or its surviving members) have carried on despite overwhelming odds and great risk to individuals. Effective performance encompasses sociological as well as interpersonal and individual aspects of morale.

Although morale as a group quality reveals itself only where it is put to the test, not every instance of effectiveness, as measured by successful performance of a task, is an index of morale. Success can be achieved by a great expenditure of resources together with a low degree of individual effectiveness. The group would to that degree be inefficient, though effective in the sense of adequate. On the other hand, a group's performance may be inadequate despite individual effectiveness and other evidence of high morale, simply because its resources and organizational structure are inadequate to the contingency. To illustrate this in the grossest fashion: two groups may exhibit the highest degree of morale in preparing to survive an anticipated strafing from the air, but if one is a group of cave dwellers and the other of desert nomads, the odds for survival are not predictable from the state of morale. On the other hand, societies may appear effective as well as efficient and yet have low morale if the participants exhibit low commitment. The apparent efficiency of some totalitarian societies that are organized is not necessarily testimony to high morale. When coercive control breaks down, artificially sustained "morale" proves brittle.

Morale, as used here, calls up an image of group enterprise in which (*a*) interpersonal attractions sustain individual esprit and (*b*) face-to-face groups act as effective conveyors of appropriate performance norms.

Demoralization

The process by which the morale of a group is undermined constitutes demoralization. It designates a progressive erosion of motivation until the norms and values of the group are no longer determining for behavior. Again there is a difference between demoralization in its individual and in its collective aspects.

A wide variety of actions and attitudes can contribute to the demoralization of an individual to a point where he no longer cares, as is shown in the various forms of political, social, or general apathy. But lack of concern for norms and values may also be manifest in precipitous actions, such as the ill-advised dumping of securities when stock market values momentarily slump, or in the confused and erratic escape activity of individuals struck by disaster. Such behavior can be adaptive for the individual: the soldier by "freezing" to avoid dangerous exposure to the fire of the well-entrenched enemy may save himself; the small-time speculator, having over-extended himself financially, remains solvent by selling at a loss. No loss of personal esprit need be involved.

Consequently the degree of personal disorganization is not a precise index of the pace at which the demoralization of a group proceeds. Personally adaptive behavior can interfere with an adaptive collective response (cf. Killian, 1952; Quarantelli, 1954). The soldiers who seek their own safety disrupt the fighting forces; the many small speculators play havoc with the price system. Such dissimilar behavior as panic flight, the dumping of securities, disorganized behavior, addiction to alcohol or drugs, looting, hysteria, or fainting can be treated as generically similar in relation to the collective effort that such behavior undermines. All are indicative of a process of demoralization, inferred from the relation of the behavior to the normative order.

Demoralization entails the disruption of two elements essential to the functioning of a group: cognitive definitions and affective ties. By cognitive definitions we mean the general expectations and intellectual schemes that people share and that, by transforming nature and society into a meaningful world, help to reduce uncertainty. Persons become disoriented when the unexpected or unfamiliar partially eclipses or shatters their basic understandings. Demoralization is fostered when things that are not supposed to happen do happen or appear about to happen.

Individuals in the group are, however, tied to each other not only by shared definitions but also by "moral" bonds. External danger that cannot be mastered or internal dissension that cannot be resolved tends to shift the balance between the controls exerted by relevant group interests and the impulse to follow more exclusive and private interests. A weakening of the affective ties that normally weld a group into a cohesive unit produces demoralization and is also an index of the degree to which it has already been demoralized. It follows that a solidary group firmly bound by mutual bonds can withstand considerably greater pressure on individuals without being disrupted or demoralized than can a group bound only by the coincidence of its members' self-interest. The less the attachment to the group, the less salience its norms have for individual conduct. Any activity in pursuit of specific and private ends contributes to demoralization, because it interferes with the attainment of collective goals and impedes the rational and ordered adaptation to a changed situation by the group as a whole.*

Defense Against Demoralization

An extreme state of demoralization, in either the individual or the group, cannot last long. Extreme demoralization in the individual who fails somehow to adapt or reintegrate precipitates mental breakdown, and a group will literally go to pieces when private and particularistic goals gain ascendancy over values and goals necessary to its persistence.

The concept of defense mechanism by which inner anxiety is managed has become indispensable in the study of personality. A person's defensive operations help to effect a reconciliation between social demands and impulsivity. Although every individual learns techniques for managing the tensions generated by the irreconcilable nature of the two sets of demands, an unsocialized neurotic potential, not under the control of symbolic activities, persists in every individual and manifests itself, on occasion, in behavior compulsively repeated, irrespective of its appropriateness or practical utility, or in attitudes tenaciously held despite disconfirming evidence.

* For a more detailed discussion of demoralization, see Lang and Lang (1961), Chapter 4.

Socially Structured Defenses. Certain institutional and social practices, rituals, beliefs, and so forth, can also be viewed as socially structured defenses against anxiety, likely to be aroused during the performance of certain roles. First, any generally accepted social arrangement by its very existence reduces uncertainty and thus helps to contain anxiety. Even ordinary social etiquette with its prescriptions for behavior facilitates the management of tension that may result if guides for conduct are lacking.

Second, institutions can serve individual members as reinforcements of their characteristic mechanisms of defense against anxiety. Jacques (1956, pp. 478-498), for example, has shown how collective bargaining arrangements were used in a factory to reinforce the defenses of participants against persecutory and depressive anxiety. Individuals who chronically vote *against* somebody rather than *for* something may likewise be expressing hostility which in other, less legitimate contexts would not be acceptable. Many such practices are regressive in that they facilitate the externalization of fantasy to reality.

Third, institutions like prisons, mental institutions, hospitals, combat units, and so forth, whose essential function inevitably means participation in situations likely to be anxiety provoking, frequently resort to routines that are externalizations of mechanisms by which participants seek to manage their anxieties. Though they are usually rationalized as necessary for achieving organizational objectives, these routines, as a matter of fact, frequently interfere with efficiency. Thus Menzies offers a careful and thoughtful evaluation of socially structured defenses incorporated in the routines of a group of nursing trainees. The death of a patient, for example, naturally aroused anxiety. Yet nurses confronted this situation day after day. The professional posture that nurses assumed tended to inhibit the development of a full person-to-person relationship between nurse and patient. But while successful, to a degree, in temporarily checking anxiety, this defense deprived nurses of an important source of satisfaction. The resultant high turnover among the student staff then interfered with the efficiency of the hospital organization (Menzies, 1960). In this way the socially structured defenses actually contributed to over-all demoralization.

Socially Sanctioned License. Most societies provide occasional opportunities for the collective indulgence of emotion that would ordinarily be contained because its release would evoke uncontrollable anxiety. Occasions on which certain excesses are openly tolerated constitute socially sanctioned license. To a point, ordinary self-restraint is momentarily cast aside, and impulses and emotions are more-or-less directly acted out. Examples range from occasions on which individuals are invited to "let off steam" to excessive orgies that are allowed to last for specified periods of time. In such instances excessive or impulsive behavior may be merely tolerated, as when demonstrations or strikes or celebrant behavior, however worrisome or even repugnant to authorities, are permitted to run their "natural" course. Temporary license can be viewed as an alternative to more threatening activity. On still other occasions, license may be officially condoned, indeed encouraged, as a ritualistic way of defending against demoralization or rebellion (see Erikson, 1950, pp. 164 ff., for a psychoanalytical approach; Gluckman, 1963, for a social anthropological approach).

Spontaneously Shared Defense. Demoralization results whenever personal or socially structured defenses fail to check anxiety, or socially sanctioned license does not suffice as a safety valve. In these circumstances new forms of collective defense often develop. The spontaneous psychological integration of individuals on the basis of emotions that are normally contained and conventionalized can thus be treated as a special kind of collective defense in a collectivity on the verge of demoralization. The concept of spontaneously shared (collective) defense is basic to any understanding of certain group responses to the threat of impending disaster. It is especially pertinent where the threat is constant and ambiguous.

Organized group defenses are aimed at anticipatory or remedial action in the event of disaster. Collective defenses are unplanned and spontaneous. Frequently they have no apparent connection with the specific threat of impending disaster and thus impede organized action intended to cope with the threat itself. Collective defense is manifested in phenomena such as riots, scapegoating, religious cultism, psychic epidemics, and so forth, all of which are associated with stress of some kind. Emotions and impulses whose open expression would bring the individual into conflict with society find an outlet in explosive activity or behavior that is shared. Thus the activity is symptomatic of the conflict between strong private motives indicative of demoralization and group roles that inhibit the tendency toward withdrawal to privacy.

The psychiatric literature contains some dramatic examples of collective symptoms formed suddenly under the influence of others. In each of these situations, the socially shared (as distinct from "structured") symptom developed spontaneously in interaction and communication. It permitted a redefinition of the situation so that submerged goals could be pursued without violating the group codes. The participants continued to act with essential solidarity. To illustrate, Strecker (1940, pp. 77 ff.) reported that a unit, which had performed in an exemplary fashion under fire, suffered within a short span of time about five hundred "gas casualties," every one of which proved, upon examination, to be of psychosomatic origin. No evidence was found of contact with gas. The various symptoms attributed by the soldiers to the effects of gas opened a route of escape from group obligations, one that was socially sanctioned and elicited sympathy. They were not malingerers. Although in terms of institutional performance the collective utilization of the symptom represents demoralization, its contagious spread is accounted for by the way in which it resolved, through an effective compromise, the conflict between individual demands and the group code. Since the individual managed to escape without violating the group code, the code was actually upheld.

During crowdlike phenomena conflicts are externalized in a way acceptable to many people. The acting out helps to estab-lish or maintain solidarity among the participants. The crowds that form spontaneously, in particular, are usually recruited from persons with needs and demands that do not receive offi-cial recognition. Submerged interests that find no legitimate expression through some form of participation can result in cleavages that disrupt communication between those in power and the "lower participants." A case in point is Caudill's (1958) study of a small mental hospital where such a situation led to "mutual withdrawal" among various categories of staff and patients. Also illustrative are the various anomic move-ments — violent street demonstrations, palace coups, gang activity — typical of many underdeveloped areas. These activi-ties express demands and interests that the political system can not absorb. The disenfranchised, demonstrating in the streets, can be thrown a bone; given a vote, they may demand more meat. Consequently, collective outbursts, viewed from the per-spective of the larger society, personify a divisive and demor-alizing tendency. At the same time, these outbursts can be used to advance certain purposes. In that case they are given official sanction and assume a more conventionalized form — witness the use of the short protest strike in some countries. One also notes that the collective paranoia of a nation in war time is considered irrational only after the nation has had a chance to "sober up." Those old enough to have been subjected to the surfeit of movies made during World War II are re-minded of this fact time and again as they watch late movies on television.

To summarize the general argument thus far: we began with a definition of morale as continued performance and coordina-tion of roles in situations of stress. Morale has individual, interpersonal, and sociological components. Demoralization in-volves the progressive weakening of affective ties and commitment to group goals and values. In a group suffering extreme demoralization, the members are either incapacitated or psychologically isolated from each other, because the conventionalized defenses that check disintegrative tendencies in a normally functioning group are no longer adequate. During periods of prolonged threat, the level of tension inevitably rises. Effective communication, leadership, and direction keep the threat from being exaggerated, thereby sustaining faith in the protective capacity of the group and the viability of its values. Constructive and coordinated preventive or remedial action depends on adequate personal and socially structured defenses.

On the other hand, collective responses that spontaneously arise on an emotional basis, though defensive for the participants, are likely, unless adequately channeled, to disrupt the group effort. Such efforts at reintegration that express the underlying tension and have negative consequences for the larger social system can be divided into three types:

(1) Collective expressions of shared emotional disturbances that do not cope with the threat except on a symbolic level, such as shared psychopathology, mass hysteria, propitiation rituals, chiliastic sects, and so forth;

(2) Reactive reassertions of group norms crystallized around hostile impulses that are displaced on targets (individuals or groups) considered outside the framework of values, such as scapegoating, aggressive crowds, and rioting;

(3) Schismatic tendencies towards mutual withdrawal and increased subgroup solidarity, such as distrust of authority, charges of favoritism, and intensification of cleavages.

Analysis of group reactions to stress, from a sociological perspective, demands assessment of the effects on group morale of each of the following: (1) cohesiveness of the group, i.e., the interpersonal fabric; (2) organizational structure; and (3) the stress situation.

This paper provides no such definitive framework; it indicates only some implications of variables in the stress situation.

67

The Stress Situation

The focus here is on stress originating in *external* disturbance (in particular, disasters such as floods, hurricanes, and
enemy attacks) rather than with stress generated internally (by
succession crises, mass unemployment, adaptations to new technology, and so forth). The distinction is sometimes hard to
uphold inasmuch as it is sometimes difficult to locate the origin
of the stress. Still the distinguishing criterion of external stress
would seem to be some identifiable source of danger originating from *without* the social system threatened.

Differences in group reaction to disaster reflect differences
in disaster characteristics: Was there a long-lasting alert or did
the disaster strike unexpectedly? Were there relevant prece-
dents in the experience of the group members? Were the
effects felt by all alike or to varying degrees by various members and subgroups? Based on the answers to these questions,
disasters can be classified as: *anticipated* or *unanticipated,*
depending on whether there was a warning period before
impact; *unprecedented* or *recurrent,* depending on whether
similar disasters have struck the population before; *undiscriminating or discriminating,* depending on how evenly its effects
are experienced. The three attributes used result in eight
categories of disasters, i.e., a two-by-two-by-two classification.

Research on the impact of disaster has shown that collective adaptations to losses incurred do vary. A disaster that is
completely unanticipated, unprecedented, and undiscriminating will in all likelihood create the greatest amount of disorganization and therefore poses the greatest threat to morale. Since it is unanticipated, it will upset cognitive expectations. If it is unprecedented, the population is not likely
to have available adequate role models for behavior. An undamaged sector capable of rendering reassurance and aid pre-
supposes some discrimination in effect. But a group struck
by an unanticipated, unprecedented, and undiscriminating
disaster is largely dependent on outside support. Individuals
still able to function tend to direct their aid to small sub-

groups — primarily to those near them. Irrespective of their heroism, however, many lose sight of the larger picture. Both resources and organizational perspectives are to a large degree introduced from the "outside."

Most disasters are neither so unexpected, so unprecedented, nor so undiscriminating in their effects. Some that pose a threat to the group as a whole may be anticipated though unprecedented — for example, a bombing raid following a declaration of war. Others, though not precisely anticipated, are not without precedent. In mining communities, for instance, certain disasters occur frequently. Though without precise warning, it is actually less a "disaster" than a recurrent problem with which communities learn to live and against which they make provision. Stress on the group is thereby minimized.

Since most disasters either are to some extent anticipated or recur more than once, some "learning" usually occurs in the predisaster period during which remedial actions can be rehearsed. In turning attention to the so-called predisaster period, one must therefore differentiate between a period of alert and a period of threat. In an unanticipated disaster, there may be some warning, but the very short interval before impact allows little time for any organizational preparation save emergency measures. Where disaster exists as a threat before it strikes, adaptations made during the predisaster period influence reactions to and ability to cope with the effects of the disaster. Where threat has existed for some time, the warning is a signal for immediate mobilization of resources held in reserve for the emergency. To be sure, the collective capacity to withstand stress is now subject to its ultimate test, but manifestations of demoralization and of collective defenses will already have occurred in the period of threat and not only in response to the impact.

A conceptual distinction between *crisis* and *attrition* seems useful here. A crisis develops as a sudden or unexpected increase in threat brings a group to a breaking point. When a breaking point is approached as a result of cumulative exposure to a threat, the stress is due primarily to attrition. Distinctions of this sort are always muddied by reality. Certainly long-standing threat can flare into a crisis when it is redefined as imminent, as happened when the "permanent" threat of a possible nuclear war between the United States and the Soviet Union suddenly metamorphosed into a real possibility during the Cuban crisis of 1962. Conversely, an alert of impending "crisis" may merely represent one more incident in a series of threats, one coming after the other. Together these crises represent an attrition situation. What is significant, however, is the differing nature of the adaptive responses, depending on whether the stress is an effect of crisis or attrition.

First, the length of the learning period in the two situations obviously differs. The longer the period of anticipation, the greater the opportunities for learning through a kind of mental and actual rehearsal of what to do when the anticipated threat materializes. In this respect, crisis situations are clearly inferior to attrition and therefore the problems of disorganization are hypothetically greater.

Second, the focus toward which adaptive responses are directed differs in the two situations. Both involve efforts to prevent and minimize the disruptive effects of threatened disaster. But attention in the crisis centers on countering demoralization directly related to disaster — assuring people that all will be done to protect them, making provisions for the re-establishment of communication and essential services. Attrition effects, by contrast, entail an accommodation to the *threat* as well. Besides learning how to prevent or counter the threatened disaster, there is the problem of learning how to "live with" the threat as such, i.e., the problem of "emotional adaptation."

Third, the prolonged anxiety characteristic of attrition also contributes toward demoralization. To say that the threat of disaster is sometimes greater than the actual disaster is almost a truism. Waiting for the bombs to fall can seem almost as unnerving as the impact of the bomb itself. It is not only sudden disaster that changes the reward structure and disrupts interpersonal ties that weld a group together. Studies of units in combat, of repeated exposure to bombing raids, and of extreme situations (such as prisons or concentration camps) indicate that continuing exposure to danger has cumulative effects that ultimately impair effectiveness. Cumulative exposure to danger can lead to denying the reality of the danger. It gives rise to protective actions that are clearly inappropriate. In the same way an exaggerated perception of the threat induces people to seek reassurance by reactive and precipitous behavior that displaces attention from the real threat.

Fourth, and apropos of reactions to the threat of disaster as distinct from its actual occurrence, the perception of probable effects as manageable and predictable tends to act as a brake on demoralization. If "danger mobilizes the emergency resources of an organism," as an analogy taken from physiology would lead us to believe, this same response can be expected from a group only as long as the threat is not seen as overwhelming. A threat defined as unmanageable induces terror that leads to demoralization. Accounts of the "airship panic" of 1913 in England or the reaction to the radio drama about the invasion of Martians illustrate inappropriate response to what was collectively defined as danger not about to be mastered.

The worst kind of threat is the generalized dread of the unknown. Preparatory responses seem possible when the extent of pain, injury, damage, or loss can be roughly estimated and the occurrence of disaster nearly pinpointed in time and place. In the absence of official pronouncements along these lines, populations are likely to externalize their own fear, thereby making the threat more specific.

"On the Beach" to "Fail-Safe"

Collective responses to the prolonged threat of nuclear war have reflected changing definitions of the nature of threat.

More specifically, American opinions on whether nuclear war can be prevented, or its consequences made "manageable," can be related to fluctuations in morale and to characteristic defenses against demoralization. This broad hypothesis could be put to empirical test. Lacking the evidence, one can perhaps go out on a limb and suggest a line of analysis.

1. One is probably on firm ground in expecting nuclear war to be widely defined as a fundamentally unmanageable disaster. It would certainly be unprecedented, and its effects — except for the knowledge gained from two low-yield bombs dropped in Japan and from nuclear testing — are not precisely predictable. The warning period would be short, at most a few hours, offering few opportunities for individual escape. The lack of fully protective shelter also means that the effects would be relatively undiscriminating.

2. Nevertheless the definitions of probable consequences (for oneself as well as for others) vary from person to person and from group to group. The greater the anxiety, the less the willingness to work through in detail the anticipated consequences. Presumably this proposition would hold both for individuals and for groups and communities with different levels of anxiety.

3. Perceptions of nuclear conflict as imminent and inevitable, or as a remote possibility that can be prevented, do not depend directly on the definition of its effects as "manageable." They are greatly influenced by events, particularly those that reflect on the degree of amity in Soviet-American relations. They also vary with degree of identification with the foreign policy pursued by the government.

4. Definitions of the effects of nuclear war as either manageable or unmanageable, and of its occurrence as either avoidable or inevitable, permit the construction of a fourfold typology of the nature of the threat. The likelihood of an instrumental response directed toward the actual danger would be greatest if the disaster was seen as *avoidable* and the dangers, should they occur, as *manageable*. This is the definition on which foreign policy is officially predicated, and one would in

particular demand such an attitude from those responsible for security measures.

But when internal opposition questions official reassurances, it can provoke other action based on the assumption that war is *inevitable* and its consequences somehow "must be" *manageable*. Uncertainty about true enemy intentions requires the maintenance of both superior resources and security. Reactive responses of all kinds can interfere with efforts to cope with the threat and promote many kinds of precipitous actions. Hence the reassertions of official policy aims are met with distrust, and the resultant schisms interfere with a unitary response. Moreover, the defenses employed may be brittle since some dangers are ignored.

A third category of response seems related to the open admission that the effects of nuclear war are *unmanageable*. There is a refusal to participate in "futile" preparation to minimize the effects should nuclear war occur, and the conviction that war can be *avoided* channels all activity toward prevention. The activities of peace groups may reflect high morale but may also express a deviant subgroup consensus that may subvert certain policy aims.

A fourth category of response is based on definitions of nuclear war as *unmanageable* and *inevitable*. Among this group, demoralization is likely to take the form of political apathy and high susceptibility, when aroused, to collective outbursts.

5. The effects on morale of the prolonged threat of nuclear holocaust are reflected in the degree of cohesiveness and willingness to join in prevention and defense efforts. The specific manifestations of demoralization and collective defense in response to what has been dubbed "atomic jitters" have depended on the existing issues and on the targets available. Examples cited to illustrate the demoralizing effects of long-standing threat have been numerous. Among them are: scattered panic reactions to unexplained noises; mass apathy in the face of civil-defense efforts to stir up interest in the fallout program; scanty publicity and lack of support for the various peace

movements; mass hysteria in the McCarthy period; scattered clashes between peace demonstrators and others intolerant of such efforts; the bruhaha over private air-raid shelter ethics. (Is it good form to shoot my neighbor if he tries to enter my fallout shelter?) But although many fads, rumors, gang and political violence have been related to anxieties generated by living with threat, their actual dependence on the existence of a prolonged threat has been difficult to pinpoint.

6. Specifically in the 1960's, however, one begins to detect a change in the perception of the threat as more "manageable" and "avoidable." Manifestations of demoralization tied to atomic threat have declined. Public reaction to the Cuban affair in 1962 indicates that the heightening of the threat promoted solidarity, however briefly.

7. If this hypothesized shift in definition has actually occurred, it can be attributed in part to the weathering of past crises. During the direct confrontation of the United States and the Soviet Union over Cuba, the threat became highly definite. It then appeared to have been displaced by concern over whether or not the Cuban bases were being dismantled. With the lessening of the crisis, specific fears aroused by the possibility that Khrushchev and Castro would refuse to comply with American demands became less salient. Furthermore, official reassurances have recently been backed by unambiguous statements of United States superiority in the arms race. The controversies over fallout-shelter programs, the test-ban treaty, open discussion over how many could be expected to survive a nuclear attack and other events have all had their subtle impact on current definitions of the nuclear threat. The shift in definition of the threat as "manageable" and "preventable" rather than "unmanageable" and "inevitable" seems well illustrated in the themes of two very popular novels concerned with nuclear disaster: *On the Beach* and *Fail-Safe*. The earlier book, by Nevil Shute, ended with the total destruction of the world. In Burdick and Wheeler's more recent best-seller, the ending was much "happier": the Russian and American leaders "prevent" total holocaust by sacrificing all New Yorkers (all

the Muscovites having already been destroyed through a "mistake"). The danger thus becomes more specific, and indiscriminate destruction becomes preventable so that all stand a chance to escape.

8. As a consequence, the anxieties aroused by the prolonged threat turn the thoughts of many people to the problem of how they, as individuals, can escape. During the Cuban crisis Khrushchev and Castro were ridiculed, but wrath was occasionally turned on peace demonstrators. Many individuals quietly made plans with their friends to evacuate. There was little public debate on the full magnitude of the threat. Observations such as these must remind us that the management of the prolonged threat and repeated crisis could interfere with an adaptive response should disaster become real. What may appear, superficially, as a turn toward solidarity is in actuality a most precarious state of morale.

References

CAUDILL, W. A. *The Psychiatric Hospital as a Small Society.* Cambridge, Mass.: Harvard University Press, 1958.

ERIKSON, E. H. *Childhood and Society.* New York: W. W. Norton, 1950.

GLUCKMAN, M. *Order and Rebellion in Tribal Africa.* New York: The Free Press of Glencoe, 1963.

JACQUES, E. Social systems as a defense against persecutory and depressive anxiety. In M. Klein et al. (Eds.), *New Directions in Psychoanalysis.* New York: Basic Books, 1956.

KILLIAN, L. M. The significance of multiple group membership in disaster. *Amer. J. Sociol.,* 1952, 57, 3–14.

LANG, K., and LANG, G. E. *Collective Dynamics.* New York: Thomas Y. Crowell, 1961.

MENZIES, I. E. P. Case-study in the functioning of social systems as a defense against anxiety. *Human Relations,* 1960, *13,* 95–121.

QUARANTELLI, E. L. Nature and conditions of panic. *Amer. J. Sociol.,* 1954, *60,* 267–275.

STOUFFER, S. A., et al. *The American Soldier.* Vol. 2. Princeton, N.J.: Princeton University Press, 1949.

STRECKER, E. A. *Beyond the Clinical Frontier.* New York: W. W. Norton. 1940.

PART THREE

REACTION PATTERNS TO THE SIGNAL

HARRY B. WILLIAMS

HUMAN FACTORS IN
WARNING-AND-RESPONSE SYSTEMS

THIS PAPER is based upon studies of natural disasters
and civil-defense false alarms. Its purpose is to tease from
these data a way of looking at warning as a system involving
the origin, coding, and transmission of information about the
existence of possible or probable danger, together with responses to, and feedback from responses to this information.
This differs from looking at warning as if it were only the
issuance of a warning message, or the transmission of such a
message, or the behavior of the sender or receiver of such a
message. The main points are: (1) whether warning is successful or not depends upon whether the people who need it
receive it, and how they react to it; (2) how people react to
warning depends upon their background experiences and their
current social and physical situations, as these factors interact
with the information they are receiving about the danger situation; and (3) the information they receive about the danger
situation, or whether they receive it at all, depends, in turn,
importantly upon the behavior of other people that are involved in the detection, interpretation, and relaying of danger
information to them.

This analysis is based upon warning systems that involve a
high degree of human activity. Only brief attention is devoted
to the hypothetical situation of warning of an impending thermonuclear attack, and none to the problem of the cold war
as a type of warning situation. Nor is account taken directly

of highly mechanized or automated systems in which the human behavioral variables discussed herein are presumably minimized. This paper simply presents a model of the warning process, conceived of *as if* it were a communication system, as it operates in natural disasters in which a period of forewarning is possible. It is hoped that the attempt to see the various elements in relation to each other has general utility.

Because of the major concern with warning considered as a system, the choice made here is to cover the major aspects of the warning process, rather than to concentrate on a few, and to cover the abstract material at the expense of additional illustration and documentation.

Warning Defined

Warning is defined for present purposes as the transmission to individuals, groups, or populations of messages which provide them with information about (1) the existence of danger, and (2) what can be done to prevent, avoid, or minimize the danger.

This definition begs an important question. Warning might be defined as the transmission of information about the existence of danger, but not information on what to do about the danger. This has, in fact, been the philosophy of some warning officials. The present definition, however, combines these elements and regards warning as a process, not as any discrete message or act.

Warning Considered as a System

Beginning 36 hours before the peak of the 1957 storm that destroyed Lower Cameron Parish, Louisiana (Hurricane Audrey), Weather Bureau messages had begun to advise people in "low exposed places" to evacuate to "higher ground." No more than two-fifths of the people heeded the warning. Between four and five hundred people were killed. Why?

If one thinks of warning only in terms of the issuance of a

message, it does not lead very far toward the answer. If one thinks of the warning issued in relation to the frame of reference of the people receiving it, he gets much further. In this case, for example, one of the factors contributing to the failure to evacuate was the use of the terms "low exposed places" and "higher ground." Most of the land in Lower Cameron Parish is at sealevel or below. It is traversed by ridges or *cheniers*, however, which run from 6 to 12 feet above sea level. In every meaningful sense in their daily lives these ridges are "high ground" to these people. When some of them left the beaches to take refuge on the *cheniers*, they had evacuated "the low exposed places," as instructed.

Thus, a given warning message may have different meanings to different people, depending upon their local circumstances and experiences.

On the other hand, if one thinks of warning only in terms of the local circumstances of the recipients, he may not get the whole picture. In the same disaster, local sources in Lake Charles put out a broadcast at 10 p.m. on the night of the disaster, saying there was no cause for alarm that night. This was done without the knowledge or approval of the Weather Bureau. It was meant, apparently, for people in Lake Charles some 60 miles away. Yet many people in Lower Cameron Parish heard it on their radios, took it as a message for them, and went to bed feeling they would not have to decide about evacuation until the next day.

Thus, misinformation may get into a warning system. Misinformation was received, on this occasion, by people for whom the message was not even intended by the sender. But this made it no less potent for the recipients. The message put into the system may depend upon the *sender's* local circumstances and frame of reference.

The 10 p.m. broadcast from Lake Charles illustrates nicely the problem of the "boundaries of systems" and how vague and permeable these may be in a disaster in an age of mass communication. One couple in Lower Cameron Parish reported that they were in the second story of their house, listening to the tuned-up radio of their car, parked below. As the water rose and drowned out the radio, the announcer was saying — from Port Arthur, Texas, some 40 miles away — that there was nothing to worry about.

The message that eventually reaches the threatened people and which, in interaction with local and background circumstances, helps to determine their reaction may be much influenced by the confidence a warning official has in the scientific information he is receiving in the first instance. It may be influenced by the policy of an agency concerning whether or when to warn people. It may be delayed, distorted, or blocked by the information, training, or emotions of some individual at a relay point, such as a telephone switchboard.

All of these points, and many more, concerning the interrelationships in a system of warning and response can be clearly, and in many cases abundantly, illustrated in actual disasters and civil defense false alerts.

It is useful to analyze warning as a system involving all the components, relationships, and processes which affect the determination and estimation of danger, the formulation or selection and the transmission of warning messages, the way people interpret and act upon warning messages, and the effect which public responses to a warning have upon (1) the next warnings issued, (2) the systems which issued the warnings, and (3) the public itself. These relationships are partly indicated in brief, schematic, and oversimplified form in Figure 1.

Warning processes involve the following steps:

1. Detection and measurement or estimation of changes in the environment which could result in a danger of one sort or another.

2. Collation and evaluation of the incoming information about environmental changes.

3. Decisions on who should be warned, about what danger, and in what way.

4. Transmission of a warning message, or messages, to those whom it has been decided to warn.

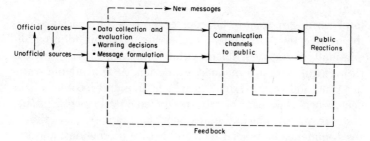

FIGURE 1. *Model of warning-and-response system.*

5. Interpretation of the warning message by the recipients and action by the recipients.
6. Feedback of information about the interpretation and actions of recipients to the issuers of warning messages.
7. New warnings, if possible and desirable, corrected in terms of responses to the first warning messages.

Other desirable feedbacks may be involved in the system: (1) feedback from the source that is issuing messages to the public to the source from which it receives the messages (e.g., so that the Weather Bureau knows whether the message it sends to the mass media is being relayed accurately) and (2) feedback concerning public reception and responses to the source issuing messages to the public (e.g., a radio or television station).

Eventually the outcomes of a given danger situation and the part that warning is believed to have played may affect the systems that issued the warnings, thus affecting warnings that may be given in future danger. The effects of the event itself, the warnings, and the public's responses may, of course, influence the public's reactions to any future similar events. These are slower, but still important, forms of feedback (which are not, for simplicity's sake, introduced into Figure 1.

Collecting Warning Data

The environment produces the initial information which must be interpreted as indicating danger and must be coded into warning messages. Of course, the type of disaster affects the opportunity to collect and issue warning information. Gradually rising river floods differ from flash floods, and hurricanes differ from tornadoes, in the length of available warning time and in the extent to which time and location of the occurrence of impact can be predicted in advance. This uncertainty about time and place may affect, among other things, the confidence an official feels in his own predictions; and this complicates his decisions on whether, when, and how to warn people. Thus nature, at the outset, affects the functioning of the warning system by the characteristics of her initial inputs.

Both official and unofficial sources may collect warning information and in many cases both may originate and transmit warning messages to the public. The United States Weather Bureau is an example *par excellence* of an official source, having responsibility, organization, specialized knowledge, and equipment for predicting dangers. Unofficial or informal sources lack this responsibility and specialization. Among unofficial sources, however, there may be persons and groups with some specialized orientation or competence concerning a given danger. Among formal community agencies, there may be some that have (or that people expect to have) responsibility for giving warning but which possess no specialized competence in predicting danger. Official and unofficial sources may interact. For example, official agencies often receive and evaluate messages from unofficial sources.

In disasters where there is a period of forewarning – and this may be a relatively short period — much warning information is spread informally. Within the populations there are usually people who are especially sensitive to certain kinds of environmental changes, and who are more capable than the population in general of detecting and interpreting signs of danger from a certain source.

In the Holland flood of 1953, some person who had responsibility or occupational orientation in connection with the water – such as a municipal workman who tended the flood boards, or a fisherman – was usually first to recognize the danger (Instituut voor Sociaal Onderzoek, 1955). Previous experience with the agent of danger also may create such sensitivity and capability.

Thus, more sensitive or capable people warn others, and informal communication processes and nets emerge for interpreting and disseminating information about changes in the environment. This process continues even into the impact period of violent disasters.[*]

Both the structure and the content of information carried in such informal nets may be influenced by predisaster social organization and culture. Thus, for example, when flood threatened people in Piedras Negras, Mexico, residents were more prone than were their neighbors across the Rio Grande, in Eagle Pass, Texas, to rely upon informal communication among kin and neighbors, and less prone to rely upon the warnings of officials or mass media (Clifford, 1955).

There is not space to elaborate further this interesting and instructive aspect of the warning problem. Needless to say, however, when there is more than one source collecting and reporting warning data, and when, as is often the case, several such sources of initial information also have access to channels that transmit their information to the public, opportunities are created for distortion, attenuation, and contradiction in warning information, as well as for redundancy. The twin arrows in Figure 1 represent these possibilities.

That these complications can create problems is obvious. The problem of evaluating the data is complicated, as is control over warning information reaching the public. On the

---

[*] NORC investigators report that when White County, Arkansas, was struck by a tornado, 33 per cent of the sample of the county as a whole reported a forewarning of more than one minute and 36 per cent reported no warning. In one area within the county, Holdingville, 53 per cent reported a forewarning of more than one minute and only 18 per cent reported no forewarning. This is attributed by the investigators to chance factors, including the presence in Holdingville of several individuals who were highly sensitized to storm cues and who tended to alert others to the danger. Much additional data on social interaction during warning, threat, and impact of disaster is included in the NORC study (Marks et al., 1954).

other hand, in a disaster such as the Holland flood, many more lives would undoubtedly have been lost had not warning been spread informally. Of the sample of survivors questioned, 41 per cent said they were warned by private means; 36 per cent were warned by official sources (Instituut voor Sociaal Onderzoek, 1955).

Collation and Evaluation of Incoming Data

When information is received, whatever the source, by a person or unit that has or assumes responsibility for issuing warnings, these data have to be collated and evaluated. Evaluation involves such questions as: Is the information reliable? If some or all of it is from unofficial sources, are these sources reliable? What do the data imply in terms of specific dangers to specific places at specific times?

In addition to the problem of weighing information from unofficial sources, the evaluator may also be faced with incompatible information from more than one official source. The acting mayor of a large American city, for example, was told by one authoritative agency that the dikes in the city would hold against a flood, and by another authoritative agency that they would not (University of Oklahoma Research Institute, 1953).

This example calls attention to another fascinating aspect of the problem of warning in many disasters: it was the acting mayor of the town who had to evaluate these data and decide whether to order evacuation of certain districts of the town. This type of responsibility often falls to the occupant of an office who has no special competence or responsibility for making decisions about probable dangers. In Holland, those who first sensed danger usually reported to the burgomaster of the village or else to some superior official in their own organization. In some cases, people seemed to feel that only the burgomaster could make a decision about warning.

When an east coast town was threatened by a hurricane in 1953, the Weather Bureau, the Coast Guard, and the State Police all felt the town should be evacuated. The decision was left in the final analysis, however, to the mayor (Rayner, 1953). The political structure often takes precedence over the systems or subsystems with specialized competence.

The Warning Decision

The discussion still relates to the upper left-hand box in Figure 1. Given data concerning the probability or possibility of danger of a certain type, at a certain place, at a certain time, someone has to decide whom, if anybody, to warn and how to warn them. Some systems are highly preplanned and may depend upon a single abstract signal, such as a siren. If the danger is unforeseen, or develops gradually, or involves a complicated rather than a single source of danger, or if the population has not previously been instructed in protective actions, then a verbal message will probably be formulated.

As has already been mentioned, unofficial sources may detect signs of danger and transmit warnings informally, or even get them into channels of mass communication or into signal systems such as the ringing of bells. Information does not always go neatly through a series of boxes labeled "evaluation," "warning decision," and so forth. However, in many situations an official warning agency or a formal agency or personage of some sort does have a large degree of control over the warnings that get issued. Furthermore, the knowledge that warning information is being transmitted informally at the same time does not detract from the responsibility of an agency like the Weather Bureau to decide what information it should issue.

The warning decision involves such questions as: (1) Is the danger really going to materialize to a certain degree at a certain place? (2) When will it strike and how much warning do people need to take protective action? (3) What will be the consequences if it strikes and there is no warning? (4) Will it do any good to give warning? Is there time to take protective action? (5) How will people behave if they are warned? (6) How will people behave if they are not warned?

On a "sticky June day" in 1953, officials in the Boston Weather Bureau first began to talk among themselves at 8 o'clock in the morning about the possibilities of a tornado. Though the situation continued to grow more threatening during the day, the term "tornado" was included in a message to the public only at 5:45 p.m. This was at about the same time that the tornado was dying out, after having struck Worcester and five other communities. Analysis of John Brooks' (1955) detailed story of this day indicates several factors that contributed to the officials' not issuing an earlier warning. Analogous factors are often found in other warning situations.

1. They could not know for sure that there would be a tornado. Their input of scientific information was not sufficiently precise.
2. They did not receive reports of actual tornadoes. (It is reported that this tornado was accompanied by so much debris and heavy wind that the vortex cloud was not actually seen by many people.)
3. On the basis of past experience, they did not expect tornadoes in that part of the country.
4. Their scientific observations, at least in the morning and around midday, were belied by their sense perceptions — the weather around them did not look so bad as the charts implied.
5. The system (i.e., the Weather Bureau), apparently as a policy [at that time], inhibited the issuance of unambiguous warnings. The forecasters were not to use the word "tornado." The system was blocked from the use of this word by fear that panic would result (at least among those who were not close to cyclone cellars) if the people were warned of a tornado.

This last point is especially interesting. The system is acting in terms of the anticipated consequences of its own output, the anticipation in this case being based upon a stereotype about how human beings act when warned of impending danger.*

Not only policies against the issuing of warning, but also ambiguity about what the policies are, can delay the issuance of warnings, as can ambiguity about who in the system has authority and responsibility to initiate such a message.

One also suspects that in the Worcester, Massachusetts, tornado and in other instances, another factor may have operated against issuance of the warning. This is what the investigators of the Dutch Flood called "the psychological inability to accept the possibility of a completely devastating disaster" (Instituut voor Sociaal Onderzoek, 1955).

Anticipation of behavioral consequences may also influence the warning decision in other ways. If the decision maker decides against issuing a warning, and death and destruction occur, will he not be blamed? May he not even be blamed unreasonably? If he decides to issue a warning and the danger does not materialize, may he not be criticized by some people for "getting people upset"?

Transmission of Warning to the Public

Warnings flow to the public through informal and unofficial channels, and this may serve useful purposes as well as create problems. In a natural disaster when an official has decided to issue warnings, they may be transmitted by a variety of means: television and radio, sirens or other signals, or police or other officials going from door to door or using loudspeakers.

Different channels of communication may have different de-

---

* Although this paper is aimed at analyzing the relationships in warning conceived as a system and not at reporting the over-all findings of disaster research, pause must be taken to note that it is a misleading stereotype. Mass panic occurs very rarely in disaster. When it does, it occurs under certain special circumstances. These are not likely to be the circumstances in most warning situations (Committee on Disaster Studies, 1955; Fritz and Williams, 1957; Quarantelli, 1954).

grees of authoritativeness or credibility for the recipients. And formal and informal channels may differ in the authoritativeness or credibility accorded them. These differences may vary in relation to the culture and social structure of the population — in one population, informal communication from kinfolk may be more readily believed than messages from officials; in another, officials may be given higher credence.

The use of multiple channels for transmitting warnings may increase the chances of reaching all the intended recipients. The resulting redundancy may be more successful in getting the message through noise and in getting it attended to. On the other hand, multiple channels increase the chances of errors.

When the message is issued by an agency such as the Weather Bureau to the transmitting medium, it has, of course, lost direct control over that message. Although there is no evidence that the wording of a message has been changed in its relay through the mass media, information can be added to or subtracted from the message by the context in which it is placed. For example, the nonverbal behavior of a television announcer reading a tornado warning has been reported by disaster researchers as carrying a message of fear and urgency beyond the verbal content of the message. Useful information may be added if, for example, a television announcer uses a map to show viewers which towns and villages are in an area demarcated as threatened by tornado.

Many warning systems involve the relay of warning messages through subpoints. The existence of these subpoints likewise increases the chances of delay, distortion, attenuation, contradiction, and even blocking of the message. There is not space to elaborate this complex problem fully. An impressive number of factors can work to delay or block the relay of the warning signal. These include structural characteristics of the communication system, lack of "memory" at key points in the system, ambiguities in the warning message itself, lack of experience and instructions for interpreting and relaying the message, pre-existing social factors such as interagency relationships, psychological expectations and emotional needs of human operators, and lack of feedback within the system.

Among the important psychological variables in the operation of a warning system involving human operators is the frequency with which the person receiving a danger message seeks confirmation before relaying it. This subjective need for feedback in a system may affect not only the relaying of the message from a given point to the intended audience, but also the system as a whole, through the overloading or bypassing of key points. It is most difficult for human beings to operate "automatically" in a warning system.

Warning Message

In the same way that different persons may react differently to the same warning message, the same person may react differently to two different messages in the same physical and social circumstances. Warning messages can be relatively clear or ambiguous, specific or general, consistent or contradictory; they can be more or less readily interpreted and understood by the audiences for which they are intended; they can have different meanings to different people and be more or less meaningful in relation to the local circumstances of the recipients.

A given warning message may actually contain much warning information or little, depending upon the extent to which it reduces the possible interpretations or alternative actions open to the recipient. In this sense, a message giving the location of the eye of a hurricane, the rate of movement of the storm, and the velocity and reading of the winds contains much less information to the people at a given place on the coast than a message that the tides will rise to a certain level and the winds will reach a certain velocity at a certain time *at that place.*

Ambiguity, contradiction, generality, and incompleteness all permit alternative explanations. Perhaps they invite them.

Of many examples, a favorite is the situation in which the inhabitants of a flood-threatened town heard the following

message from a sound truck: "An all-time record flood is going to inundate the city. You must evacuate immediately.
(Pause) The — — — Theater is presenting two exciting features tonight. Be sure to see these pictures at the — — —
Theater tonight" (Clifford, 1955).

The fellow who broadcast this wondrously contrived invita-
tion to confusion and disbelief must have unthinkingly relayed two different messages — one previously received from
the theater management and one received more recently from
civic officials. The situation was not allowed to continue long,
but it illustrates how various and diverse elements in the situation may operate to affect the messages the public receives
and thus influence public response.

Incompatible messages can cancel or devaluate warning information. In a false alert situation, the alert signal was
sounded in some localities but not in neighboring localities.
A person on the border of two such communities received
two messages — "alert" and "no alert."

It may be helpful to conceptualize *all* the messages issued
during the potential danger period as *one* message. Suppose a
radio listener hears a special bulletin stating that there is a
possibility of a tornado in his area and then later hears the
regular forecast which states that tomorrow will be fair and
warmer and the expected high temperature is 80 degrees. The
first half of "the" message said tornadoes are possible; the
second half — by saying nothing at all about tornadoes and
talking about normal weather conditions — may have said,
to the listener, that the danger was past.

These considerations are especially important when it is
considered that most people would rather believe they are
safe than in danger. If the warning information is ambiguous,
they are, by and large, more likely to make the optimistic interpretation. If it is further considered that the character of
the warning messages ultimately issued may be affected by the
factors previously discussed concerning official and unofficial
sources of warning, the collection and evaluation of the data,
the decision about warning, the transmissions of messages to

the public, and the characteristics of warning nets and their relay points, then the value of considering warning as a system is indicated.

Public Reaction to Warning

The attempt to consider the various aspects of warning as a system does not leave ample space to consider the respectable body of literature and unpublished material, both theoretical and empirical, which now exists on public responses in warning situations.

A large variety of factors and pieces of information may enter into the way a person interprets a danger situation and, therefore, how he responds.

Following are some statements of victims of Hurricane Audrey:* "At ten o'clock that night they told the people to go to bed and get a good night's sleep at their homes, the storm would not strike until late Thursday evening or Thursday night." "We kept hearin' in Galveston there was a storm. We thought, well, gee, they've skipped us, this is the worst it's gonna be." "Oh, I told them, it's gonna be just like 1918. It can't get no worse." "Wednesday I put sticks in the edge of the water and watched them. The water didn't come no higher on them." "Never did think of leaving. We listened to TV and it seemed like it wasn't so rough."

Often the same person gives several such explanations in the same interview. They may seem logically inconsistent, and certainly they are often meteorologically inconsistent, but there is a certain psychological consistency. One factor, one piece of information, or one bit of experience seems to be added to another until an answer comes out. These people in Hurricane Audrey — as in other disasters — were taking a number of messages and trying to make them add up into

---

* All the direct quotations from Hurricane Audrey reproduced herein were collected for the Disaster Research Group by staff members Charles E. Fritz and Jeannette F. Rayner or by collaborators Hiram J. Friedsam, A. S. Foley, or Harry E. Moore.

one message that said to them clearly either "stay" or "get out."

The way an individual responds to warning is apparently a function of the way he defines the situation. This definition seems to include the following factors: strength of threat (how likely is the danger to materialize, and how serious will be the loss if it does?), the time element (how long will it be before one has to decide, and how long will it require to take effective protective action?), the cost of taking protective actions (economic, psychological, social), the presumed effectiveness of available countermeasures (will they do any good against the threat?) (see Withey, 1962).

These factors are interrelated — e.g., if the strength of the threat is great enough, the cost is given less weight.

It is not implied that this response is a conscious, coldly calculating process. Unconscious and irrational factors may enter. Repressive denial and even perceptual distortion of incoming information may occur. In any event, as indicated earlier, most people would rather believe they are safe than in danger. If the warning information is not clear or is contravened by other information — such as, for example, disbelief by influential people in the group receiving the warning — the definition of the situation is likely at least to lead to delay in action while further information is sought. Often it leads to no action. The burden of proof seems to be on the warning system — except in those situations where it has been specifically and carefully designed, taught, and practiced in relation to a conceivable, clearly defined danger and defined courses of protective action.

The definition of the situation seems to be influenced by a number of sets of factors. These include the warning messages received from one or more sources and through one or more channels. As suggested earlier, the clarity and consistency of the message influence the responses, as do the credibility and authoritativeness of the sources from which the warnings come.

Another set of inputs is informal social communication involving the current actions, opinions, and information of other people. In a study of Federal employees exposed to a false air-raid warning, seventy-five people who were present reported that they "talked it over with others."* This is consistent with the studies of natural disasters where there was a period of forewarning. This process of social interaction can lead to greater or to less belief in the validity of the warning. The Federal employee study suggests that this process can be utilized and its outcome affected by preplanning and training.

Another set of inputs is personal observation. People look at the skies or the river, for example, and try to form their own judgment of the seriousness of the situation. They also look at the behavior of others to see whether they seem to be taking it seriously.

These inputs are evaluated and interpreted in relation to the individual's and group's previous experience with the same or similar dangers, and in relation to current and immediately preceding social, personal, and physical situations. For example, action is influenced by whether one is separated from loved ones and whether there seems to be a chance to get to them before the danger strikes.

Social and cultural background variables influence people's interpretations. For example, do they belong to a culture in which momentous decisions — such as evacuating one's home — are usually made only on the advice, or with the sanction, of family elders?

Except where action must be taken very quickly, the interpretation of warning and the decision on how to act usually involve seeking additional information from the other sources, official or unofficial, or both. Where it is possible, a decision may involve the actual testing of possible courses of action. In short, interpretation of and reaction to warning is not a

---

* The only published material from this study is contained in Mack and Baker (1961). The original sources, which are also relied upon in this presentation, are unpublished. They are Williams and Baker (1959) and Baker (1959).

simple or automatic process, except in those situations where reflexive action, or at least very rapid action, is required. It is a complex and, if time and a group of people are involved, usually a highly social process.

Feedback to the Warning Source

When warnings have been issued, the issuing source needs to know what effects the warnings have had: Are they being received as intended? Are they being interpreted as intended? What are people doing about them?

It is often extremely difficult to get this feedback information in a disaster situation. There are examples of the issuing of new messages based upon knowledge that the public needed such information. A brilliant example is a city official who, believing that the people were not getting the message on how high the river would rise, went out and painted a yellow band along the store fronts at the predicted high-water mark.

Most disaster and false-alert studies, however, reveal little or no attempt by warning officials to seek feedback and issue new information accordingly. There are few indications that they have thought of it. In many cases there would be time to issue new messages if the desire and the means were available. The model we have used and experience with disaster suggest that it would be both valid and useful to regard warning as at least potentially a circular communication process, rather than simply a linear process.

Feedback continues to occur after the disaster is over. (It may even occur in the form of study by "disaster researchers.") This slow feedback may and does result in changes in the official warning systems and in other systems involved in the presumed effectiveness or ineffectiveness of the warning. There is also, and this is important, feedback to the public that permits it to evaluate the effects of its own actions or lack of action in response to the warnings. More is said of this below.

Some Implications for Building Effective Warning Systems

Experience in natural disasters leads to the conclusion that it is difficult to warn people successfully against impending danger when they have not experienced the predicted danger in recent years and when they cannot directly perceive the signs of danger. There have been relatively effective as well as relatively ineffective warnings, however, and this fact leads to the further conclusion that the success of the warning process can be improved.

Hurricane Donna wreaked one billion dollars' worth of damage in 1960 and cost 17 lives. Hurricane Diane, which had struck nearly the same area in 1955, "did half the damage and killed ten times as many people." Much of the credit, according to an editorial in *Science* (1960), belongs to the improved warning procedures, involving precise information that permitted a person to know whether *he* and *his* house would be in danger, what roads could be safely taken for evacuation, and other specific, useful information.

As indicated previously, no more than two-fifths of the residents of Lower Cameron Parish evacuated before Hurricane Audrey struck in 1957. The next year 75 per cent evacuated in the path of tropical storm Ella, even though Weather Bureau advisories did not at that time advise evacuation. When Hurricane Carla occurred in 1961, 96.6 per cent of the persons interviewed had evacuated the area (Moore et al., 1963).

This experience, as well as other studies, seemed to show clearly that experience that punishes or results in a "near miss" is a great teacher (MacCurdy, 1943; Janis, 1951).

There were other factors, however. Cameron Parish had developed an elaborate plan of evacuation after Hurricane Audrey. Compared to other areas sampled by Moore et al. (1963) in their study of Hurricane Carla, many more of the Cameron Parish residents knew about an evacuation plan and many more said they had been ordered or advised to evacuate.

Thus clarity and specificity of information and instructions about the danger and about the steps to be taken to avoid it seem to increase the probability of effective warning. The existence of a plan of action, known to the populace, seems to increase the effectiveness of warning. Prior thought by the public about conceivable dangers — such as that a dam might burst — also seems to increase the effectiveness (Danzig, Thayer, and Galanter, 1958).

Prior training and practice among the populace and the presence of trained, organized leadership at the time of warning also add to the effectiveness of warning. Studies of reactions to false air-raid warnings in two cities, and among federal employees in Washington, are revealing (Katz, 1960; Mack and Baker, 1961; Scott; Williams and Baker, 1959; Baker, 1959).

In the three samples interviewed, about the same percentage of respondents reported hearing the signals, and roughly the same percentage (from 20 to 33 per cent) believed that the attack might be real. Yet among the federal employees 55 per cent took some sort of protective action, even though it may have been minor action, whereas only 3 and 10 per cent in the two cities took any action. Although other factors were also involved, the evidence strongly suggests that prior instruction and practice in signal recognition and civil-defense procedures, and the existence of civil-defense plans and trained wardens, accounted for much of the difference. This conclusion is strongly supported by comparison of the actions at different locations among the federal agencies in the same study: the following of planned procedures was associated with previous instruction, practice in emergency procedures, and the influence of wardens. This study showed also that people's initial interpretation of a warning signal could be changed — in the direction of taking it more seriously — if they had authoritative sources of additional information or informed co-workers to consult, and that they could be moved to take protective action even though they were not convinced that a real attack was imminent.

The application of these findings to the hypothetical case of warning of an impending thermonuclear attack is risky at best. But certain points emerge with sufficient clarity to warrant emphasis. First is the recognition that *signals* of some sort are not, by themselves, the same thing as a *warning*. Warning, as Charles E. Fritz has said (personal communication), should be a "call to action," not just a sign of danger. This holds true even for an "alert" message, which should convey not just information that there is a possible danger and that one should "stay alert," but also information as to what he should stay alert *to* (e.g., the radio) and *for* (e.g., one or more clearly defined courses of action to be taken when and if certain specific further information is received).

When there is little time to take action after a warning is received, or when means are not available to disseminate instructions for action, the information about *what* to do must be in the hands of the population before the warning signal is given. The warning signal then becomes a message that says, *now* is the time to do it.

The major implication, then, in the writer's judgment, is that the success of a warning about impending thermonuclear attack would be directly related to the extent to which warning is an integral part of carefully planned emergency procedures.* The occurrence of warning signals without some understanding of the action to be taken when they are heard is as useless as having emergency procedures without being able to tell people when to use them.

The great teacher, experience, is not available for warning of thermonuclear attack, but it has been shown that other measures can be taken which probably would increase the success of warnings. Prior instruction in signal recognition and emergency procedures, practice, and a network of trained

---

* This point, in the writer's opinion, applies to most of the major problems of human behavior in attack: "Coping with the problem of human behavior in nuclear attack is not something esoteric and not something different from planning and making ready a total functioning system for national survival and recovery" (Williams, 1960).

leaders and wardens* are methods which have been effective and which can be developed and used in the absence of the real danger. No one can say what percentage of the population could be trained and led to react appropriately to warning signals, but it does appear that this percentage could be substantially increased.

Again, however, the extent of this improvement will be substantially affected by the extent to which emergency procedures actually are available to people. The extent to which they use the procedures, in turn, will be affected not only by their understanding of them, but also by their belief that they do in fact afford some protection. (However, the evidence also indicates that, once they have decided the danger is real, many people will take protective measures which they previously scoffed at.)

Within the area of warning itself, two additional points bear brief mention. One is improvement of the signals. Studies have revealed technical difficulties (e.g., a rotating siren emitting a "steady blast" was heard as a "wailing tone"). They have also revealed that one reason people have often given for not taking action in response to air-raid warnings is that they thought it was a practice signal, or a testing of the signal. Means need to be devised to train people in signal recognition, as well as means of testing signal devices, in order to combat this tendency for repeated hearing of the signal to lead to extinction of its value as a "call to action."

The second point is that people seek and seem to need confirmation of a warning of great danger. When people get a message saying "this is it!" they seem to need a second message which says, "yes, this really *is* it!" This applies to personnel within the warning system as well as to the populace. Persons at relay points, for example, are prone to try to contact the source from which they received the signal to

---

* Elliot Danzig and colleagues (in an unpublished study of a civil-defense drill) showed that personnel such as headwaitresses, bellboys, and elevator operators — called "gatekeepers" by the investigators — could probably be trained for informal leadership roles in a warning situation.

inquire if it is indeed "the real thing" before they relay it. Seventy-five per cent of the Federal employees studied and 77 per cent of the Chicago residents studied sought further information when they heard the sirens. In Oakland, three-fourths of those who thought, even for a moment, that the signal might not be a practice tried to get some further information to confirm the warning. Whether it would be better, in different situations, to try to train these needs out of people, to provide a means of conveying confirmatory second messages, or some combination of the two is a matter that should be studied intensively.

This brief discussion provides only a bare introduction to the problems of devising a successful system of warning against impending attack. The main point is to call attention again to the need for regarding and analyzing warning as a system.

It is customary to close papers with a call for more research. In no instance is this call more valid than in the present subject. Not only is this subject of vital importance, it is also more open to research than are many other problems of disaster behavior. There does not have to be an enemy attack to study many of the problems of warning. A substantial body of research exists upon which to build more rigorous approaches.* The research should include: (1) systems analysis, wherein all the interrelated parts of broad warning systems are traced out and analyzed in relation to each other and to all the foreseeable contingencies; (2) studies and, where possible, tests of known problems of attack warning, such as signal improvement and signal recognition, and the need and possibilities for confirmation of warning; (3) systematic research on the technical, psychological, social, cultural, economic, and situational variables which influence public responses to warnings; (4) studies of the behavior of human

---

* A recent example is the work of Moore et al. (1963) in utilizing Hurricane Carla to test hypotheses derived by Mack and Baker (1961) from an analysis of the false-alert studies in Oakland, Chicago, and Washington.

beings who are parts of warning systems, and how their behavior affects the outputs of those systems; (5) studies of the effectiveness of warnings in each major disaster or threat of disaster and, above all, any additional false air-raid warnings, so as to provide immediate and reliable evaluation of changes being made in the warning systems and to identify any new problems or variables that occur.

References and Suggested Readings

BAKER, G. W. "Operation 4:30: A Survey of Responses to the Washington, D. C. False Air Raid Warning (Technical Report)." Washington, D. C.: National Academy of Sciences — National Research Council, Disaster Research Group, 1959. Prepared for the Office of Civil and Defense Mobilization.

BATES, F. L., FOGLEMAN, C. W., PARENTON, V. J., PITTMAN, R. H., and TRACY, G. S. "The Social and Psychological Consequences of a Natural Disaster: A Longitudinal Study of Hurricane Audrey." Washington, D. C.: National Academy of Sciences — National Research Council, Disaster Study No. 18, 1963.

BLUM, R. H. and KLASS, B. "A Study of Public Response to Disaster Warnings." Menlo Park, California: Stanford Research Institute, 1956.

BROOKS, J. A Reporter at Large: Five-ten on a sticky June day. *The New Yorker*, May 28, 1955, pp. 39 ff.

CLIFFORD, R. A. "Informal Group Activities in the Rio Grande Flood. A Report to the Committee on Disaster Studies." Michigan State College and The University of Texas, 1955. Mimeographed.

CLIFFORD, R. A. "The Rio Grande Flood: A Comparative Study of Border Communities in Disaster." Washington, D. C.: National Academy of Sciences — National Research Council, Disaster Study No. 7, 1956.

Committee on Disaster Studies. *The Problem of Panic.* Washington, D. C.: U.S. Government Printing Office, 1955 (FCDA Technical Bulletin TB-19-2).

DANZIG, E. R., THAYER, P. W., and GALANTER, LILA R. "The Effects of a Threatening Rumor on a Disaster-Stricken Community." Washington, D. C.: National Academy of Sciences — National Research Council, Disaster Study No. 10, 1958.

FRITZ, C. E., and WILLIAMS, H. B. The human being in disasters: A research perspective. *Ann. Amer. Acad. Polit. Soc. Sci.,* 1957 *309,* 42–51.

Instituut voor Sociaal Onderzoek van het Nederlandse Volk. "Studies in Holland Flood Disaster." 4 vols. Amsterdam and Washington, D. C.: Instituut voor Social Onderzoek van het Nederlandse Volk and National Academy of Sciences — National Research Council, Committee on Disaster Studies, 1955.

JANIS, I. L. *Air War and Emotional Stress: Psychological Studies of Bombing and Civil Defense.* New York: McGraw-Hill, 1951.

JANIS, I. L. Psychological effects of warnings. In G. W. Baker and D. W. Chapman (Eds.), *Man and Society in Disaster.* New York: Basic Books, 1962, pp. 55–92.

KATZ, E. "Joy in Mudville: Public Reaction to the Surprise Sounding of Chicago's Air Raid Sirens." Chicago: National Opinion Research Center, 1960. Mimeographed.

KILLIAN, L. M. "Evacuation of Panama City Before 'Hurricane Florence.' " Washington, D. C.: National Academy of Sciences – National Research Council, Committee on Disaster Studies, 1954. Mimeographed.

MACCURDY, J. T. *The Structure of Morale.* New York: Macmillan, 1943.

MACK, R. W., and BAKER, G. W. "The Occasion Instant: The Structure of Social Responses to Unanticipated Air Raid Warnings." Washington, D. C.: National Academy of Sciences – National Research Council, Disaster Study No. 15, 1961.

MARKS, E. S., FRITZ, C. E., and others. "Human Reactions in Disaster Situations." 3 vols. Chicago: National Opinion Research Center, 1954. Typewritten.

MOORE, H. E. *Tornadoes over Texas: A Study of Waco and San Angelo in Disaster.* Austin: University of Texas Press, 1958.

MOORE, H. E., BATES, F. L., LAYMAN, M. V. and PARENTON, V. J. "Before the Wind: A Study of the Response to Hurricane Carla." Washington, D. C.: National Academy of Sciences – National Research Council, Disaster Study No. 19, 1963.

QUARANTELLI, E. L. "A Study of Panic: Its Nature, Types, and Conditions." Unpublished Master's Thesis, University of Chicago, 1953;

QUARANTELLI, E. L. The nature and conditions of panic. *Amer. J. Sociol.,* 1954, *60,* 267–275.

RAYNER, JEANNETTE F. "Hurricane Barbara: A Study of the Evacuation of Ocean City, Maryland, August 1953," Washington, D. C.: National Academy of Sciences – National Research Council, Committee on Disaster Studies, 1953. Mimeographed.

Science. Editorial, October 1960, No. 3432.

SCOTT, W. A. "Public Reactions to a Surprise Civil Defense Alert in Oakland, California." Survey Research Center, Institute for Social Research, University of Michigan, undated.

SPIEGEL, J. P. Psychological transactions in situations of acute stress. In *Symposium on Stress (16–19 March 1953).* Washington, D. C.: Army Medical Service Graduate School, Walter Reed Army Medical Center, 1953, pp. 103–115.

University of Oklahoma Research Institute. "The Kansas City Flood and Fire of 1951." Chevy Chase, Maryland: Operations Research Office, The Johns Hopkins University, Technical Memorandum ORO-T-203, 1953.

WILLIAMS, H. B. Some functions of communication in crisis behavior. *Human Organization,* 1957, *16* (2), 15–19.

WILLIAMS, H. B. The human factor in national survival. *Canad. Army J.,* 1960, *14* (4), 24–31.

WILLIAMS, H. B., and BAKER, G. W. "Operation 4:30: A Survey of Responses to the Washington, D. C. False Air Raid Warning (Summary Report)." Washington, D. C.: National Academy of Sciences – National Research Council, Disaster Research Group, 1959. Prepared for the Office of Civil and Defense Mobilization.

WITHEY, S. B. Reaction to uncertain threat. In G. W. Baker and D. W. Chapman, *Man and Society in Disaster.* New York: Basic Books, 1962, pp. 93–123.

STEPHEN B. WITHEY

SEQUENTIAL ACCOMMODATIONS
TO THREAT

AT ONE TIME or another organisms face sustained stress, and quite a bit is known about the forms of adaptive response. Those organisms that are advanced enough to respond to distant early warnings also face frequent threats. There is a considerable temptation to regard these responses to threat as somehow overlapping reactions to more present danger. Perhaps there is some similarity or parallel between patterns of adjustive effort that are aroused by distal conditions and those that are reactive to proximal dangers.

There is no reason to assume that any similarity in the responses to stress and to threat would entail a physiological identity. There could be a behavioral parallel in anticipatory responses. The similarity could exist in a structural or functional analysis of cognitive functions. One might search even more abstract levels for equivalence of processes.

A traditional approach to stress behavior regards reactions as a series of increasingly expensive mechanisms of defense, expensive in that increasingly they slow down the rate of recovery and increasingly they invade the critical resources of the organism that are needed for survival. These mechanisms or tactics of defense are initiated serially (with overlap in their maintenance) as preliminary measures fail to handle the demands created by the stressor. Eventually stress is alleviated by the success of some defense in the hierarchy of defense tactics or the cessation of stress conditions owing to environmental factors.

Ashby (1952) proposes some elements of such a model when he refers to step-functions in adaptive sequences. Basowitz and his collaborators (1955) and others report finding a hierarchy of stress sensitivity among biochemical variables, and at least analogously, Karl Menninger (1954 *a, b*) proposes an ordering of disintegrative functions in the ego's homeostatic regulator activity that is increasingly disruptive to what is called "normal" functioning.

Rioch (1955) reports a sequential pattern of gross behavior in a cat under stress in which the stress is not increased but is steadily maintained:

If you take cats and pinch their tails, the friendly cat will take a look and it's okay. We had one who patted me on the foot while I was pinching its tail. If you go on . . . all of a sudden, there is a change, a rapid shift, and the cat takes one swipe. The swipe is at the hand with the forceps, then on the forceps, then where the forceps touch the tail. Then, if you don't stop, . . . the cat is making nice accurate movements with one part of its body. [Then] it goes into total action, screaming, biting, etc. This is very effective (for the cat), unless you have gloves and forceps. This goes on for a time, then you get a further change. The cat stops attacking and tries to pull away with all its earlier responses. This goes on, then it changes, the cat falling flat in panic. As far as cats go, there is a series of steps which can be definitely separated. For the time relationship, there is a very sharp curve, and one can get this with no change in the input . . . just the continuation of the input is going to make a difference in the capacity of [the organism] to withstand it.

As one might expect from a systems-theory orientation, there is a parallel or analogy in the military defenses of a state. A minor threat may be handled initially by a small expeditionary force, or military aid, neither of which is very disturbing to the life of the defending nation. If the threat is not alleviated, a further commitment is made. This commitment grows. More personnel and greater resources are assigned. If the threat still continues, extremely expensive defenses are brought into play as casualties rise; the economy swings into arms production in major proportions, and defense becomes an expensive preoccupation of the total system.

Whether these sequences end in victory or defeat, whether they are adaptive or inadaptive, objectively valid or subjectively misleading, is not always clear or certain. Sometimes only the course of events will tell. But both courses demand an increasing commitment of resources, both are increasingly expensive, and both involve step-function shifts in defensive posture.

The processes are obviously not identical. If there are similarities, they are true of only certain characteristics of a sequence. There are certain biochemical correlates of the fear of pain, and these are not identical with certain biochemical correlates of the fear of shame. Also, some unusual things are threatening. Change can be threatening. Monkeys react violently to an unfamiliar arrangement of familiar stimuli. Boredom can become unendurable and monotony can be torture.

Hebb (1949), in addition to drawing attention to "pain" stimulation that is innately disruptive of cortical activity, and to chemical changes of the blood content that alter the rate of neural firing, also considers the stress created by the occurrence of a neural firing of incompatible nerve networks and also the absence of sensory facilitation (sensory change and sensory feedback) that has in the past contributed to certain neural network activity. Thus it is difficult to separate clearly fear, uncertainty, and the threat of change from pain, deprivation, and other stress, even though they are obviously not all the same thing. Within a theoretical framework dealing with adaptation, they might somehow all be encompassed.

The following example is not valid since a driver and a car are not as interdependent as a brain and its body, but one can imagine strain on the engine that may stop a car, and one can also imagine uncertainties and fears on the part of the driver that may be equally incapacitating if the driver feels lost, uncertain, or afraid of where he is going. Both driver and car require the maintenance of some more-or-less normative level of operation within certain limits of stress.

The work of Bruner (1951) and Festinger (1957) in cognition has recently contributed considerably to our knowledge of how we construct our way of looking at the world and ourselves in the face of ambiguities, conflict, uncertainty, threat, and stress. What one might call "cognitive stress" — competing and irreconcilable cognitions — or the cognizing of threat or stress in fear or anxiety is usually reduced by changing the *environment* in actuality, or by the way one interprets it, or by altering *oneself* in terms of what one does or how one evaluates oneself. A parallelism in defense mechanisms between those that seem to alter the *environment* and those that seem to alter the *self* was noted years ago by Anna Freud (1946). There is also evidence on the preference of certain personalties for one or the other type. There is some similarity in what we do adaptively to cope with problems, such as, for instance, when we do not invest our emotional resources in distant danger, and what we do defensively when we underestimate a danger so as not to get emotionally disturbed by it. The processes are both similar and different.

Stress frequently exists over a comparatively short span of time. Perhaps it is for this reason that the study of stress reactions has included the notion of changing and extended adaptation, as initial failures at adaptation aroused more severe and expensive mechanisms. Threat often extends over a longer period of time. It sometimes takes longer to determine the failure of a particular reactive behavior, and people who are trying to help may be confronted with one particular stage of coping or defensive behavior. Some defenses are "successful" because threats do not materialize.

Let us assume that a warning (a threat) of impending danger is received. The first response is usually one of verification, what might be called a "say-that-again" or "did-you-hear-that?" response. If the message is verified, a second stage is usually one of authentication, a check on the truth of the warning or the authority of the transmitter. The vast majority of people who have been exposed to a warning of impending nuclear attack have discounted its authenticity, rationalizing it away as a short circuit, mistake, practice alarm, rehearsal, etc. After all, what is communicated in a warning is what cannot be contradicted in disbelief!

If a warning is authenticated, it still needs to be elaborated. One needs to know its nature, probability, locus, timing, types of effects, and severity. The search for information can result in definition, inattention, distortion, and selection, or purposefully maintained uncertainty. Usually something can be done. Information about a threat is evaluated in terms of the threat's manageability, escapability, postponability, survivability, and even one's tolerance for enduring it. At this point there is usually some commitment to a posture, position, or response to the threat.

Failure can then be recognized only under certain circumstances. Information to which one tries to be inattentive may continue to force its attentions. There may be a real change in the threat conditions. The efficacy of a defensive behavior may be destroyed. Consideration may lead one to regard a behavior as inadequate or uncertainly effective. The avoidance behavior itself may be threatening. One may be denied the path that one thought was open.

The mere fact of having to shift to a new adaptive or defensive response, in a sense, redefines the threat. Part of the redefinition is one's potency in dealing with it. Many threats create an initial feeling of camaraderie in exposure to a common fate. Increased seriousness of the threat leads to a recruitment of allies and a mobilization of resources, duties, and commitments on the part of others. Continued threat leads to greater organization and a tolerance of central authority. If this is ineffective, scapegoating may occur; and if it is inadequate, social disorganization sets in and is replaced by social organization of units, cliques, gangs, and so forth, at a smaller level. If these are inadequate, a state of every-man-for-himself signifies complete disorganization and extreme threat.

These items are not new. The idea that they all signify some sequential order has some novelty. Tactical sequences, problem-solving steps, and defense mechanisms have been known for a long time. Much of what is reported can be classified as an accounting of rationalizations, intellectualizations, impersonalizations, suppression, affective denial, and so forth. What is added is the notion that these accommodations or defenses are sequentially predictable from a definition of the situation and a knowledge of what has been confirmed or disconfirmed in the threat information, and what relationship of the self to the threat is defined. The effort to maintain cognitive priorities suggests a similar or analogous process in cognition and cognitive reorganization to the processes of successive or sequential defense in physical reaction to stress, or the successive stages of disorganization of the ego. There is, for instance, an analogous similarity in the brain's efforts to maintain the picture of the self and the body's efforts to maintain the functioning of critical organs at the expense of other bodily functions.

It is interesting to suggest that there is a systematic mathematical model for the patterning of defenses and coping mechanisms in threat situations. There appear to be divergent paths, but there is considerable evidence that "stations" on these tracks show considerable similarity.

Much of this line of thinking has been developed out of the research on how individuals and exposed groups react to personal threat and warnings of impending natural disasters. The threat of nuclear war should offer a classical test since conditions have changed, with the threat maintained by episodic crises, and yet without actual incident or onset. Unfortunately, no research seems to have studied the same individuals and their reactions over time. There is no panel study of the public's reactions to the threat of nuclear war. A series of representative national samples do not offer any adequate verification of this line of thinking, since individuals would be at various stages of adaptation sequences at various points in time and would stay at individual points for various durations. This would result in a distribution of responses to threat in the population at some one point in time that would indicate little, if anything, about previous or ensuing accommodations to the threat.

Confronted with the threat of nuclear war a decade ago, one would guess, in this frame of reference, that the public would have tended to discount the probability of war and its local impact. This the public did! Faced with an increase in the severity and extent of weapons effects that denied people the escape contained in the idea that "I'd-be-safe-here," there should have been an increasing number of people who indicated the increased *un*likelihood of war. This has happened! Furthermore, it has happened every time there has been an indication of an enlargement of weapons effects.

There are differences among the public in estimates of the severity of a nuclear attack, in its likelihood, and in its timing if it does come. There is variety in estimates of how war might start — whether by accident, by escalation in a web of circumstances, or by aggressive intent. But these are not independent. To commit one's belief to one likelihood is to facilitate belief in certain others. One's interpretation of Russian character and intentions influences one's notions of how a war might be started — or is it vice versa? — and also commits one to certain defenses or security measures rather than others. This tangle of cognitive knots cannot easily be combed, and at present we must look at the knots in somewhat isolated fashion.

Where a familiar or it-will-pass "explanation" cannot be maintained, the next step appears to be one of probing and scanning for unusual reasons or partial cues for discounting or discrediting the reality of nuclear threat. For years the public overestimated the defense capabilities of the military.

Where disbelief cannot be maintained, distortion can be introduced. There is a defense in time — the danger will happen later than expected. There is also a defense in space — the danger will be worse elsewhere.

There is also a defense that tries to maintain uncertainty and therefore limit action. As a result there is a dike against the hazards and fears of premature commitment. Although few people regard shelter building as either a deterrent or a provocation to war, a large majority of those who have *no* access to shelters feel that, if shelters are built, it must be that attack is somewhat more probable. On the other hand, among those who have built or favor a shelter, there are a variety of perspectives on, for instance, the likely calendar for an attack, that suggest that they have minimized their need for the shelter after its construction.

If a threat cannot be denied, there is likely to be an increased sensitization to the danger, so that cues to danger result in overreaction and emotional and sometimes precipitous behavior. Where threat cannot be discounted, aggressive and projective behaviors begin to develop and scapegoating, polarizing of antagonists, and other hate and fear situations are generated.

There are partially adaptive behaviors in which minor steps are enlarged into adequate security measures. There is denial and resignation and apathetic rejection of information. There is also impersonalization in which much of the meaning of threat is bled, and the white skeleton of numbers is the focus of attention. There is even reversal, in which one manages to regard the danger as not so bad after all — and, in fact, once you get used to it, things might even be better than now.

It is possible to look at these zigzags of threatened men trying to escape a turn of fortune as somewhat abnormal, escapist, nonadaptive, defensive mechanisms. And some of them may be just that. On the other hand, it is difficult to be certain. If we look at mechanisms that are usually categorized as adaptive or coping mechanisms, we see some striking similarities.

Some people make the threat of nuclear war manageable, for them, by regarding themselves as outside of a probable target area. Some of them are probably right but others are most probably wrong. Many nonowners of shelters are found to have a fair amount of confidence in negotiations, reciprocal reduction in tensions, and similar measures. Are they probably right or probably wrong in this way of making the threat manageable for themselves?

Most of the supporters of arms control and disarmament measures have already managed somehow to acquire a position in which they tend to regard the likelihood of conflict as relatively low and its timing, if it does occur, under present trends, as somewhat distant. Most of those few people who favor pre-emptive attack have somehow acquired a perspective in which they see the likelihood of enemy attack as high and imminent.

Those who favor shelter programs tend to overestimate their worth somewhat, and those who oppose such programs tend to underestimate their value somewhat. Those who own shelters tend to feel that shelter programs operate as a slight deterrent. Those who do not own shelters tend to feel that a shelter program is irrelevant to deterrence.

Those who see war as highly imminent tend to see their area of residence as less disastrously hit than other areas of the U.S. Those who tend to emphasize policy measures that will prohibit the occurrence of war tend to see war as more disastrous than those who tend, rather, to emphasize defense against the possibility of nuclear attack. Even notions about the likelihood of a war's being started by accident, by escalation, or by intent appear to be related to the preferential choice of preventive versus defensive measures.

Many of these perspectives, advocated policies, and behaviors are rational and adaptive. The point is that for an individual they tend to show a sort of logic, consistency, harmony, and cohesion. Some of these perspectives and their attendant behaviors may turn out to be successful in stopping or minimizing the danger. Some of them may lead in unsuccessful directions. Some may not lead to anything more than intrapsychic escapes. But much of the raw material of interpretations of events, forecasts of trends, evaluations of potential hazard or security can be manipulated — they are not certainties — and they *are* manipulated in the effort to make

Stephen B. Withey

the threat socially and personally manageable. There is evidence, however, that the interpretations, judgments, and commitments of positions regarding the threat of nuclear war are not well tested in experience. From what little evidence we have, it is difficult to abstract the real course of success or failure. Perhaps the very sequences of reactions that have got us to this point have developed committed positions and complexities that are as difficult to handle as the core threat of nuclear attack itself. It is too bad that more research effort has not been focused, as yet, on the course of reactions to crises, to changing weapons technologies, to shifting political alignments, and so forth, as evidenced by individuals over a period of years.

References

ASHBY, W. R. *Design for a Brain.* New York: John Wiley, 1952.
BASOWITZ, H., PERSKY, H., KORCHIN, S. V., and GRINKER, R. R. *Anxiety and Stress.* New York: McGraw-Hill, 1955.
BRUNER, J. S. Personality dynamics and the process of perceiving. In R. R. Blake and G. V. Ramsey (Eds.), *Perception: An Approach to Personality.* New York: Ronald Press, 1951.
FESTINGER, L. *A Theory of Cognitive Dissonance.* Evanston, Ill.: Row, Peterson, 1957.
FREUD, A. *Ego and Mechanisms of Defense.* New York: International Universities Press, 1946.
HEBB, D. O. *The Organization of Behavior: A Neuropsychological Theory.* New York: John Wiley, 1949.
MENNINGER, K. Psychological aspects of the organism under stress. *J. Amer. Psychoanal. Assoc.,* 1954 *a,* 2, 67–104, 280–309.
MENNINGER, K. Regulatory devices of the ego under major stress. *Int. J. Psycho-Anal.,* 1954 *b,* 35, 412–420.
RIOCH, D. In "Conference on Theories of Human Behavior in Extreme Situations, February 12–13, 1955, Poughkeepsie, New York." Unpublished minutes, National Academy of Sciences — National Research Council, Committee on Disaster Studies, 1955.
WITHEY, S. B. Reaction to uncertain threat. In G. W. Baker and D. W. Chapman (Eds.), *Man and Society in Disaster.* New York: Basic Books, 1962.

PART FOUR

THE FEAR OF
NUCLEAR ANNIHILATION

LESTER GRINSPOON

FALLOUT SHELTERS
AND THE UNACCEPTABILITY
OF DISQUIETING FACTS

THE IMPOSING THREAT of nuclear war with its unimaginable potential for destruction and suffering has been met with a variety of reactions, from the involvement in a fallout shelter program at one extreme, to apathy at the other. This paper consists first of an examination of some of the psychological ramifications of fallout shelters, particularly individual or family shelters, and second of an exploration of why it is that, in the face of such a serious threat, so few people have built shelters or become involved in any kind of activity which would seem to reduce this threat.

There has been much debate and concern about the efficacy of fallout shelters in relation to physical survival, but relatively little attention has been given to the prospects for psychological survival. In general, people seem to take it for granted that if they can preserve their bodies intact their psyches will also remain undamaged. Researchers, however, have made various attempts to study situations which have some relevancy. These include studies of situations in which people have been snowbound overnight in a restaurant, confined to a submarine during a lengthy cruise, confined to a shelter during World War II, isolated for long periods of time, and subjected to several natural disasters (Fritz, Rayner, and Guskin, 1958; Rayner, 1960; Rohrer, 1959; Powell, Rayner, and Finesinger, 1953; Demerath and Wallace, 1957).

117

More recently, direct studies of different-sized groups in fall-out shelters have been conducted (AP Dispatch; Altman et al., 1960). The crucial experiment, however, that of studying people under conditions which closely simulate those of life in a fallout shelter during and after nuclear holocaust, cannot be performed.

When one considers the vast qualitative and quantitative differences between these simulated situations and an actual nuclear holocaust, one might well question the validity of formulations derived from natural disasters or from experiments. To use an analogy, we can make certain predictions about the effects of a specific drug or a combination of drugs when given in physiologic doses, but when they are given in doses of an entirely different magnitude, these predictions have no validity. Any prediction of the psychological responses to life in a shelter during and after a nuclear holocaust, even on the basis of the most thorough research which can be done today, is highly conjectural at best. It is safe to say, however, that individuals would suffer some kinds of traumata which might precipitate various types of transient or long-lasting mental disorders. I will attempt to outline some of the kinds of traumata that might afflict human beings during such an unprecedented disaster. Such an outline is based on the assumption that, at the very least, these traumata would be experienced, but it does not take into account their degree or configuration.

Threat to Life

No simulated fallout shelter experience can possibly assess the traumatic effects of the threats to life that a nuclear holocaust would present to the survivors. It is well known that people whose lives are threatened, especially over long periods, are likely to suffer psychological disintegration.

Separation, Fear of Loss, and Loss

Because an attack could come at any time during the day

or night, and because there would be such a limited warning time, it is unlikely that all members of a family would be in in a shelter together. In a suburban family, the head of the household might be "downtown" at the time of a holocaust; the children might be in school. If one considers other emotionally important people beyond the immediate family, it is almost inevitable that everyone would experience some degree of separation, fear of loss, or actual loss. Just as there would be wide individual variation in the extent of loss, so there would be great variation in the ability to tolerate loss; but for a number of people, loss and multiple loss would constitute a devastating threat to emotional well-being.

Helplessness

The utter impotence which many survivors would feel under such circumstances may be compared with the helplessness of an abandoned infant. These people would be severely limited in the ways in which they could help themselves. Such feelings of helplessness are extremely threatening to the average adult. Closely related are the limitations which would be imposed on the individual's ability to act. Activity, as a means of relieving anxiety, is a well-established fact. During the London blitz, those who served as air raid wardens suffered fewer breakdowns than those who were confined to shelters during raids.

Indefinite Duration of Danger

People can endure a great deal of hardship if they can sustain hope that the hardship is limited and temporary. Thus, in World War II, it was discovered that there was less likelihood of mental breakdown if a flyer was told he could return home after 25 missions. After a nuclear catastrophe there would in reality be no conceivable end to the kinds of suffering that survivors would have to endure. And sooner or later this reality would threaten sustaining fantasies in a way that would be overwhelming to many egos.

Fear of Radiation and Other Unknown Dangers

People in a fallout shelter would be trying to protect themselves from the dangers of something they could not see, hear, smell, feel, or taste. Then, depending on their knowledge of radiation hazards and the extent of their suggestibility, they might develop innumerable psychogenic symptoms. They would not know whether or to what extent the hazard existed, how long it would exist, or what to do about it.

The Threat of Having to Defend Oneself and One's Family

Associated with the real or fantasied threat of outsiders breaking into the shelter is the need of having to defend against such attack, presumably through some sort of violent action. There has been talk of equipping shelters with guns, yet little thought has been given to how well equipped emotionally the occupants would be to use such weapons. So sudden and so devastating would the disruption of relationships be, that a neighbor who formerly might have been quite welcome to borrow a cup of sugar would now be viewed as a dangerous enemy.

The Threat of Sickness and Death

The possibility of sickness caused by the bacteriologic and chemical weapons and the increased risk of infection consequent to diminished resistance, which is in turn due to radiation and unhygienic living conditions, make the likelihood of physical sickness in such a situation quite high. It should be recognized that the risk to mental health would be equally high. Serious illness under the best of conditions is always a threat to the individual's mental health. Under these conditions, where there would be no doctors or medical facilities, this threat would be greatly magnified.

Speculations about the World Outside

During the days and weeks underground, people would be limited only by their imaginations in their speculations about the world outside which they would have to face. Their fantasy about this world, and what it would demand of them in order to maintain life, would at the very least provoke extreme anxiety.

We know there are people who have an extraordinary capacity to endure incredible threats and suffering with minimal detectable psychological disturbances. On the other hand, there are those whose psychic structure is so delicately balanced that a seemingly trivial event can precipitate an acute emotional disturbance. Between these two extremes is the great majority of people whose individual mental makeup is more or less equipped to handle the psychological insults that civilized man must endure. How many would be able to cope successfully with the kinds of problems they would suddenly encounter in a shelter during and after a nuclear holocaust is highly speculative. To put it another way, how many people could withstand the sudden necessity to cope with kinds of problems that are comparable to none in their present experience, but are nearer to those with which man must have had to deal at the dawn of his history? Indeed, the people most likely to be able to cope successfully with the new world might be those whom we consider most primitive in their psychological makeup today. In conclusion, it would seem that we must give serious attention to the possibility that relatively few of the physical survivors in an atomic wasteland would be psychologically healthy enough even to reconstitute themselves, let alone their society.

The fact is, relatively few people have built fallout shelters. The reason for this is not, it is believed, the result of a rational choice. That is, people did not and do not first acquaint themselves with data which bear on the possibility of the shelter's providing physical survival or psychological survival and then make a rational decision not to build. I believe that they do not build fallout shelters or, for that matter, appear to do much of anything that would seem to minimize the nuclear threat because they have not become meaningfully involved with some of the disquieting facts of the present world situation.

Interestingly enough, the fallout shelter movement, which culminated in considerable national discussion, was never translated into large-scale action, although government agencies and citizens' groups made sporadic attempts to mobilize it. It has now fairly well subsided. This change from activism to apathy cannot be considered the consequence of lessening international tension. As a matter of fact, national controversy about shelter programs reached its highest point before the Cuban crisis in 1962. This nuclear confrontation, which probably brought the world closest to the brink of a nuclear war, was not associated with increased shelter activity, but rather with the continuance of its de-emphasis and a shift towards disarmament in some circles. The most prominent reaction, however, after the Cuban crisis subsided, can be described as public apathy and denial of future threat. An authoritative survey conducted even before the Cuban crisis sought reasons for personal unhappiness in the United States. It reported that problems on the community, national, or world level were mentioned by only 13 per cent of the population, and that of this 13 per cent, only 4 per cent expressed unhappiness about problems of world tension and the possibility of war (Gurin, Veroff, and Feld, 1960, p. 28).

How do we explain this seeming lack of concern? Are we to believe simply that the facts are not available to people and the mass media have conspired to hide the truth? It is tempting to explain the lack of concern by the inadequacies of the mass media, but such an explanation cannot be reconciled with the fact that there is a handful of people, without any special resources, who fully appreciate the present state of the world. The truth about the nature and risk of thermonuclear war is available; it is not recognized because it is not acceptable. People cannot risk being overwhelmed by the anxiety which might accompany a full cognitive and affective grasp of the present world situation and its implications for the future. It serves no useful purpose for a man to accept this truth if it leads only to the development of very disquieting feelings, feelings which interfere with his capacity to be productive, to enjoy life, and to maintain his mental equilibrium.

This remarkable ability to avoid accepting certain compelling facts suggests that the individual is employing some active psychological processes to protect himself against uncomfortable feelings. These conscious and unconscious ego mechanisms which maintain man's internal peace are protective and adaptive. They defend and protect the individual against intrapsychic, obnoxious mental elements; and although they are often spoken of as though they were protecting directly against external noxious stimuli, they do so only secondarily, insofar as these stimuli are translated by the individual into internal noxious elements.

Intellectualization

The psychological defense of intellectualization is invariably used by those working on peace research, as well as by those making preparations for war. This is the defense of the expert, the man who has an excellent understanding of facts and technical details. Intellectualization is the way he makes use of this knowledge to keep emotional distance from the realities that the details represent. Intellectualization is as necessary to strategic thinkers in their shop talks as it is to doctors in theirs.

Dogmatism

The use of dogmatism may be another means of disallowing disquieting facts. Essential to this mechanism is an airtight system of beliefs which provides an individual with all the answers; thereby he avoids uncertainty or the accept-ance of truths that threaten him with anxiety he cannot man-age. New facts, however much they must be distorted, are merely integrated into this system.

Rationalization

The ubiquitous defense, rationalization, accounts for atti-tudes such as: "No one's going to be mad enough to start an H-bomb war," "I'm sure the President (Premier) and all those generals know more about it than we do," "It's so ter-rible it'll never be used," "After all, perhaps it's God's will . . . ." Such rationalizations serve to protect the individual from a genuine engagement with the indisputable facts. Yet it is difficult to conceive of a person managing for a single day without rationalization. How else could he indulge him-self in ways he cannot afford or eat what he knows he should not?

Displacement

Displacement is one of the most important defenses pro-tecting the individual against involvement with the facts of the threat of World War III. Displacement is the unconscious process whereby people transfer affect from its real source (in this case the threat of nuclear war) to substitute objects. Displaced anxiety about war may, to some extent, account for the hyperpatriot's concern about "the enemy." Dis-placement enables people to attach affect to substitute ob-jects and thus allows for alternate paths of discharge.

A case in point may be the fluoridation issue. The conse-quences of exposure to Strontium 90 and other harmful radio-nucleides cause surprisingly little concern, although medical intelligence warns of both short and long-term effects, i.e., carcinogenesis and increased genetic mutations. Contrast this general complacency about Strontium 90 with the strong pub-lic reaction against fluoridation in many communities in this country. In Worcester, Massachusetts, in November 1963, for instance, despite the emphatic recommendations by dental and public health authorities in favor of fluoridation, residents vetoed fluoridation by four to one. They opposed fluoridation with the argument that no one should be forced to ingest any artificial substance, no matter how beneficial it might prove, and that people *en masse* should not be exposed to an agent over which they have no control. The equally vociferous arguments in favor of fluoridation held that the risks were nonexistent or exceedingly small and were greatly outweighed by the benefits.

It is proposed that some of the concern both for and against fluoridation may be displaced feeling about fallout. This displacement is facilitated by the fact that the fluoridation of a community's water supply and the pollution of its atmosphere with fallout have many similarities. Neither substance can be felt, seen, heard, tasted, or smelled. In both instances, people are faced with an imperceptible substance, the ingestion of which they cannot avoid. One might add, parenthetically, that if the fluoridation unit had been described as attractively as "sunshine unit" describes Strontium 90, its proponents might have been able to dispel some of the voters' anxiety.

It must be acknowledged that the mechanism of displacement works both ways; not only is anxiety about the possibility of war displaced, but also the fantasy of war itself may serve as a substitute object for the anxiety of personal internal conflicts. For many people who become actively engaged in war-peace issues, the underlying need may be to deal with their own internal conflcts by substituting the much more remote international conflct. Here, involvement may be largely determined by displacement. On the other hand, because the possibility of World War III may, by displacement, be made the external substitute for a fantasy of destruction against internal objects, it must be denied in order to prevent the anxiety associated with achievement of the fantasy aims. One would expect individuals in whom displacement is operating in this manner to express little interest in the international conflict.

Isolation

Increasingly characteristic of our society is the separation of fact from feeling. Archibald MacLeish has said:

... Knowledge without feeling is not knowledge, and can only lead to public irresponsibility and indifference, conceivably to ruin. . . . When the fact is dissociated from the feel of the fact . . . that people, that civilization is in danger (1959).

This "knowledge without feeling" involves the use of isolation, another mechanism people employ to protect themselves against disquieting feelings. When a man can acknowledge the fact that a continuing arms race might very well lead to a war which might annihilate millions of human beings, without experiencing any more affect than he would on contemplating the effects of DDT upon a population of fruit flies, he is probably making use of the defense of isolation. In this way people can be quite facile in saying that they and their loved ones would lose their lives in the event of a nuclear war. They are speaking of death, but as something isolated from the feelings associated with the concept of total annihilation. In other words, they are speaking of an abstraction, of something which has no real connection with themselves. One might perhaps somewhat fancifully speculate that this defense of isolation is becoming institutionalized in our rapidly developing reliance on computers and cybernetics. But like other defenses, isolation has essential adaptive properties, such as those which make it possible for a doctor to see a nude woman as a patient or a corpse as a subject of study.

Denial

The most primitive and one of the most important of the defense mechanisms is denial. When a person can ignore or dismiss internal or external events whose perception is painful, he is using this mechanism. Reluctance to acknowledge the loss of a loved one and avoidance of contemplating one's own death are common examples of denial.

Daniel Defoe, in describing how the people of London in 1664 would not accept the increase in recent deaths listed in the Parish Bills as evidence of the plague's return, was chronicling widespread denial. We can recall how only a few decades ago people in the immediate vicinity of concentration camps seemed strikingly unaware of their existence. And today we can observe among ourselves the widespread denial of the possibility of nuclear war. Despite its magnitude, its imminence, and the omnipresent hazard of accident and conflict, the threat of war is particularly easy to deny because of several unique characteristics. In the first place, the threat seems remote because of the distance between the weapons and the potential victims. The increased range of weapons has increased psychological distance, although, in fact, technological advances have decreased delivery time. Secondly, the nature of the act of destruction, simply pushing a button, is so far removed from conventional physical aggression that it, too, contributes to psychological distance.

But like the previously mentioned mechanisms, the use of denial is not necessarily pathological; it may be mustered in the service of adaptation. It would be far more difficult to travel by air, to undergo surgery, or to perform many other acts of daily life, were it not for denial.

This is by no means an exhaustive treatment of the mental mechanisms which individuals use to defend themselves against intolerable fantasies and feelings stimulated by disturbing truths. There are others, and, though all are spoken of as defense mechanisms, what should be emphasized is their adaptive function, for they are important means by which people orient themselves in their daily tasks and protect themselves from whatever threatens to upset their routine. In the face of nearly 40,000 traffic deaths and 3,345,000 injuries

yearly* they make it possible for people to drive without experiencing overwhelming anxiety. In the face of the Surgeon
General's recent warning about the serious hazards of smoking, they make it possible for millions to continue to smoke
with a minimum of disquietude (Advisory Committee to the
Surgeon General, 1964). Likewise, they enable people to go
about their daily lives without much concern for the threats
of thermonuclear, chemical, and bacteriological warfare.

It has been argued by some that solutions to the difficult
and dangerous problems which beset the world would be
more readily found and implemented if whole populations
really appreciated the nature of the present risks. They maintain that means must be found to *make* people aware, and
they suggest that showing movies of twenty-megaton bursts
during prime television time would be one way of arousing
people from apathy. But this endeavor might well prove
disastrous, inasmuch as it might only overwhelm people's defenses and leave them burdened with intolerable feelings of
anxiety with which they might have no way of coping constructively. Contrary to expectations, the activities which
those with unmanageable anxiety might seize upon could well
result in just the opposite of lessening world tension. There
is, in fact, some experimental evidence that shows that fear-
bearing communications decrease the recipient's capacity for
adaptive response (Janis, 1959; Janis and Feshbach, 1953, 1954).

The truth alone is not enough. In the psychotherapeutic
relationship, for example, a therapist would not offer an
interpretation which his patient was not prepared to deal
with, no matter how "true" his interpretation might be. It
is his responsibility to understand the possible consequences
of his interpretation, what it will mean to this patient in this
relationship at this time. The psychotherapeutic relationship
may, in fact, serve as a model situation wherein disturbing
truths can be made acceptable. On the strength of their relationship with a responsible and trusted therapist, a group of

* According to "Wheels of misfortune," in the *Massachusetts Physician,*
3 November 1963, 22, 64.

patients or a single patient can accept truths from him which they might not otherwise be able to deal with constructively.

Another model requires the availability of a program or activity which promises to modify the disquieting facts. Here the belief that there is something they can do about an otherwise intolerable situation enables people to come closer to a fuller appreciation of its existence. One can conceive of a model which, in some respects, represents a hybridization of the two. A respected and trusted leader would provide the means, or at least a belief in the means, by which the facts might be altered, and not simply attempt to call the disturbing facts to his people's attention. He would, so to speak, take with one hand and give with the other. The fallout shelter program was offered as the means of altering the unacceptable facts; it foundered because it was perceived as the harbinger of those facts. But for some people, whose defenses were to a greater or lesser extent overwhelmed, the involvement with building a fallout shelter undoubtedly served as an anxiety-relieving activity.

What happens when the means of keeping disquieting facts at bay have suddenly been broken through? For a while a person may suffer anxious and depressive feelings which may be incapacitating to some degree. It is possible that for some these feelings may precipitate serious mental illness; however, it is expected that most would either reconstitute their defense mechanisms, much as a self-sealing tire seals up after a puncture, or they would embrace some anxiety-relieving program or activity, such as building fallout shelters, in an effort to alter the unacceptable facts. Perhaps what actually takes place is an admixture of restitution of old defenses and adoption of new ideas and activities. The new programs or activities may be either in the intellectual sphere, such as in peace research, or they may be largely action-oriented, such as the fallout shelter programs. While they may be adaptive for some of the individuals concerned, they may be adaptive or maladaptive with regard to the development of a peaceful world.

References

Advisory Committee to the Surgeon General of the Public Health Service. "Report on Smoking and Health." Public Health Service Publication No. 1103, Department of Health, Education, and Welfare, Washington, D. C., 1964.

ALTMAN, J. W., SMITH, R. W., MEYERS, R. L., MCKENNA, F. S., and BRYSON, S. "Psychological and Social Adjustment in a Simulated Shelter: A Research Report." American Institute for Research, 1960. Reprinted by Office of Civil and Defense Mobilization.

Associated Press Dispatch. *The New York Times,* February 18, 1962, p. 69.

DEFOE, DANIEL. *A Journal of the Plague Year and Other Pieces.* New York: Doubleday, Doran, 1935 (first published in 1722).

DEMERATH, J. J., and WALLACE, A. F. C. (Eds.). Human adaptation to disaster. *Human Organization,* Summer 1957, *16* (2), Special issue.

FRITZ, C. E., RAYNER, J. F., and GUSKIN, S. L. "Behavior in an Emergency Shelter: A Field Study of 800 Persons Stranded in a Highway Restaurant During a Heavy Snowstorm." Washington, D. C.: National Academy of Sciences — National Research Council, May 1958.

GURIN, G., VEROFF, J., and FELD, S. *Americans View Their Mental Health.* New York: Basic Books, 1960.

JANIS, I. L. Motivational factors in the resolution of decisional conflicts. In *Nebraska Symposium on Motivation.* Lincoln: University of Nebraska Press, 1959, pp. 198–231.

JANIS, I. L., and FESHBACH, S. Effect of fear-arousing communications. *J. Abnorm. Soc. Psychol.* 1953, *48,* 78-92.

JANIS, I. L., and FESHBACH, S. Personality differences associated with responsiveness to fear-arousing communications. *J. Personality,* 1954, *23,* 166.

MACLEISH, ARCHIBALD. The poet and the press. *Atlantic Monthly,* March 1959, 40–46.

POWELL, J. W., RAYNER, J. F., and FINESINGER, J. E. Responses to disaster in American cultural groups. In *Symposium on Stress.* Washington, D. C.: Army Medical Service Graduate School, Walter Reed Army Medical Center, 1953, pp. 174–193.

RAYNER, J. F. "An Analysis of Several Surveys Relative to Problems of Shelter Habitability." Washington, D. C.: National Academy of Sciences — National Research Council, January 1960.

ROHRER, J. B. "Studies of Human Adjustment to Polar Isolation and Implications of Those Studies for Living in Fallout Shelters." Washington, D. C.: Georgetown University Medical School, July 1959.

Wheels of misfortune. *Massachusetts Physician,* 3 November 1963, *22,* 64.

ROY W. MENNINGER

ATTITUDES TOWARD INTERNATIONAL CRISIS IN RELATION TO PERSONALITY STRUCTURE

THE VIEW that a person's attitudes about his environment can be demonstrably related to his personality structure is the basis in clinical psychology for a great variety of projective tests (Murray, 1938; Frank, 1948). Attempts to define social attitudes in terms of personality characteristics (cognitive and affective) have been made by Frenkel-Brunswik (1948; Frenkel-Brunswik and Sanford, 1946) initially as an exploration of the bases of anti-Semitism, and later in a comprehensive study of ideology and personality with Adorno, Sanford, and Levinson (Adorno et al., 1950).

These investigations produced the widely used "F-Scale" and the clinical picture of the "authoritarian personality." Typically, individuals with a high score on the F-Scale also manifested marked ethnocentrism, prejudice, and political conservatism, and were characterized by dependent, authority-oriented, exploitive relationships with others. On the basis of interviews with such persons, the authors concluded that these behavioral manifestations in relation to authority, to minority groups, and to deviations from conventionality are the expression of unresolved conflicts created by specific childhood experiences (Frenkel-Brunswik, 1954).

The most crucial result of these exhaustive studies lay in the demonstration of a coherence and internal consistency

131

in the beliefs and attitudes of people "... ranging from the most intimate features of family and sex adjustment through relationships to other people in general, to religion and to social and political philosophy" (Adorno et al., 1950, p. 971).

Additional studies have attempted to extend the methodology of assessing ideology in relation to personality (Campbell and McCandless, 1951; Mussen and Wyszynski, 1952; Inkeles and Levinson, 1954; Levinson and Huffman, 1954; Rokeach, 1960). While these studies have contributed to an understanding of social and personal belief systems (ethnocentrism, conventionalism, discipline and authority, open- and closed-mindedness), the conceptions of personality on which the studies were based were limited to trait enumerations, attitudes, personality attributes, symptoms or isolated dynamisms, e.g., "parental ambivalence"). Seldom were such assessments tied to a comprehensive theory of personality.

Psychiatrists and psychoanalysts have studied ideology in such forms as prejudice (Kris, 1946; Ackerman and Jahoda, 1948), Negro race hatred (Sterba, 1947; Kurth, 1950; Bird, 1957; the Group for the Advancement of Psychiatry, 1957) and political ideology (Erikson, 1942; Dicks, 1950). These studies confirmed the projective hypothesis, setting down in detail the intricate manner in which early experience and consequent unconscious conflicts, through the establishment of persisting character traits, materially influenced behavior in widely differing social settings.

Efforts to relate the complexities of human attitudes to the important but psychologically more remote areas of foreign affairs, international tensions, and the problems of war and peace are exemplified by Klineberg (1950). Theoretical papers (Scott, 1958; Gladstone, 1962) and correlational studies relating international ideology to interpersonal ideology (Scott, 1960; Rosenberg, 1957), authoritarianism (MacKinnon and Centers, 1956), and pacifism, belligerence and threat (Gladstone, 1955; Gladstone and Taylor, 1958), though provocative, have been difficult to integrate with concepts of personality development. Christiansen (1959) sought to establish and test hypotheses that might account for the relationship in extensive researches on attitudes toward foreign affairs as a function of personality.

Relying heavily on psychoanalytic conceptions of personality organization, Christiansen used various test devices (questionnaires, projective tests, attitude scales) to assess the relative importance of intrapsychic and interpersonal conflicts to attitudes about foreign affairs. His findings suggest that "... attitudes toward foreign affairs seem to be correlated with nationalism, with individual psychodynamic conflicts and with manifest reactions in everyday conflict situations. ... whereas there appeared to be no correlation worth mentioning with regard to personal insecurity and international knowledge" (p. 232).

In the context of the projective hypothesis and its assumptions about the person-environment relationship, the author examined a group of patients in a small private psychiatric hospital, comparing their responses to a foreign affairs questionnaire with clinical psychiatric data which had been obtained on each patient as part of the diagnostic evaluation and treatment process. The reaction of the group to the Cuban crisis in October 1962 provided an opportunity to inquire into the impact of this crisis, with special reference to whether, or in what way, that episode was perceived as threatening, and whether such reactions could be related to personality structure.

Method

Each of sixteen unselected patients was interviewed for 30 minutes. Ten open-ended questions were presented, with additional discussion or inquiry as suggested by the responses. The questions were:

1. In your view, what is the most serious problem facing the world?
2. In your view, what is the worst threat to the United States?

3. Which of these (or what) worries you most about current international affairs?
4. In your view, is nuclear war likely, very likely, or unlikely?
5. How might it start?
6. What is your reaction to what President Kennedy did about Cuba?
7. What is our best next move?
8. What should the United Nations do (a) about Cuba? (b) about the Cold War?
9. What, in your view, is most needed to ease Cold War tensions?
10. Do you consider yourself more or less worried about these problems than most people you know?

In the initial survey of sixteen patients, the age ranged from 16 to 59 (average, 21.8 years). Characterologic diagnoses were limited largely to infantile (8) and schizoid (6) personalities. Clinical symptoms included schizophrenic reactions (5), adjustment reactions of adolescence (4), depressive syndromes (3), obsessive-compulsive syndromes (2), hysterical reaction (1), and anxiety reaction (1). All were open-ward patients in treatment programs that required their active cooperation.

Findings

Their first responses to the questions presented were stereotyped and conventional, differing little from opinions expressed in the daily newspapers. For example, "Our position is being hacked away"; "We must draw the line"; "We should stand up for our rights"; "We should have done something like this (the Cuban blockade) long ago"; "The worst danger is the possibility of nuclear war and annihilation." Only two of the sixteen persons mentioned matters they defined as threats which did not touch upon Cuba, the Cold War, or a possible hot war. Fifteen of the sixteen either agreed with President Kennedy's move to blockade Cuba, or felt he had done the only thing that could be done; the sixteenth was too obsessive to commit himself.

Eleven of the sixteen mentioned nuclear war as a major threat, either to the world, or to this country, or to both. An additional four spoke first of other dangers ("religious indifference," "Russia is challenging our power in Cuba," "Colored versus the whites"), but acknowledged nuclear war as a danger when asked specifically. Only the sixteenth said he was "not worried about the bomb," although the fact that this statement was offered spontaneously suggests that his denial contained its own affirmation.

These and similar responses illustrated the presence of a capacity for reality testing in these patients and demonstrated a notable similarity of *initial* response which bore no relationship to the diagnoses of the respondents. Furthermore, their replies indicated that the Cuban crisis had a palpable impact on these patients, and that all of them were aware of the destructive potential of nuclear war. The fact that they were hospitalized psychiatric patients appeared to have no effect on their replies.

Beneath this stereotyped response "layer," however, they manifested gross differences in their *styles of response:* manner of expression, points of emphasis, use of language, and rationales for points of view.

The protocols of ten patients in the initial group of sixteen provided data for a more detailed examination of the relationship between their responses and the clinical assessments of their personality structure. This group of ten was composed of two characterologically distinct groups of five patients each.

Infantile-Personality Group

One group included patients with personality structures variously labeled "infantile personality," or "immature character," whose predominant features were impulsiveness and egocentricity (narcissism). Their self-interest was evident in

135

tendencies to interpret or evaluate events and people in highly (and usually inappropriately) personal ways, to demand immediate gratification, and to react to any frustration with anger amounting to destructive rage. Distortions of truth and deceit in attempts to gratify their wishes were not uncommon. Impulsive behavior frequently led to antisocial activities, both aggressive and sexual in nature. The four women and one man in this group (Andy, Bess, Connie, Doris, and Ella) ranged in age from 18 to 31 (average 22.6) years.

Their questionnaire responses abundantly illustrated the patterns of reaction so characteristic of the infantile personality. Excerpts from their interview protocols, related to the clinical assessments, appear in the following summaries.

1. Andy, a 23-year-old adolescent, responded to the interview with gusto. He believed the biggest problem facing the world was "keeping peace" and the biggest threat facing this country was the risk of "total annihilation by Russia or a satellite." Indeed, he felt war was "always a mistake, and very likely [to occur], but not for at least a year," and that when it came, it would start "by direct illegal attack." Likelihood of war was so great that "it makes me feel like saying 'to hell with treatment'; I should just get out and have fun while I can, but . . ."

In a discussion about the Cold War, he emphatically declared that "having a parley with K is malarkey, since how can we be sure Russia's not building up while we talk?" Seeming to forget his earlier comments on the grave danger of war he said, "Both countries have to state their aims clearly, then if one of them doesn't agree, why, then, go to war! The United States can't stand a Cold War like this much longer; one has to show the other who's boss, even by war, if necessary."

His suggestions for improving matters had the same impetuous, directive quality: "We should get an alliance between the Soviet Union, United States, China, and have Europe unite, in which all agree to give up their nuclear arms. All four groups would designate one man who would run it like scientific research. That would give you more voices to have a say in what happens." At the same time, he felt that "the United Nations counts for nothing; it serves no purpose at all." While ostensibly outlining a cooperative plan, he spoke of it in autocratic terms, and rejected the United Nations (which was something like what he himself suggested) as if he felt it lacked the absolute authority he believed necessary for keeping the peace.

He noted that his wish to "get out and have fun" was the very problem which brought him first to treatment. This reaction suggested that he perceived the threat of nuclear war as roughly similar to the many provocations which had pushed him to irresponsible and impulsive behavior in earlier years. Moreover, his feelings of apprehension about the possibilities of war, in spite of their genuineness, had an isolated quality, an absence of visible effect on the rest of his ideas (illustrated by his alacrity later in the interview to employ war if necessary). His comments about determining "who's boss" with a ready resort to war, his disdain for "talk," and his view that the United States cannot stand (the tensions of) a Cold War much longer, seemed to be expressions of his own impulsive, sporadically assaultive, and destructive behavioral pattern.

2. Bess was a defiant teen-ager with a history of many emotional crises, sexual promiscuity, lying, and gross disobedience. There was much evidence of severe chronic conflict with her rather autocratic father.

She answered questions with unusual vigor and directness. Acknowledging that the risk of open conflict (and nuclear war) was the gravest threat and insisting that no one wanted war, she nonetheless emphasized "not backing down" (referring to our stance vis-à-vis Russia during the Cuban crisis). She declared that "Kennedy should have done it months ago; it is about time we took a stand; we should have called Russia's bluff before. We shouldn't back down. We could have avoided (this crisis) if we had taken a stand earlier." The phrases "taking a stand," "calling a bluff," "not backing down," were repeated throughout her comments, and carried a strong message of challenge and determination. Her intense call for firmness suggested that she saw the Russian-American confrontation over Cuba as a personal test of autonomy. The capacity of this reality situation to evoke strong reactions similar to those marking her own struggle tended to obscure for her ways in which the international crisis was different, and, more importantly, the grave risks of the international crisis.

Her comments alternated in recommending first firm action, then "understanding and agreement," which were followed by urgings that we "not back down," and saying that the situation would improve "only through talks and student exchanges on a large scale." Her failure to integrate ideas and convictions into a sensible whole is common in adolescents in mild form, but it was also typical of her chaotic, unorganized, impulse-ridden emotional life. Her emphasis on talking as a means to agreement was noteworthy; her physician ruefully commented on her use of an amazing verbal dexterity to distort reality, explain away her misbehavior, and avoid responsibility for it.

3. Connie was an immature adolescent caught between her need to please and be accepted and her wish to rebel. Her answers reflected an intensely personal reaction to the international crisis over Cuba. She felt, for example, that "Cuba is more serious than Berlin because it is closer to us," although she recognized that overt conflict in either place might lead to nuclear catastrophe. In her comments about the President's decision to blockade Cuba, she indicated her personal involvement: "I am *very* proud and *very, very* happy that we are standing up for our rights." Similarly, the aspect of the crisis that made it "the worst situation the United States has ever been in" was not the danger of all-out war, or the threat to the country, but that now "they could bomb New Orleans" (her home).

Her responses were heavily action-oriented and stated in an imperative way with all the indignation of personal outrage: "We should *definitely* do something; Russia should *not* have bases in Cuba; Cuba should *not* be a Russian pawn; we should do as we did in the Philippines."

Her demands for action contrast sharply with her own characteristic reactions to critical or threatening situations with passive aggression and irresponsibility (absence, carelessness, nonperformance) rather than direct action. Her need to be liked and popular led her to a passive expression of rebellion rather than a more aggressive approach which might risk the loss of the interest of others. Her emphatic action-oriented answers to the questionnaire, viewed in the context of her passive aggressive manner, were evidently a vicarious expression of what she wished she might do. This conflict between the wish to be directly aggressive and the fear of the consequences of doing so was exquisitely expressed in her comment (in response to a question about what move would improve matters): "Assuming I had the support of the rest of the world, I would definitely invade Cuba and throw Castro and the other Communists out. Russia couldn't do anything (to us) if the others were behind us."

4. Doris considered that the worst threat to the world was not merely nuclear war, but the "possibility of two powers drawing us into war, as much as all of us don't want it." She spoke of

Communist aggression as a threat to this country, but discussed it in ambiguous terms. She felt that this threat must be dealt with "in the best possible way. We must keep face in the world view. Now that we've taken a stand (over Cuba) we should deal in a satisfactory way to bring about peace," leaving the definition of "the best way" quite unspecified. Associating more explicitly to the "threat," she said, the most frightening thing "is the manner in which Russia deals with everyone. They don't say what they do. They are underhanded, while we are in the open. We always have to be on our guard."

She felt good about President Kennedy's stand on Cuba, saying, "the United States stood up for its rights. We are entirely justified. The whole world thought so."

Lessening of world tensions could occur, she felt, if it were possible "to get world leaders together to agree to stop using arms and between countries for settling disputes." She felt this had not happened because "Russia won't let in the inspectors."

Doris was 17 years old and required hospitalization for control of severe temper tantrums and arguments with her mother which had led to an increasing breakdown in her school performance. Her perception of the "worst threat" as the risk of being "drawn into war by two powers," and her conviction that improvement depended on getting the leaders to agree to stop using arms parallels her statement that her earliest memories were of her parents fighting or deceiving her. Her perceiving the struggle in terms of "two powers" might also refer to the more immediate problem of continual covert conflict between herself and the hospital staff.

Her emphasis on the secretiveness and "under-handedness" of Russia and her contrasting statements about our operating "in the open" as well as her view of the necessity of "keeping face" had an impressive parallel in her own behavior. She was variously described by her physician as "maintaining an inexpressive face," "having a need to put on many faces, since she does not know what she is really like," of not being able "to show openness in treatment," and manifesting many indications of a wish to "fool" people by a "mature, sophisticated, intellectual façade." Her deviousness and tendency to withhold information presented serious management problems in her treatment and contrasted curiously with her projective view of these features as being characteristic of others (notably Russia). Her physician noted, moreover, that she had "lost face" when she changed her mind about a recent significant decision.

5. Ella said the worst problem was that "people will fail to learn to live with each other and respect each other's rights, without having to take from each other. I feel there will be no outbreak of war because of this terrible fear that we would retaliate. War would only happen from someone who took matters into his own hands. We have so much power. I keep wishing we lived back when weapons were limited. Just how long will this fear of destroying each other last?"

These comments suggested that she felt that the threat of severe punishment (retaliation) would control undesirable behavior (war) — at least for the time being — but that even this restraint could be undermined by the actions of an irresponsible third party. Her use of "we" further hinted at her feeling that the threat and the retaliation might come from within. She began with a naive hope and concluded with a nostalgic wish for a return to the past, where things were simpler and "weapons were limited."

Her reactions were in line with the findings of the psychiatric examination, which indicated that she was particularly sensitive to any hint that people might not like her, and fearful that she might be unwanted and unloved. She was an obedient, childlike person who was apprehensive of transgression by herself or others. She was preoccupied by thoughts of harming herself and fearful that she might impulsively act upon them. As a child she had experienced much threat of punishment and physical abuse.

Schizoid-Paranoid Personality Group

The second group of five patients (Fred, George, Harry, Ian, and Joe) corresponded to the general characterological rubric of "schizoid-paranoid personality." The predominant feature of these patients was a marked isolation from others, associated with varying degrees of suspiciousness and covert apprehension. All were reluctant to make specific replies to the questions, pleading uncertainty, ignorance or doubt, even though most tended to be articulate in less demanding circumstances. None was frankly psychotic, and several manifested symptoms such as obsessive-compulsive reactions or anxiety reactions. Their ages ranged from 21 to 38 years (average: 29.4).

Excerpts from their protocols demonstrated a relationship

to character structure, as illustrated in the following summaries.

6. Fred was 23 and uncertain about his own identity. This was
enhanced by strong dependent wishes for others to manage his
life. He was often overwhelmed by the opinions of others and
could develop a sense of independence only by resisting threatening influences of those who threatened him. His views of others
were often distorted by suspiciousness, which made his existence
seem a constant struggle to conciliate or push away powerful
figures who he felt were trying to control him.

This complex struggle was reflected in his comments to the
questionnaire. He felt that the most serious problem confronting the country was the danger that "we'll lose out; our position
will be chopped at, hacked away." This contention was consistent with his strong support of the position taken by the President: "I felt *good* about that; it made a bond between us and
many others." His limited perception of the confrontation as an
experience similar to his own, but bigger, was borne out in his
failure to consider the risks of war. War, in his view, if it started
at all, might be the result of an accident (". . . like the geese in
the radar screen"). He did not see war a likely result of the Cuban
crisis.

He suggested that "a clarification of the aims of the West [is
most needed to improve matters] so there can be some trust."
He added that "Russia must feel continually on the defensive,"
introducing an unexpected hint of some identification with Russia as the underdog, contrasting with his saying earlier that the
United States was the one likely to get "hacked away and
chopped up." This switch in his allegiance was comparable to his
alternating pattern of provoking those in authority, then concili-
ating them by complying with their demands on him, much as
though he attempted to handle conflict with others by alternating
his participation from one side to the other.

7. George was a pedantic, mildly eccentric youth with pre-
tentions of scholarship. The clinical picture suggested a schizophrenic reaction; yet with his carefully integrated façade and
superior intelligence (I.Q. 136) he had maintained a tenuous adjustment. Efforts to influence his decisions he perceived as efforts
to control him, and they often led to angry outbursts and further retreat to a protective but lonely isolation.

His response to a question about the worst threat facing the
world was to condemn "religious indifference, since this is most

basic. Our search for national purpose would be amusing if it were not so serious. After all, the fight with Communism is essentially a religious struggle."

Such a description of the most significant threat to the world, whatever its determinants in reality, was also a reflection of his preoccupation with church history, ritual, and worship. Most of his daily activities centered around this interest, to the exclusion of all else. He was aware of the possibility of nuclear war and the devastating result of one, saying "nuclear war is unlikely since even the victor will get nothing," but this comment came in direct response to a question about the chances for war. His lack of emphasis suggested that he did not consider the threat of war a grave one.

His principal target for criticism was the lack of morality in this country. Speaking of the result of religious indifference, he observed that "the United States has more on its side, but we are not presenting our best features. We allow ourselves to be put on the defensive: colonialism versus Hungary; we fight our allies instead of Russia. We must make clear that we will not betray our allies and work for liberty and justice. This is stated, but not done." His position was more one of irritation with the West than apprehension about or anger with Russia. He saw the dangers as lying within the moral and religious structure of his own country, rather than in threats of attack from without.

His preoccupation with the status of domestic strengths was the counterpart and perhaps an expression of his own precarious psychic structure. His pedantry, his formalism, and his interest in religious ritual appeared to be devices employed against the felt danger of inner breakdown. For him, this risk and its social parallel of "religious indifference" were far more real threats than Communism, thermonuclear war, or the population explosion.

8. Harry was an extremely withdrawn, bright man of 35 with a slim hold on reality and a distinct potential for disturbed thinking under stress. Clinically, he was severely disabled by intellectualizing, mannerisms, and obsessional indecision to the point of being unable to complete his education, hold a job, or even deal with simple social situations. His responses showed his obsessive intellectualizing in long pauses, complicated circumlocutions and a great reluctance to be definite.

Some answers to the questionnaire suggested his suspiciousness; he felt, for example, that the "most obvious threat to the United States was insidious subversion." By this, he referred to his view that "the Soviet Union has made inroads in Latin

America over long periods of time, insidious, but nevertheless overwhelming, with serious communist activity at trade union levels. With gradual entrenchment and infiltration in Latin America and Europe, [they might] gather strength, then manifest themselves in an overt episode and finally overt war."

In spite of his obsessiveness, he demonstrated some capacity for thoughtful judgment, noting that "it's a tight spot to be in; not triggering off a nuclear war yet maintaining a defensive position." This comment also expressed in metaphor a core issue of his own: the struggle to maintain control over his aggressive impulses. His intellectualization served to keep distance between himself and his environment. Although it was severely strained in anxious situations, he was surprisingly capable of reasoned thought.

He guessed that the threat of nuclear war might move the Soviet Union to bargain for other areas in its long-range interests, perhaps making an exchange for Berlin. He thought the Soviets might be trying to gain leverage: pulling this obvious "burlesque" activity in Cuba only to push out again elsewhere. He concluded that Russia might be willing to bargain for advantages elsewhere in exchange for "regressing" in Cuba.

His recasting the crisis into a barter operation illustrated his use of intellectualization to control the anxiety stirred up by the threatening crisis.

9. Ian was a severely inhibited, highly intellectualizing, obsessive-compulsive, 32-year-old with a marked dependence on his parents. His announced problems included his judgment that, "I have never had a goal, purpose, or preference; I am merely going through life like a somnambulist, living a pointless, joyless, weird kind of existence. My life is empty."

He thought atomic warfare was the worst threat to the world, but that, though possible, it was not likely. He thought war could start as a result of some nation making a move that required a warlike response from another, but he stressed the more likely possibility that war would start as a result of "some accident . . . or something irresponsible, not considering everything involved." Continuing this theme of war starting from impulse or bad judgment, he noted that "the Chinese have less [self-] control than the Soviet Union, and, with the proliferation of weapons in countries like France, Cuba, and others, there is a possibility that people will be less thinking and more rash."

Ian's attitudes toward others, especially those he considered more powerful than himself, were passive dependent ones, alternating compliance with covert rebellion, and mixed with hostility. His defensive efforts of obsessive thinking, compulsive ritual, and passivity seemed partly intended to suppress action impulses that would risk various but unspecified dangers, to project them outward onto these 'others,' and to anticipate that they rather than he might "lose control" and act impulsively. His marked dependence on others enhanced his sensitivity to their intentions and actions bearing on him and highlighted his suspiciousness.

His view of the greatest threat to this country was that "the Soviet Union has ideological weapons that we don't have — a certain purpose." He noted that "we lack a conscious sense of national purpose evident in some countries," and moreover "we do not talk about the virtues of capitalistic society with the same enthusiasm that the Communists do. This lack of our goal and presence of theirs enables them to be more purposeful in their exploitation of the rest of the world."

In these comments, he recited (attributing it to the whole nation) a complaint he had previously listed as his own — and continued by noting that lack of purpose constituted a significant weakness. He saw himself as worthless and emasculated and seemed to believe that his own society was liable to the same consequences.

His opinions revealed a certain admiration for the strong, powerful, and potentially dangerous enemy, perhaps reflecting a covert wish to identify himself more closely with the "dangerous one" and suggested that his passive dependence concealed serious sado-masochistic conflicts. These inferences were borne out by strong evidences of conflicts in the psychological testing.

10. Interviewed at the height of the Cuban crisis, Joe said he thought this was the greatest threat to the world, since it marked "the first time America and Russia have clashed together." He described the crisis, not as a prelude to holocaust, but as if it were a "pushing match" between neighborhood bullies in which one "draws the line and pushes until the other backs down." He did not see war as likely at that time, the tensions and dangers of an international clash notwithstanding. Although he did suggest that "an attempt to board a Russian ship might touch off a nuclear war, if resisted," he felt war was unlikely for another 10 years if started intentionally, and likely to be accidental ("from someone manning a missile base, or human error of some sort") if it happened before that time. He made no reference to war as a consequence of some foreign action.

His view of the greatest threat to America was its lack of strength: "I don't believe we're as strong as our leaders give us to believe. I was in the CIC in the Army and saw the many discrepancies between reality and what it said on paper." He thought

Russia was stronger than we, having more powerful rocket boosters and with destructive power greater than American missiles. He believed a second danger was the excessive power of unions, saying they used their economic power to buy votes to support the Communist party.

These comments were consonant with observations by the examining psychiatrist, who said that "his prevailing façade is one of bland affability, beneath which he conceals a deep-seated sense of inadequacy, jealousy, injustice, and basic suspiciousness. With authority figures in general, he expects to be kept ill-informed and to be unjustly maligned."

Psychological testing suggested that "the patient's major problem appears to revolve around a difficulty in managing explosive hostile impulses." He frequently reacted to unexpected events with hostile outbursts. Coupled with his anxiety about his own weakness, his distorted perceptions led to hostile distorted attacks on his physician for what he felt were efforts to "make things rough and turn me into a weakling without any fight left." His apprehension about his explosive impulses may have determined his view that war, if it came, would be accidental, but it is not clear how his denial of the obvious risks in the critical Cuban confrontation related to his self-perceptions.

His view of himself as weak and inadequate, and of others as more powerful, was reflected in his comments about the relative strengths of Russia and the United States. His view of Russia as stronger carried no question or doubt of its truth and implied a certain admiration for this greater power.

Discussion

The infantile-personality group tended to view the international crisis in highly personal terms. Their opinions about it were usually expressed with great emphasis and little hesitation, and were often couched in phrases which also characterized acute personal problems: "keeping face," "don't back down," "take a stand." They appeared to see the international crisis as a blown-up version of personal crises in their past experience. The underlying issue in many of their personal crises appeared to be a defiant but ambivalent struggle with powerful authority figures who could be neither ignored nor subdued. In some instances, there were hints in their views of the crisis of current struggles of adjustment to hospital routine and with the physicians.

For several of these patients, interpersonal conflict appeared to serve a number of psychodynamic functions. To persons uncertain of their own identity and of the limits of their own autonomy, conflict provided a test of these limits, though at considerable cost to the patients and to their environment. At the same time, conflict offered a means of separating themselves from the real or fancied control by the powerful figures in their lives, while allowing them still to maintain contact. Lastly, conflict was an outlet for the expression of aggression and hostility, though again in frequently expensive ways. The use of conflict for such multiple functions by these immature personalities may explain their ready perception of the international crisis as if it were their own.

Perhaps the most striking characteristic of these infantile patients was the impulsive quality of their acts and a blatant disregard for the consequences. Such patterns of behavior are both a reflection of meager ego development with inadequate mechanisms for the management of impulses, and a failure to move beyond the primary narcissism of infancy to the establishment of object relationships. As a result, these infantile patients tend to be victimized by the eruption of aggressive (and sexual) impulses, are seldom able to tolerate delay or frustration, and are seldom influenced by more reasonable considerations.

Their inability to invest in anything outside themselves blinds them to the impact of their behavior on others and prevents the development of empathy that would enable them to see the world through eyes other than their own.

The split between the impulse for action and the recognition of the consequences of such action was evident in their responses, and an indication of the assimilation of the international crisis into their own egocentric framework. Andy, for example, noted the great dangers of nuclear war, then ignored his own comments with a later statement that it might take war "to show who's boss." Such a contradiction between feelings and judgment illustrated the pressures of poorly managed impulses and the tendency to reinterpret reality in narcissistic terms. The combined pressure exerted by the pressure of feelings and the impulse to act swept away rational judgment and whatever influence it might have had, and cogently demonstrated the critical personality conflict of these patients.

The similarity of the reactions of this group to the struggles commonly associated with adolescence is obvious, and it is consistent with the relative youthfulness of this group (as compared with the other). In many respects, the reactions of marked immaturity shown by these patients are caricatures of normal adolescence.

A second and less common pattern evident in this group was the expression of feelings of personal helplessness. Neither Doris nor Ella demonstrated the rebelliousness and negativism which characterized the other members of their group, nor did the others express feelings of helplessness as openly as these two. The reciprocal nature of these observations is suggestive, but its significance is not made clear by the available information.

Members of the schizoid-paranoid personality group showed none of the reaction patterns characteristic of the infantile group except for Fred, an adolescent in the midst of an identity crisis. He showed indications of infantile conflicts as well as schizoid-paranoid reactions. In contrast to the directness and vigor of expression seen in members of the infantile group, these patients spoke much more hesitantly and with a marked reluctance to commit themselves to an unequivocal statement. They frequently used a variety of circumlocutions, awkward or ambiguous phrases, and cautious demurrals ("I don't want to sound dogmatic...."). They more often referred to concerns not international in nature, and in two instances (George and Joe) considered issues threatening which were not relevant to the Cuban crisis itself (religious indifference, union subversion).

A characteristic of the responses of members of this group was the tendency to attack some element within our own society (religious indifference, military weakness, union subversion, lack of national purpose) rather than external power (the Soviet Union). This perception of inner danger or weakness was frequently accompanied by comments which conveyed a sense of admiration for the Soviet Union. Its sense of purpose, its enthusiasm, and even its rocket boosters were favorably contrasted to our own.

An adequate understanding of the personal meanings of these identifications would depend on further information about the underlying fantasies. The admiration for the strong, powerful "enemy" might be based on an identification with the aggressor, and the criticism of one's own country might reflect a self-perception of weakness. The operation of the paranoid mechanism in several of these patients suggests that the self-criticism they expressed (in terms of failings of their country) may symbolically represent an attempt to defend themselves against and to separate themselves from the absorbing, enervating (and emasculating) control of maternal authority. Whatever the dynamics of the sequence may be, the consistency of the pattern in the members of this group was noteworthy.

In the responses of two members of this group (and observed in none of the other) was a curious side-stepping of a direct conclusion. Both Fred and Joe saw the Cuban crisis as a world-threatening event, implying the imminence of catastrophe; yet both avoided expressing the obvious conclusion that war might eventuate. Both suggested that, if it came at all, it would be accidental (e.g., arising from an error or accident unassociated with the crisis). A variant of this view was expressed by a third member of this group (Ian), who thought that war might come as a result of irresponsibility (in contrast to the calculated risk-taking of the Cuban crisis). One may infer this to be an example of denial, a mechanism used extensively by this group in the management of conflict situations and impulse control.

Three of the five patients in the schizoid-paranoid group (Harry, Ian, and Joe), as well as the two nonrebellious members of the infantile group (Doris and Ella), expressed concern that war, if it began, would be the result of accident. This view was variously put in terms of irresponsible action of someone, error, or "mistake." Each of these views could be understood as a judgment that the crucial event was "beyond our control."

Expressed in terms of "control," this fear of "accident" may be comparable to a fear of impulsive breakthrough of an aggressive wish within the mental apparatus of these patients. Other evidence suggests that such a breakthrough — an "accident" — was perceived as threatening by these patients, as something "beyond our control." One would assume that this fear of loss of control was partly responsible for their patterns of inhibition, ritualism, withdrawal, and other devices intended to minimize the risk of impulsive expression of aggression.

A further inquiry into the unconscious meanings of such reality events as the Cuban crisis should yield a more comprehensive understanding of the manner in which such experiences are perceived by the individual, of how they are integrated into previous and current experience, and, finally, how they are used as a basis for verbal or motor activity.

The unconscious fantasies which the Cuban crisis provoked might be demonstrably related to unconscious fantasies about persons and events within one's immediate environment, and might, in turn, reflect the significant unconscious conflicts that motivate one's affective life. What part such unconscious conflicts may play in the complex process of assessing and responding to international issues remains to be clarified through further study.

Summary

An examination of the responses to a questionnaire on international affairs, in the light of clinical psychiatric data about the respondents, suggested these observations:

1. These patients tended to perceive the reality of the Cuban crisis and the risks of nuclear war as major threats, and

in terms quite similar to those used by persons not hospitalized or under psychiatric treatment. Their psychiatric status did not produce characteristically different judgments about what was perceived as threatening.

2. The *style of response* (expressiveness, points of special emphasis, implications drawn, language used, and the rationales for points of view) did appear to be consistent with and characteristic of underlying personality structure. Examples from two groups of personologic types (infantile personality and schizoid-paranoid personality) were examined in some detail.

3. The consistency between styles of response and personality structure suggests that a fuller examination of the unconscious meanings of such events as the Cuban Crisis would amplify and further clarify the role of important unconscious conflicts in the determination of attitudes about international affairs. Such a study is a logical extension of this pilot inquiry.

References

ACKERMAN, N., and JAHODA, M. The dynamic basis of anti-Semitic attitudes. *Psychoanal. Quart.* 1948, *17*, 240–260.

ADORNO, T. W., FRENKEL-BRUNSWIK, ELSE, LEVINSON, D., and SANFORD, R. N. *The Authoritarian Personality.* New York: Harper, 1950.

BIRD, B. A consideration of the etiology of prejudice. *Amer. Psychoanal. Assoc. J.* 1957, 5, 490–513.

CAMPBELL, D. T., and McCANDLESS, B. R. Ethnocentrism, xenophobia and personality. *Human Relations,* 1951, *4*, 185–192.

CHRISTIANSEN, B. *Attitudes towards Foreign Affairs as a Function of Personality.* Oslo: Oslo University Press, 1959.

DICKS, H. V. Personality traits and national socialist ideology. *Human Relations,* 1950, *3*, 111–154.

ERIKSON, E. H. Hitler's imagery and German youth. *Psychiatry,* 1942, *5*, 475–493.

FRANK, L. K. *Projective Methods.* Springfield, Ill.: C. C. Thomas, 1948.

FRENKEL-BRUNSWIK, ELSE. A study of prejudice in children. *Human Relations,* 1948, *1*, 295–306.

FRENKEL-BRUNSWIK, ELSE. Further explorations by a contributor to "The Authoritarian Personality." In R. Christie and M. Jahoda (Eds.), *Studies in the Scope and Method of "The Authoritarian Personality."* Glencoe, Illinois: Free Press, 1954, pp. 226–275.

FRENKEL-BRUNSWIK, ELSE, and SANFORD, R. N. The anti-Semitic personality: A research report. In E. Simmel (Ed.), *Anti-Semitism: A Social Disease*. New York: International Universities Press, 1946, pp. 96–124.

GLADSTONE, A. I. The possibility of predicting reactions to international events. *J. Soc. Issues*, 1955, *11*, 21–28.

GLADSTONE, A. I. Relationship orientation and the processes leading toward war. *Background*, 1962 *6*, 13–25.

GLADSTONE, A. I., and TAYLOR, M. A. Threat-related attitudes and reactions to communications about international events. *J. Conflict Resolution*, 1958, *2*, 17–28.

Group for the Advancement of Psychiatry. "Psychiatric Aspects of School Desegregation." Report formulated by the Committee on Social Issues, 1957.

INKELES, A., and LEVINSON, D. National character: The study of modal personality and sociocultural systems. In G. Lindzey (Ed.) *Handbook of Social Psychology*. Cambridge, Mass.: Addison-Wesley, 1954.

KLINEBERG, O. *Tensions Affecting International Understanding*. New York: Social Science Research Council, 1950.

KRIS, E. Notes on the psychology of prejudice. *Engl. J.*, 1946, *25*, 304–308.

KURTH, GERTRUD. Politics: Unconscious factors in social prejudice and mass movements. In H. Herma and Gertrud Kurth (Eds.), *Elements in Psychoanalysis*. Cleveland: World Publishing Co., 1950, pp. 297–309.

LEVINSON, D. Authoritarian personality and foreign policy. *J. Conflict Resolution*, 1957, *1*, 37–47.

LEVINSON, D. J. and HUFFMAN, PHYLLIS E. Traditional family ideology and its relation to personality. *J. Personality*, 1954–55, *23*, 251–273.

MACKINNON, W. J. and CENTERS, R. Authoritarianism and internationalism. *Publ. Opin. Quart.* 1956, *20*, 621–630.

MURRAY, H. A. *Explorations in Personality*. New York: Oxford University Press, 1938.

MUSSEN, P. H. and WYSZYNSKI, ANNE B. Personality and political participation. *Human Relations*, 1952, *5*, 65–82.

ROKEACH, M. *The Open and Closed Mind*. New York: Basic Books, 1960.

ROSENBERG, M. Misanthropy and attitutdes toward international affairs. *J. Conflict Resolution*, 1957, *1*, 340–345.

SCOTT, W. A. Rationality and non-rationality of international attitudes. *J. Conflict Resolution*, 1958, *2*, 8–16.

SCOTT, W. A. International ideology and interpersonal ideology. *Publ. Opin. Quart.*, 1960, *24*, 419–435.

STERBA, R. Some psychological factors in Negro race hatred and in anti-Negro riots. In G. Roheim (Ed.), *Psychoanalysis and the Social Sciences*. Vol. 1. New York: International Universities Press, 1947.

ROBERT JAY LIFTON

PSYCHOLOGICAL EFFECTS OF THE ATOMIC BOMB IN HIROSHIMA: THE THEME OF DEATH *

HIROSHIMA commands our attention now, 18 years after its exposure to the atomic bomb, perhaps even more insistently than when the event actually occurred.[1]† We are compelled by the universal threat of nuclear weapons to study the impact of such weapons upon their first human victims, ever mindful of the relevance of this question to our own future and to all of human survival. Much research has already been done concerning the physical consequences of the Hiroshima and Nagasaki disasters, particularly in relationship to their unique new feature of delayed radiation effects.[2] But little attention has been paid to psychological and social elements, though these might well be said to be at present the most vivid legacies of the first atomic bomb.[3]

My own interest in these problems developed during the course of two years of research, conducted in Tokyo and Kyoto from 1960 to 1962, on the relationship of individual character and historical change in Japanese youth.[4] I was struck by the significance which the encounter with nuclear weapons had for the Japanese as a whole, even for young Japanese who could hardly remember the event. Also involved in my undertaking a study in Hiroshima were my concern with the psy-

* An article based on the paper delivered at the AAAS Symposium on Human Reactions to the Threat of Disaster has appeared in *Daedalus,* Summer 1963, 462–497. Reprinted courtesy of Houghton Mifflin Company,

† A section of notes will be found at the end of this article.

chological aspects of war and peace, as well as a previous interest in the behavior of individuals and groups under extreme conditions.[5]

I began the work in April 1962, through two brief visits to Hiroshima, followed by four and one-half months of residence there. My approach was primarily that of individual interviews with two groups of atomic bomb survivors: thirty-three chosen at random from the list of more than 90,000 survivors (*hibakusha*)[6] kept at the Hiroshima University Research Institute for Nuclear Medicine and Biology; and an additional group of forty-two survivors specially selected because of their prominence in dealing with A-bomb problems or their capacity to articulate their experiences — including physicians, university professors, city officials, politicians, writers and poets, and leaders of survivor organizations and peace movements. I also sought out all those in Hiroshima (mostly Japanese, but also Americans and Europeans) who could tell me anything about the complex array of group emotions and social problems which had arisen in the city over the 17 years that had elapsed since the disaster.

I was aware of the delicacy of my situation as an American psychiatrist conducting this study, and I relied heavily upon the continuous support and assistance of Japanese groups within the Hiroshima community, so that all meetings and interviews were arranged through their introductions. In the case of the randomly selected group, my first contact with each survivor was made through a personal visit to the home, accompanied by a Japanese social worker from Hiroshima University. My previous experience in Japan, including the ability to speak a certain amount of Japanese, was helpful in eliciting the many forms of cooperation so crucial for the work; but perhaps of greatest importance was my conveying to both colleagues and research subjects a sense of my personal motivation in undertaking the work, the hope that a systematic study of this kind might clarify important problems often spoken about loosely, and thereby in a small way contribute to the mastery of nuclear weapons and the avoidance of their use.

Interviews were generally about 2 hours long, and I tried to see each research subject twice, though I saw some three or four times, and others just once. I tape recorded all sessions with subjects of the randomly selected group, and did so with many of those in the special group as well, always with the subject's consent. Interviews were conducted in Japanese,[7] and a research assistant was always present to interpret. After making an initial appraisal of the problems involved, I decided to focus my questions upon three general dimensions of the problem: first, the recollection of the experience itself and its inner meaning 17 years later;[8] second, residual concerns and fears, especially those relating to delayed radiation effects; and third, the survivor's sense of self and society, or of special group identity. But subjects were encouraged to associate freely to these topics, and to any feelings or ideas stimulated by them. And in gathering these data I sought always to evaluate to what degree exposure to the atomic bomb in Hiroshima resembles psychological and social patterns common to all disasters, as described in the general literature on disaster, and in what ways it might be a unique experience. What follows is a preliminary statement on work in progress, a composite description of some of the basic trends I have observed.

The Experience Recalled

The degree to which one anticipates a disaster has important bearing upon the way in which one responds, and the predominant tone in the descriptions I heard was that of extreme surprise and unpreparedness. Since it was wartime, people did of course expect conventional bombing; there had been regularly occurring air-raid warnings because of planes passing over Hiroshima, though only an occasional stray bomb had actually been dropped on the city. While military censorship prevented most people from fully understanding Japan's desperate wartime plight, they were aware that the situation was serious. Many, in fact, wondered at Hiroshima's relatively untouched state, despite its obvious strategic significance (as a major staging area for Japan's military operations in China and Southeast Asia, with a large military population), in contrast to the devastation by American air raids of the nearby naval base at Kure. Some attributed this to inexplicable good fortune; others thought that Hiroshima was being intentionally spared because of the large number of Japanese from the Hiroshima area who had emigrated to America. But there was also general apprehension, the feeling that there was something dangerous about Hiroshima's strangely intact state, and that the Americans must be preparing something extraordinarily big for the city (though this latter thought could have been partly a retrospective construction). And at 8:15 A.M. on August 6, 1945, the moment the bomb fell, most people were in a particularly relaxed state, since, following a brief air-raid warning, the all-clear had just been sounded. People thus had a false sense of immediate security, as well as a total incapacity to imagine the nature of the weapon that was about to strike them.[9]

It was only those at some distance from the bomb's hypocenter who could clearly distinguish the sequence of the great flash of light in the sky accompanied by the lacerating heat of the fireball, followed by the sound and force of the blast, and then by the impressive multicolored "mushroom cloud" rising above the city. Two thousand meters is generally considered to be a crucial radius for high mortality (from heat, blast, and radiation), for susceptibility to delayed radiation effects, and for near-total destruction of buildings and other structures. But many were killed outside of this radius, and indeed the number of deaths from the bomb — variously estimated from 63,000 to 240,000 or more — is still unknown. Falling in the center of a flat city made up largely of wooden residential and commercial structures, the bomb is reported to have destroyed or badly damaged (through blast and fire) more than two-thirds of all buildings within 5000 meters, an area roughly encompassing the city limits, so that all of Hiroshima became immediately involved in the atomic disaster.[10]

Those within the 2000-meter radius could not clearly recall their initial perceptions: many simply remember what they thought to be a flash — or else a sudden sensation of heat — followed by an indeterminate period of unconsciousness; others only recall being thrown across a room, or knocked down, then finding themselves pinned under debris of buildings.

The most striking psychological feature of this immediate experience was the sense of a sudden and absolute shift from normal existence to an overwhelming encounter with death. This is described by a young shopkeeper's assistant, who was 13 years old at the time the bomb fell, and 1400 meters from the hypocenter:

I was a little ill ... so I stayed at home that day.... There had been an air-raid warning and then an all-clear. I felt relieved and lay down on the bed with my younger brother.... Then it happened. It came very suddenly.... It felt something like an electric short — a bluish sparkling light.... There was a noise, and I felt great heat — even inside of the house. When I came to, I was underneath the destroyed house.... I didn't know anything about the atomic bomb so I thought that some bomb had fallen directly upon me ... and then when I felt that our house had been directly hit I became furious.... There were roof tiles and walls — everything black — entirely covering me. So I screamed for help.... And from all around I heard moans and screaming, and then I felt a kind of danger to myself.... I thought that I too was going to die in that way. I felt this way at that moment because I was absolutely unable to do anything at all by my own power. ... I didn't know where I was or what I was under.... I couldn't hear voices of my family. I didn't know how I could be rescued. I felt I was going to suffocate and then die, without knowing exactly what had happened to me. This was the kind of expectation I had. ...

I stress this sudden encounter with death because I believe that it initiates, from this first moment of contact with the atomic bomb, an emotional theme within the victim which remains with him indefinitely: the sense of a more-or-less permanent encounter with death.

This early impact enveloped the city in an aura of weirdness and unreality — as recalled by an elderly electrician, who at the time of the bomb was in his mid-forties, working at a railroad junction 5000 meters from the hypocenter.

I was setting up a pole. . . . near a switch in the railroad tracks. . . . I heard a tremendous noise. There was a flash . . . a kind of flash I had never seen before which I can't describe. . . . My face felt hot and I put my hands over my eyes and rushed under a locomotive that was nearby. I crawled in between the wheels, and then there was an enormous boom and the locomotive shook. I was frightened, so I crawled out. . . . I couldn't tell what happened. . . . For about five minutes I saw nobody, and then I saw someone coming out from an air-raid shelter who told me that the youngest one of our workers had been injured by falling piles . . . so I put the injured man on the back of my bicycle and tried to take him to the dispensary. Then I saw that almost all of the people in that area were crowded into the dispensary, and since there was also a hospital nearby, I went there. But that too was already full. . . . So the only thing to do was go into [the center of] Hiroshima. But I couldn't move my bicycle because of all the people coming out from Hiroshima and blocking the way. . . . I saw that they were all naked and I wondered what was the matter with them. . . . When we spoke to people they said that they had been hit by something they didn't understand. . . . We were desperately looking for a doctor or a hospital but we couldn't seem to have any success. . . . We walked toward Hiroshima, still carrying our tools. . . . Then in Hiroshima there was no place either — it had become an empty field — so I carried him to a place near our company office where injured people were lying inside, asking for water. But there was no water and there was no way to help them and I myself didn't know what kind of treatment I should give to this man or to the others. I had to let them die right before my eyes. . . . By then we were cut off from escape, because the fire was beginning to spread out and we couldn't move — we were together with the dead people in the building — only we were not really inside of the building because the building itself had been destroyed, so that we were really outdoors, and we spent the night there. . . .

This rote and essentially ineffectual behavior was characteristic for many, during the first few hours, in those situations where any attempt at all could be made to maintain a group cooperative effort; people were generally more effective in helping members of their immediate families, or in saving

Robert Jay Lifton

themselves. This same electrician, an unusually conscientious man, kept at his post at the railroad over a period of several weeks, leaving only for brief periods to take care of his family. Again his description of the scene of death and near-death takes on a dreamlike quality:

There were dead bodies everywhere.... There was practically no room for me to put my feet on the floor.... At that time I couldn't figure out the reason why all these people were suffering, or what illness it was that had struck them down.... I was the only person taking care of the place as all of the rest of the people had gone.... Other people came in looking for food or to use the toilet.... There was no one to sell tickets in the station, nothing ... and since trains weren't running I didn't have much work to do.... There was no light at all and we were just like sleepwalkers....

And a middle-aged teacher, who was also on the outskirts of the city about 5000 meters from the hypocenter, describes his awe at the destruction he witnessed:

I climbed Hijiyama Mountain and looked down. I saw that Hiroshima had disappeared.... I was shocked by the sight.... What I felt then and still feel now I just can't explain with words. Of course I saw many dreadful scenes after that — but that experience, looking down and finding nothing left of Hiroshima — was so shocking that I simply can't express what I felt. I could see Koi [a suburb at the opposite end of the city] and a few buildings standing.... But Hiroshima didn't exist — that was mainly what I saw — Hiroshima just didn't exist.

And a young university professor, 2500 meters from the hypocenter at the time, sums up these feelings of weird, awesome unreality in a frequently expressed image of hell:

Everything I saw made a deep impression — a park nearby covered with dead bodies waiting to be cremated ... very badly injured people evacuated in my direction.... Perhaps the most impressive thing I saw were girls, very young girls, not only with their clothes torn off but with their skin peeled off as well. ... My immediate thought was that this was like the hell I had always read about.... I had never seen anything which resembled it before, but I thought that should there be a hell, this was it — the Buddhist hell, where we were taught that people who could not attain salvation always went. . . . And I imagined that all of these people I was seeing were in the hell I had read about.

But human beings are unable to remain open to emotional experience of this intensity for any length of time, and very quickly — sometimes within minutes — there began to occur what we may term *psychic closing off:* that is, people simply ceased to feel.

For instance, a male social worker, then in his twenties and in military service in Hiroshima, was temporarily on leave at his home just outside the city; he rushed back into the city soon after the bomb fell, in accordance with his military duty, only to find that his unit had been entirely wiped out. A certain amount of military order was quickly re-established, and a policy of immediate mass cremation of dead bodies was instituted in order to prevent widespread disease, and in accordance with Japanese custom. As a noncommissioned officer and one of the few able-bodied men left, he was put in charge of this work of disposing of corpses, which he found he could accomplish with little difficulty:

After a while they became just like objects or goods that we handled in a very businesslike way. . . . Of course I didn't regard them simply as pieces of wood — they were dead bodies — but if we had been sentimental we couldn't have done the work. . . . We had no emotions. . . . Because of the succession of experiences I had been through I was temporarily without feeling. . . . At times I went about the work with great energy, realizing that no one but myself could do it.

He contrasted his own feelings with the terror experienced by an outsider just entering the disaster area:

Everything at that time was part of an extraordinary situation. . . . For instance, I remember that on the ninth or tenth of August, it was an extremely dark night . . . I saw blue phosphorescent flames rising from the dead bodies — and there were plenty of them. These were quite different from the orange flames coming from the burning buildings. . . . These blue phosphorescent flames are what we Japanese look upon as spirits rising from dead bodies — in former days we called them fireballs[11] — and yet at that time I had no sense of fear, not a bit, but merely thought, "those dead bodies are still burning." . . . But to people who had just come from the outside, those flames looked very strange. . . . One of those nights I met a soldier who had just returned to the city, and I walked along with him. . . . He noticed these unusual fireballs and asked me what they were. I told him that they were the flames coming from dead bodies. The soldier suddenly became extremely frightened, fell down on the ground, and was unable to move. . . . Yet I at that time had a state of mind in which I feared nothing. Though if I were to see those flames now I might be quite frightened. . . .

Relatively few people were involved in the disposal of dead bodies, but virtually all those I interviewed nonetheless experienced a similar form of psychic closing off in response to what they saw and felt, and particularly in response to their over-all exposure to death. Thus many told how horrified they were when they first encountered corpses in strange array, or extremely disfigured faces, but now, after a period of time as they saw more and more of these, they felt nothing. Psychic closing off would last sometimes for a few hours, and sometimes for days or even months and merge into longer-term feelings of depression and despair.

But even the deep and unconscious psychological defensive maneuvers involved in psychic closing off were ultimately unable to afford full protection to the survivor from the painful sights and stimuli impinging upon him. It was, moreover, a defense not devoid of its own psychological cost. Thus the same social worker, in a later interview, questioned his own use of the word "businesslike" to describe his attitude toward dead bodies, and emphasized the pity and sympathy he felt while handling the remains of men from his unit and the pains he took to console family members who came for these remains; he even recalled feeling frightened at night when passing the spot where he worked at cremation by day. He was in effect telling me that not only was his psychic closing off imperfect, but that he was horrified — felt ashamed and guilty — at having behaved in a way which he now thought callous. For he had indulged in activities which were ordinarily, for him, strongly taboo, and had done so with an energy, perhaps even an enthusiasm, which must have mobilized within him primitive emotions of a frightening nature.

The middle-aged teacher who had expressed such awe at the disappearance of Hiroshima reveals the way in which feelings of shame and guilt, and especially shame and guilt toward the dead, break through the defense of psychic closing off and painfully assert themselves:

> I went to look for my family. Somehow I became a pitiless person, because if I had pity I would not have been able to walk through the city, to walk over those dead bodies. The most impressive thing was the expression in peoples' eyes — bodies badly injured which had turned black — their eyes looking for someone to come and help them. They looked at me and knew that I was stronger than they. . . . I was looking for my family and looking carefully at everyone I met to see if he or she was a family member — but the eyes — the emptiness — the helpless expression — were something I will never forget. . . . I often had to go to the same place more than once. I would wish that the same family would not still be there. . . . I saw disappointment in their eyes. They looked at me with great expectation, staring right through me. It was very hard to be stared at by those eyes. . . .

He felt, in other words, accused by the eyes of the anonymous dead and dying, of wrongdoing and transgression (a sense of guilt) — for not helping them, for letting them die, for "selfishly" remaining alive and strong; and "exposed" and "seen through" by the same eyes for these identical failings (a sense of shame).[12]

There were also many episodes of more focused guilt toward specific family members whom one was unable to help, and for whose death one felt responsible. For instance, the shopkeeper's assistant mentioned above was finally rescued from the debris of his destroyed house by his mother, but she was too weakened by her own injuries to be able to walk very far with him. Soon they were surrounded by fire, and he (a boy of 13) did not feel he had the strength to sustain her weight, and became convinced that they would both die unless he took some other action. So he put her down and ran for help, but the neighbor he summoned could not get through to the woman because of the flames, and the boy learned shortly afterward that his mother died in precisely the place he had left her. His lasting sense of guilt was reflected in his frequent experience, from that time onward, of hearing his mother's voice ringing in his ears calling for help.

A middle-aged businessman related a similarly guilt-stimulating sequence. His work had taken him briefly to the south of Japan and he had returned to Hiroshima during the early morning hours of August 6. Having been up all night, he was not too responsive when his 12-year-old son came into his room to ask his father to remove a nail from his shoe so that he could put them on and go to school. The father, wishing to get the job quickly over with, placed a piece of leather above the tip of the nail and promised he would take the whole nail out when the boy returned in the afternoon. As in the case of many youngsters who were sent to factories to do "voluntary labor" as a substitute for their school work, the boy's body was never found — and the father, after a desperately fruitless search for his son throughout the city, was left with the lingering self-accusation that the nail he had failed to remove might have impeded the boy's escape from the fire.

Most survivors focus upon one incident, one sight, or one particular *ultimate horror* with which they strongly identify themselves, and which left them with a profound sense of pity, guilt, and shame. Thus the social worker describes an event which he feels affected him even more than his crematory activities:

On the evening of August 6, the city was so hot from the fire that I could not easily enter it, but I finally managed to do so by taking a path along the river. As I walked along the bank near the present Yokogawa bridge, I saw the bodies of a mother and her child. . . . That is, I thought I saw dead bodies, but the child was still alive — still breathing, though with difficulty. . . . . I filled the cover of my lunch box with water and gave it to the child but it was so weak it could not drink. I knew that people were frequently passing that spot . . . and I hoped that one of these people would take the child — as I had to go back to my own unit. Of course I helped many people all through that day . . . but the image of this child stayed on my mind and remains as a strong impression even now. . . . Later when I was again in that same area I hoped that I might be able to find the child . . . and I looked for it among all the dead children collected at a place nearby. . . . Even before the war I had planned to go into social work but this experience led me to go into my present work with children — as the memory of that mother and child by Yoko-gawa bridge has never left me, especially since the child was still alive when I saw it.

These expressions of ultimate horror can be related to direct personal experience of loss (for instance, the businessman who had failed to remove the nail from his son's shoe remained preoccupied with pathetic children staring imploringly at him), as well as to enduring individual emotional themes. Most of them involved women and children, universal symbols of purity and vulnerability, particularly in Japanese culture. And, inevitably, the ultimate horror was directly related to death or dying.

Contamination and Disease

Survivors told me of three rumors which circulated widely in Hiroshima just after the bomb. The first was that for a period of 75 years Hiroshima would be uninhabitable — no one would be able to live there. This rumor was a direct expression of the *fear of deadly and protracted contamination from a mysterious poison believed to have been emitted by the frightening new weapon.* (As one survivor put it, "The ordinary people spoke of poison, the intellectuals spoke of radiation.")

Even more frequently expressed, and I believe with greater emotion, was a second rumor: trees and grass would never again grow in Hiroshima; from that day on the city would be unable to sustain vegetation of any kind. This seemed to suggest *an ultimate form of desolation even beyond that of hu-*

man death: nature was drying up altogether, the ultimate source of life was being extinguished — a form of symbolism particularly powerful in Japanese culture with its focus upon natural aesthetics and its view of nature as both enveloping and energizing all of human life.

The third rumor, less frequently mentioned to me but one which also had wide currency in various versions, was that all those who had been exposed to the bomb in Hiroshima would be dead within three years. This more naked death symbolism was directly related to the appearance of frightening symptoms of toxic radiation effects. For almost immediately after the bomb and during the following days and weeks people began to experience, and notice in others, symptoms of a strange form of illness: nausea, vomiting, and loss of appetite; diarrhea with large amounts of blood in the stools; fever and weakness; purple spots on various parts of the body from bleeding into the skin (purpura); inflammation and ulceration of the mouth, throat, and gums (oropharyngeal lesions and gingivitis); bleeding from the mouth, gums, nose, throat, rectum, and urinary tract (hemorrhagic manifestations); loss of hair from the scalp and other parts of the body (epilation); extremely low white-blood-cell counts when these were taken (leucopenia); and in many cases a progressive course until death.[13] These symptoms and fatalities aroused in the minds of the people of Hiroshima a special terror, *an image of a weapon which not only kills and destroys on a colossal scale but also leaves behind in the bodies of those exposed to it deadly influences which may emerge at any time and strike down their victims.* This image was made particularly vivid by the delayed appearance of these radiation effects, two to four weeks after the bomb fell, sometimes in people who had previously seemed to be in perfect health.

The shopkeeper's assistant, both of whose parents were killed by the bomb, describes his reactions to the death of two additional close family members from these toxic radiation effects:

My grandmother was taking care of my younger brother on the 14th of August when I left, and when I returned on the 15th she had many spots all over her body. Two or three days later she died. . . . My younger brother, who . . . was just a [five-month-old] baby, was without breast milk — so we fed him thin rice gruel. . . . But on the 10th of October he suddenly began to look very ill, though I had not then noticed any spots on his body. . . . Then on the next day he began to look a little better, and I thought he was going to survive. I was very pleased, as he was the only family member I had left, and I took him to a doctor — but on the way to the doctor he died. And at that time we found that there were two large spots on his bottom. . . . I heard it said that all these people would die within three years . . . so I thought, "sooner or later I too will die". . . . I felt weak and very lonely — with no hope at all . . . and since I had seen so many people's eyebrows falling out, their hair falling out, bleeding from their teeth — I found myself always nervously touching my hair like this [he demonstrated by rubbing his head]. . . . I never knew when some sign of the disease would show itself. . . . And living in the countryside then with my relatives, people who came to visit would tell us these things and then the villagers also talked about them — telling stories of this man or that man who visited us a few days ago, returned to Hiroshima, and died within a week. . . . I couldn't tell whether these stories were true or not, but I believed them then. And I also heard that when the *hibakusha* came to evacuate to the village where I was, they died there one by one. . . . This loneliness, and the fear . . . the physical fear . . . has been with me always. . . . It is not something temporary, as I still have it now. . . .

Here we find a link between this early sense of ubiquitous death from radiation effects, and later anxieties about death and illness. In a smilar tone, a middle-aged writer describes his daughter's sudden illness and death:

My daughter was working with her classmates at a place 1000 meters from the hypocenter. . . . I was able to meet her the next day at a friend's house. She had no burns and only minor external wounds so I took her with me to my country house. She was quite all right for a while but on the 4th of September she suddenly became sick. . . . The symptoms of her disease were different from those of a normal disease. . . . She had spots all over her body. . . . Her hair began to fall out. She vomited small clumps of blood many times. Finally she began to bleed all over her mouth. And at times her fever was very high. I felt this was a very strange and horrible disease. . . . We didn't know what it was. I thought it was a kind of epidemic — something like cholera. So I told the rest of my family not to touch her and to disinfect all utensils and everything she used. . . . We were all afraid of it and even the doctor didn't know what it was. . . . After ten days of agony and torture she died on September 14. . . . I thought it was very cruel that my daughter, who had nothing to do with the war, had to be killed in this way. . . .

Survivors were thus affected not only by the fact of people dying around them but by the way in which they died: a gruesome form of rapid bodily deterioration which seemed unrelated to more usual and "decent" forms of death.

We have seen how these initial physical fears could readily turn into lifetime bodily concerns. And during the years that followed, these fears and concerns became greatly magnified by another development: the growing awareness among the people of Hiroshima that medical studies were demonstrating an abnormally high rate of leukemia among survivors of the atomic bomb. The increased incidence was first noted in 1948 and reached a peak between 1950 and 1952; it has been greatest in those exposed closest to the hypocenter so that for those within 1000 meters the increase of leukemia has been between 10 and 50 times the normal. Since 1952 the rate has diminished, but it is still higher than in unexposed populations, and fears which have been aroused remain strong. While symptoms of leukemia are not exactly the same as those of acute radiation effects, the two conditions share enough in common — the dreaded "purple spots" and other forms of hemorrhage, laboratory findings of abnormalities of the blood, progressive weakness and fever and (inevitably in leukemia, and often enough in acute irradiation) ultimate death — that these tend to merge, psychologically speaking, into a diffuse fear of bodily annihilation and death.[14]

Moreover, Hiroshima survivors are aware of the general concern and controversy about genetic effects of the atomic bomb, and most express fear about possible harmful effects upon subsequent generations — a very serious emotional concern anywhere, but particularly so in an East Asian culture which stresses family lineage and the continuity of generations as man's central purpose in life and (at least symbolically) his means of achieving immortality. The Hiroshima people know that radiation *can* produce congenital abnormalities (as has been widely demonstrated in laboratory animals); and abnormalities have frequently been reported among the offspring of survivors — sometimes in very lurid journalistic terms, sometimes in more restrained medical reports. Actually, systematic studies of the problem have so far revealed no higher incidence of abnormalities in survivors' offspring than in those of control populations, so that scientific findings regarding genetic effects have been essentially negative. However, there has been one uncomfortably positive genetic finding, that of disturbances in sex ratio of offspring: men exposed to a significant degree of radiation tend to have relatively fewer daughters, whereas exposed women tend to have fewer sons, because, it is believed, of sex-linked lethal mutations involving the X chromosome — a finding whose significance is difficult to evaluate. Moreover, there are Japanese physicians who believe that there has been an increase in various forms of internal (and therefore invisible) congenital abnormalities in children of survivors, despite the absence so far of convincing scientific evidence.[15]

Another factor here is the definite damage from radiation experienced by children exposed *in utero*, including many stillbirths and abortions, as well as a high incidence of microcephaly with and without mental retardation. (These occurred almost exclusively in pregnancies which had not advanced beyond four months.) This is, of course, a direct effect of radiation upon sensitive, rapidly growing fetal tissues, and, scientifically speaking, has nothing to do with genetic problems. But laymen often fail to make this distinction; to them the witnessing of children born with abnormally small heads and retarded minds was apt to be looked upon as still another example of the bomb's awesome capacity to inflict a physical curse upon its victims and their offspring.

There are also other areas of concern regarding delayed radiation effects. There has been a definite increase in cataracts and related eye conditions, which was not stressed to me by survivors as so great a source of emotional concern as the other problems mentioned, but has been nonetheless far from negligible. There is evidence, though not yet decisive, that the incidence of various forms of cancer has increased among survivors; if confirmed, this could be an extremely serious problem, since it involves fatal disease entities much more frequent in their normal occurrence than leukemia. There is also some evidence of impairment in the growth and development of children, though this is contested by some on the grounds of inadequately accounting for social and economic factors. And there is a large group of divergent conditions — including anemias and liver and blood diseases, endocrine and skin disorders, impairment of central nervous system (particularly midbrain) function, and premature aging — which have been attributed by various investigators to radiation effects, though none of them has shown increased incidence in large-scale studies involving control populations. Even more difficult to evaluate is a frequently reported borderline condition of general weakness and debilitation also believed — by a very large number of survivors and by some physicians as well — to be caused by delayed radiation effects.

These fears about general health and genetic effects have inevitably affected marriage arrangements (which are usually made in Japan by families with the help of a go-between), in which survivors are frequently thought to encounter discrimination, particularly when involved in arrangements with families outside of Hiroshima.

A company employee in his thirties, who was 2000 meters from the bomb's hypocenter when it fell, described to me virtually all these bodily and genetic concerns in a voice that betrayed considerable anxiety:

Even when I have an illness which is not at all serious — as for instance when I had very mild liver trouble — I have fears about its cause. Of course if it is just an ordinary condition there is nothing to worry about, but if it has a direct connection to radio-activity, then I might not be able to expect to recover. At such times I feel myself very delicate. . . . This happened two or three years ago. I was working very hard and drinking a great deal of *sake* at night in connection with business appointments and I also had to make many strenuous trips. So my condition might have been partly related to my using up so much energy in all of these things. . . . The whole thing is not fully clear to me. . . . But the results of statistical study show that those who were exposed to the bomb are more likely to have illnesses — not only of the liver, but various kinds of new growths, such as cancer or blood diseases. My blood was examined several times but no special changes were discovered. . . . When my marriage arrangements were made we discussed all these things in a direct fashion. Everyone knows that there are some effects, but in my case it was the eleventh year after the bomb and I discussed my physical condition during all of that time. From that, and also from the fact that I was exposed to the bomb while inside of a building and taken immediately to the suburbs, and then remained quite a while outside of the city — judging from all of these facts, it was concluded that there was very little to fear concerning my condition. . . . But in general, there is a great concern that people who were exposed to the bomb might become ill five or ten years later or at any time in the future. . . . Also when my children were born, I found myself worrying about things that ordinary people don't worry about, such as the possibility that they might inherit some terrible disease from me. . . . I heard that the likelihood of our giving birth to deformed children is greater than in the case of ordinary people . . . and at that time my white blood cell count was rather low. . . . I felt fatigue in the summertime and had a blood count done three or four times. . . . I was afraid it could be related to the bomb, and was greatly worried. . . . Then after the child was born, even though he wasn't a deformed child, I still worried that something might happen to him afterwards. . . . With the second child too I was not entirely free of such worries. . . . I am still not sure what might happen and I worry that the effects of radioactivity might be lingering in some way. . . .

Here we see a young man carrying on effectively in his life, essentially healthy, with normal children, and yet continually plagued by underlying anxieties — about his general health, then about marriage arrangements, and then in relationship to the birth of each of his children. Each hurdle is passed, but there is little relief; like many survivors, he experiences an inner sense of being doomed for posterity.

And a young clerk, also exposed about 2000 meters from the hypocenter, but having the additional disadvantage of retaining a keloid scar resulting from facial burns, expresses similar emotions in still stronger fashion:

> Frankly speaking, even now I have fear. . . . Even today people die in the hospitals from A-bomb disease, and when I hear about this I worry that I too might sooner or later have the same thing happen to me. . . . I have a special feeling that I am different from ordinary people . . . that I have the mark of wounds — as if I were a cripple. . . . I imagine a person who has an arm or a leg missing might feel the same way. . . . It is not a matter of lacking something externally, but rather something like a handicap — something mental which does not show — the feeling that I am mentally different from ordinary people . . . so when I hear about people who die from A-bomb disease or who have operations because of this illness, then I feel that I am the same kind of person as they. . . .

The survivor's identification with the dead and the maimed initiates a vicious circle on the psychosomatic plane of existence: he is likely to associate the mildest everyday injury or sickness with possible radiation effects; and anything he relates to radiation effects becomes associated with death. The process is accentuated by the strong Japanese cultural focus upon bodily symptoms as expressions of anxiety and conflict. Thus the all-encompassing term "A-bomb sickness" or "A-bomb disease" (*genbakushō*) has evolved, referring on the one hand to such fatal conditions as the early acute radiation effects and later cases of leukemia, and on the other hand to the vague borderline area of fatigue, general weakness, sensitivity to hot weather, suspected anemia, susceptibility to colds or stomach trouble, and general nervousness — all of which are frequent complaints of survivors, and which many associate with radiation effects.[16] Not only does the expression "A-bomb disease" have wide popular currency but it has frequently been used by local physicians as a convenient category for a condition otherwise hard to classify, and at the same time as a means of making it possible for the patient to derive certain medical and economic benefits.

These benefits also loom large in the picture.[17] Doctors and survivors, as well as politicians and city officials, are caught in a conflict between humanitarian provision for medical need, and the dangers (expressed to me particularly by Japanese physicians) of encouraging the development in survivors of hypochondriasis, general weakness and dependency — or what is sometimes called "A-bomb neurosis." During the years immediately after the war, when medical care was most needed, very little adequate treatment was available, as the national medical law providing for survivors was not enacted until 1957. But since that time a series of laws and amendments have been passed with increasingly comprehensive medical coverage, particularly for those in the "special survivors" group (those nearest the hypocenter at the time of the bomb and those who have shown evidence of medical conditions considered to be related to A-bomb effects). In the last few years the category of "special survivors" has been steadily enlarged: distance from the hypocenter, as a criterion for eligibility, has been extended from 2000 to 3000 meters; and qualifying illnesses — originally limited to such conditions as leukemia, ophthalmic diseases, and various blood and liver disorders, all of which were considered to be related to radiation effects — have been extended to include illnesses not considered to be necessarily directly caused by radiation but possibly aggravated by the over-all atomic bomb experience, such as cancer, heart disease, endocrine and kidney disorders, arteriosclerosis, hypertension, and others.

Maximum medical and economic benefits, however, can be obtained only by those "certified" (through a special medical procedure) to have illnesses specifically related to the atomic bomb; but some physicians believe that this "certification" — which can sometimes be given for such minor conditions as ordinary anemia (as well as for more serious illnesses) — tends to stamp one psychologically as a lifetime A-bomb patient. The rationale of these laws is to provide maximum help for survivors and to give them the benefit of the doubt about matters which are not entirely scientifically resolved. But there remains a great deal of controversy over them. In addition to those who feel that the laws foster an exaggerated preoccupation with atomic bomb effects (not only among doctors, but also among city officials, ordinary people, and even survivors themselves), there are other survivors who criticize them as being still insufficiently comprehensive, as having overly complicated categories and subcategories which in the end deny full care for certain conditions.

My own impression in studying this problem is that, since "A-bomb disease" is at this historical juncture as much a spiritual as a physical condition (as our young clerk made so clear) — and one which touches at every point upon the problem of death — it is difficult for any law or medical program to provide a cure.

The general psychological atmosphere in Hiroshima — and particularly that generated by the effects of the mass media — also has great bearing upon those psychosomatic problems. As one would expect, the whole subject of the atomic bomb and its delayed radiation effects has been continuous front-page news — within the limits of the restrictions upon publicizing these matters imposed by the American Occupation from 1945-1952,[18] and without such restrictions thereafter. Confronted with a subject so emotionally charged for the people of Hiroshima — its intensity constantly reinforced by world events and particularly by nuclear weapons testing — newspapers in Hiroshima and elsewhere in Japan have dealt with it dramatically, particularly in circulating the concept of "A-bomb disease." Mass media are caught in a moral dilemma in some ways similar to what I have already described for physicians, city officials, and the survivors themselves: there is, on the one hand, the urge to give full publicity to the horrors of nuclear weapons through vivid description of the effects and suspected effects of atomic bomb radiation, thereby serving warning to the world and also expressing a form of sympathy to survivors through recognition of their plight; and on the other hand, the growing awareness that lurid reports of illness and death have a profoundly disturbing effect upon survivors. Responsible media have struggled to reconcile these conflicting moral pressures and achieve balanced treatment of an unprecedentedly difficult problem; others have been guided mainly by commercial considerations. In any case, the people of Hiroshima have been constantly confronted with frightening descriptions of patients dying in the "A-bomb hospital" (a medical center built specifically for the treatment of conditions related to the bomb) of "A-bomb disease." In the majority of cases the relationship of the fatal condition to delayed radiation effects is equivocal, but this is usually not made clear, nor does it in any way lessen the enormous impact of these reports upon individual survivors.[19] Also furthering this impact have been the activities of peace movements and various ideological and political groups — ranging from those whose universalistic dedication to peace and opposition to the testing of nuclear weapons leads them to circulate the effects of the bomb on a humanistic basis, to others who seek narrower political goals from the unique Hiroshima atmosphere.

What I wish to stress is the manner in which these diverse passions — compounded of moral concern, sympathetic identification, various forms of fear, hostility, political conviction, personal ambition, and journalistic sensationalism — interact with the psychosomatic preoccupations of survivors. But I would also emphasize that these passions are by no means simply manufactured ones; they are the inevitable expression of the impact of a disaster of this magnitude upon basic human conflicts and anxieties. And whatever the medical exaggerations, they are built upon an underlying lethal reality of acute and delayed radiation effects, and upon the genuine possibility of still undiscovered forms of bodily harm.

Yet, in bodily terms or otherwise, human beings vary

greatly in their capacity to absorb an experience of this kind. And one's feelings of health or invalidism — as well as one's symbolic attitude toward the bomb — have much to do with individual emotions and life patterns. This is made clear by a middle-aged female artist who experienced the bomb just 1500 meters from the hypocenter, and during subsequent years suffered continuously from a variety of bodily symptoms of indefinite origin, as well as from general unhappiness in marital and family relationships:

> It looks as though marriage and the normal life one leads with marriage is good for the health. . . . Among A-bomb victims, those that are married and well established with their families have fewer complaints. Of course, even those who are settled in their families remember the incident. But on the whole they are much better off and feel better . . . their attitude is, *"shoganai"* (it can't be helped). "It is useless to look back on old memories," they keep saying. They are simply interested in their immediate problems of marriage and everyday life. They look forward rather than backward. . . . Those without families, on the other hand, keep remembering everything. Clinging to their memories, they keep repeating the experience. . . . They curse the whole world — including what happened in the past and what is happening now. Some of them even say, "I hope that atomic bombs will be dropped again and then the whole world will suffer the same way I am suffering now."

This kind of hostility is likely to occur together with psychosomatic complaints, and particularly in those people who feel that their life had been blighted by the atomic bomb — those who lost close family members or who in one way or another feel themselves unable to recover from the experience. The cosmic nature of the emotion — its curse upon (and perhaps even a wish for total annihilation of) the whole world — resembles in some ways the retaliatory emotions of hurt children. But it contains additional elements of personal recollection: the experience of "world destruction" at the time of the bomb. And it is a projection into the future: the even greater world destruction one can envisage as a consequence of a repetition of the use of nuclear weapons.

Unwanted Identity

It is clear by now that exposure to the atomic bomb changed the survivor's status as a human being, in his own eyes as well as those of others. Both through his immediate experience and its consequences over the years, he became a member of a new group; he assumed the identity of the *hibakusha*, of one who has undergone the atomic bomb. When I asked survivors to associate freely to the word *hibakusha*, and to explain their feelings about it, they invariably conveyed to me the sense of having been compelled to take on this special category of existence, by which they felt permanently bound, however they might wish to free themselves from it. The shopkeeper's assistant expresses this in simple terms characteristic for many:

Well . . . because I am a *hibakusha* . . . how shall I say it—I wish others would not look at me with special eyes . . . perhaps *hibakusha* are mentally — or both physically and mentally — different from others . . . but I myself do not want to be treated in any special way because I am a *hibakusha*. . . .

To be a *hibakusha* thus separates one from the rest of humankind. It means, as expressed by a young female clerical worker left with a keloid from her atomic-bomb exposure at 1600 meters, a sense of having been forsaken.

I don't like people to use that word [*hibakusha*]. . . . Of course there are some who, through being considered *hibakusha*, want to receive special coddling [*amaeru*]. . . . But I like to stand up as an individual. When I was younger they used to call us "atomic bomb maidens". . . . More recently they call us *hibakusha*. . . . I don't like this special view of us. . . . Usually when people refer to young girls, they will say girls or daughters, or some person's daughter . . . but to refer to us as atomic bomb maidens is a way of discrimination. . . . It is a way of abandoning us. . . .

What she is saying, and what many said to me in different ways, is that the experience, with all its consequences, is so profound that it can virtually, so to speak, become the person; others then see one *only* as a *hibakusha* bearing the taint of death, and therefore, in the deepest sense, turn away. And even the special attentions — the various forms of emotional succor — which the survivor may be tempted to seek cannot be satisfying because such succor is ultimately perceived as inauthentic.

A European priest, one of the relatively few non-Japanese *hibakusha,* expresses these sentiments gently but sardonically:

> I always say — if everyone looks at me because I received the Nobel Prize, that's O.K., but if my only virtue is that I was 1000 meters from the atomic bomb center and I'm still alive — I don't want to be famous for that.

Hibakusha look upon themselves as underprivileged in other ways too. Not only are they literally a minority group (one-fifth of the city's population), but they are generally considered to be at the lower socioeconomic levels of society and have even at times been compared to the *burakumin,* or outcast group.[20] For once it was realized that Hiroshima was not permanently contaminated after all, not only did the survivors attempt to rebuild their homes, but hordes of outsiders — some from overseas areas, some from the industrial Osaka region, some of them black marketeers and members of gangs who saw special opportunity beckoning, all of them both physically and culturally more vigorous than the atomic-bombed, traditionalistic Hiroshima population — poured into the city and became perhaps the main beneficiaries of the economic boom which later developed. Survivors have encountered discrimination not only in marriage but also in employment, as it was felt that they could not work as hard as ordinary people and tended to need more time off because of illness and fatigue. Of course, survivors regularly work and marry; but many do so with a sense of having, as *hibakusha,* impaired capacity for both. They strongly resent the popular image of the *hibakusha* which accentuates their limitations, but at the same time accept much of it as their own self-image. Thus, concerning occupational competition, older survivors often feel that they have lacked the over-all energy to assimilate their economic, spiritual, and possibly physical blows sufficiently to be the equal of ordinary people; and young survivors, even if they feel themselves to possess normal energy, often fear that being identified by others as a *hibakusha* might similarly interfere with their occupational standing. Concerning marriage, the sense of impairment can include the need to have one's A-bomb experience more-or-less "cleared" by a go-between (as we have seen), fears about having abnormal children, or sometimes about the ability to have children at all,[21] and occasionally, in males, diminished sexual potency (thought of as organic, but probably psychogenic in origin).

However well or poorly a survivor is functioning in his life, the word *hibakusha* evokes an image of the dead and the dying. The young clerk, for instance, when he hears the word, thinks either of the experience itself ("...Although I wasn't myself too badly injured I saw many people who were ... and I think ... of the look on their faces ... camps full of these people, their breasts burned and red....") or, as we have already heard him describe, of the aftereffects: "When I hear about people who die from A-bomb disease or who have operations because of this illness, then I feel that I am the same kind of person as they...."

We are again confronted with the survivor's intimate identification with the dead; we find, in fact, that it tends to pervade the entire *hibakusha* identity. *For survivors seem not only to have experienced the atomic disaster, but to have imbibed it and incorporated it into their beings, including all of its elements of horror, evil, and particularly of death.* They feel compelled virtually to merge with those who died, not only with close family members but with a more anonymous group of "the dead." And they judge, and indeed judge harshly, their own behavior and that of other survivors on the basis of the degree of respect it demonstrates toward the dead. They condemn, for instance, the widespread tendency (which, as Japanese, they are at the same time attracted to) of making the anniversary of the bomb an occasion for a gay festival — because they see this as an insult to the dead. Similarly they are extraordinarily suspicious of all individual and group attempts to take any form of action related to the atomic bomb experience, even when done for the apparent purpose of helping survivors or furthering international peace. And they are, if anything, more critical of a survivor prominent in such programs than they are of "outsiders," constantly accusing such a person of "selling his name," "selling the bomb," or "selling Hiroshima." The causes for their suspiciousness are many — including a pervasive Japanese cultural tendency to be critical of the man who shows unconventional initiative (as expressed in the popular saying, "A nail that sticks out will be hammered down"), as well as an awareness of how readily the Hiroshima situation can be "used" by ambitious leaders. But there is an ultimate inner feeling that any such activities and programs are "impure," that they violate the sanctity of the dead. For in relationship to the atomic bomb disaster, it is only the dead who, in the eyes of survivors, remain pure; and any self- or group assertion can readily be seen as an insult to the dead.

The *hibakusha* identity, then, in a significant symbolic sense, becomes an identity of the dead. Created partly by the particularly intense Japanese capacity for identification, and partly by the special quality of guilt over surviving, it takes shape through the following inner sequence: I almost died; I should have died; I did die, or at least am not really alive; or if I am alive it is impure of me to be so; and anything I do which affirms life is also impure and an insult to the dead, who alone are pure.[22]

Finally, this imposed identity of the atomic bomb survivor is greatly affected by his historical perceptions (whether clear or fragmentary) of the original experience, including its bearing upon the present world situation. The dominant emotion here is the sense of having been made into "guinea pigs," not only because of being studied by research groups (particularly American research groups) interested in determining the effects of delayed radiation, but more fundamentally because of having been victimized by the first "experiment" (a word many of them use in referring to the event) with nuclear weapons. They are affected by a realization, articulated in various ways, that they have experienced something ultimate in man-made disasters; and at the same time by the feeling that the world's continuing development and testing of the offending weapons deprives their experience of meaning. Thus, while frequently suspicious of organized campaigns against nuclear testing, they almost invariably experience anxiety and rage when such testing is conducted, recall the horrors they have been through, and express bitter frustration at the world's unwillingness to heed their warnings. And we have seen how this anger can at times be converted into thoughts of cosmic retaliation. There remains, of course, a residuum of hostility toward America and Americans for having dropped the bomb, but such hostility has been tempered over the years and softened by Japanese cultural restraints — except, as we have also seen, in individuals who experienced personal losses and blows to self-esteem from which they have been unable to recover. More than in relationship to the dropping of the bomb itself (which many said they could understand as a product, however horrible, of war), survivors tend to express hostility in response to what they feel to be callousness toward their plight, or toward those who died; and also in response to nuclear weapons testing. Thus, in singling out President Truman as an object of hatred, as some do, it is not only because he ordered that the bomb be used, but also because he was assertively unapologetic about having done so.[23]

Survivors tend to be strongly ambivalent about serving as symbols for the rest of the world, and this ambivalence is expressed in Hiroshima's excruciating conflict about whether or not to tear down the so-called "A-bomb dome" (or "peace dome") — the prominent ruins of a dome-shaped exhibition hall located almost directly at the hypocenter. The dome has so far been permitted to stand as a reminder of the experience, and its picture has been featured in countless books and pamphlets dealing, from every point of view, with the A-bomb problem. Three different sets of attitudes on the question were expressed to me. The first, let it remain permanently so that people (especially outsiders) will remember what we have been through and take steps to prevent repetitions of such disasters. The second, tear it down (for any of the following reasons) — it does no good, as no one pays any attention to it; we should adopt the Buddhist attitude of resignation toward the experience; the dome is inauthentic, does not adequately convey what we really experience, and is not in fact directly at the hypocenter; it is too painful a reminder for *us* (the *hibakusha*) to have to look at every day (perhaps the most strongly-felt objection); and we should look ahead to the future rather than back to the unpleasant past. And the third, let it be permitted neither to stand indefinitely nor to be torn down, but instead to be left as it is until it begins to crumble of its own, and then simply removed — a rather ingenious (and perhaps characteristically Japanese) compromise solution to the dilemma, which the city administration has proposed. Most survivors simultaneously feel various conflicting elements of the first and second sets of attitudes, and sometimes of all three. The inner conflict is something like this: for the sake of the dead, and of our own sense of worth, we must give our experience significance by enabling it to serve wider moral purposes; but to do so — to be living symbols of massive death — not only is unbearably painful but also tends ultimately to be insincere and to insult, rather than comfort, the dead.

Beyond Hiroshima

We return to the question we raised at the beginning: Does Hiroshima follow the standard patterns delineated for other disasters, or is it — in an experiential sense — a new order of event? We must say first that the usual emotional patterns of disaster [24] are very much present in what I have already described. One can break down the experience into the usual sequence of anticipation, impact, and aftermath; one can recognize such standard individual psychological features as various forms of denial, the "illusion of centrality" (or the feeling of each person that he was at the very center of the disaster's path),[25] the apathy of the "disaster syndrome" resulting from the sudden loss of the sense of safety and even omnipotence with which we usually conduct our lives, and the conflict between self-preservation and wider human responsibility which culminates in feelings of guilt and shame; even some of the later social and psychological conflicts in the affected population are familiar.[26] Yet we have also seen convincing evidence that the Hiroshima experience,[27] no less in the psychological than in the physical sphere, transcends in many important ways that of the ordinary disaster. I shall try to suggest what I think are some of the important ways in which this is true. And when these special psychological qualities of the experience of the atomic bomb have been more fully elaborated — beyond the preliminary outlines of this paper — I believe that they will, in turn, shed light on general disaster patterns, and, of greater importance, on human nature and its vicissitudes at our present historical juncture. We may then come to see Hiroshima for what it was and is: both a direct continuation of the long and checkered history of human struggle, and at the same time a plunge into a new and tragic dimension.

The first of these psychological elements is one we have already referred to, the continuous encounter with death. When we consider the sequence of this encounter — its turbulent onset at the moment the bomb fell, its shocking reappearance in association with delayed radiation effects, and its prolonged expression in the group identity of the doomed and nearly dead — we are struck by the fact that it is an interminable encounter. There is, psychologically speaking, no end point, no resolution. This continuous and unresolvable encounter with death, then, is a unique feature of the atomic bomb disaster. Its significance for the individual survivor varies greatly, according to such factors as his previous character traits, his distance from the hypocenter at the time the bomb fell, fatalities in his immediate family, and many other features of his bomb experience and subsequent life pattern. There is little doubt that most survivors lead reasonably effective personal, family, and occupational lives. But each retains, though in varying degree, emotional elements of this special relationship to death.

In the light of the Hiroshima experience we should also consider the possibility that in other disasters or extreme situations there may also be more significant inner encounters with death, immediate or longer-term, than we have heretofore supposed. Psychiatrists and social scientists investigating these matters are hampered by the same factors that interfere with everyone else's approach to the subject: first, by our inability to imagine death, which deprives us, as psychiatrists, of our usual reliance upon empathy and leaves us always at several psychological removes from experiential understanding; and second, by the elaborate circle of denial — the profound inner need of human beings to make believe that they will never die — in which we too are enclosed. But these universal psychological barriers to thought about death become much greater in relation to a nuclear disaster, where the enormity of the scale of killing and the impersonal nature of the technology are still further impediments to comprehension. No wonder, then, that the world resists full knowledge of the Hiroshima and Nagasaki experiences and expends relatively little energy in comprehending their full significance. And beyond Hiroshima, these same impediments tragically block and distort our perceptions of the general consequences of nuclear weapons. They also raise an important question relevent for the continuous debate about the desirability of preparedness for possible nuclear attacks: if the human imagination is so limited in its capacity to deal with death, and particularly death on a vast scale, can individuals ever be significantly "prepared" for a nuclear disaster?

The Hiroshima experience thus compels us, particularly as psychiatrists, to give more thought to psychic perceptions of death and dying.[28] Here I would particularly stress the psychological importance of identification with the dead — not merely the identification with a particular loved one, as in an ordinary mourning experience, but rather, as we have observed in atomic bomb survivors, a lasting sense of affiliation with death itself. This affiliation creates in turn an enduring element, both within, and standing in judgment of, the self — a process closely related to the experience of shame.[29] Also of great importance is the *style of dying*, real or symbolic, the way in which one anticipates death and the significance with which one can relate oneself to this anticipation. Among those I interviewed in Hiroshima, many found solace in the characteristically Japanese (partly Buddhist) attitude of resignation, but virtually none were able to build a framework of meaning around their overwhelming immersion in death. However, philosophically they might accept the horrors of war, they had an underlying sense of having been victimized and experimented upon by a horrible device, all to no avail in a world that has derived no profit from their sufferings.

And this sense of purposeless death suggests the second special feature of the atomic disaster: *a vast breakdown of faith in the larger human matrix supporting each individual life, and therefore a loss of faith (or trust) in the structure of existence.* This is partly due to the original exposure to death and destruction on such an extraordinary scale, an "end-of-the-world" experience resembling the actualization of the wildest psychotic delusion; partly because of the shame and guilt patterns which, initiated during the experience itself, turned into longer-lasting preoccupations with human selfishness (preoccupations expressed to me by a large number of survivors); and partly due also to the retention of a sense of having encountered an ultimate form of *man-made* destruction. Phrased in another way, the atomic bomb destroyed the complex equilibrium which ordinarily mediates and integrates the great variety of cultural patterns and individual emotions that maintain any society, large or small. One must, of course, take into account here the disruption accompanying the extensive social change which has occurred all over Japan immediately following World War II; and one must also recognize the impressive re-emergence of Hiroshima as an actively functioning city. Nevertheless, this profound loss of confidence in human social ties remains within survivors as a derivative of the atomic bomb experience.

A third psychological feature of particular importance in the Hiroshima disaster is what I have called *psychic closing off*. Resembling the psychological defense of denial and the behavioral state of apathy, psychic closing off is nonetheless a distinctive pattern of response to overwhelmingly threatening stimuli. Within a matter of moments, as we have seen in the examples cited, a person may not only cease to react to these threatening stimuli, but in so doing may, equally suddenly, violate the most profound values and taboos of his cultural and his personal life. Though the response may be highly adaptive — and may very often be a means of emotional self-preservation — it can vary in its proportions to the extent of almost resembling at times a psychotic mechanism. Since psychic closing off, at least in the form it took in Hiroshima, is specifically related to the problem of death, it raises the question of the degree to which various forms of psychosis may also be responses to the symbolic fear of death or bodily annihilation.

The psychic closing off created by the Hiroshima disaster is not limited to the victims themselves, but extends to those who, like myself, attempt to study the event. Thus, although I had had previous research experience with people who had been exposed to extreme situations, I found that at the beginning of my work in Hiroshima the completion of each interview would leave me profoundly shocked and emotionally spent. But as the work progressed and I heard more and more of these accounts, their effects upon me greatly lessened. My awareness of my scientific function — my listening carefully for specific kinds of information and constantly formulating categories of response — enhanced the psychic closing off necessary to me for the task of conducting the research, as is true for a wide variety of human efforts that deal with problems in which death is a factor. It is the vast ramification of psychic closing off, rather than the phenomenon itself, that is unique to nuclear disaster, so much so that all who become in any way involved in the problem find themselves facing a nearly automatic tendency to close themselves off from what is most disturbing in the evidence at hand.

Finally, there is the question of *psychological mastery of the nuclear disaster experience*. Central to this problem is the task of dealing with feelings of shame and guilt of the most profound nature: the sense that one has, however unwittingly, participated in this total human breakdown in which (in Martin Buber's words) "the human order of being is injured."[30] That such feelings of self-condemnation — much like those usually termed "existential guilt" — should be experienced by the *victims* of a nuclear disaster is perhaps the most extreme of its many tragic ironies. Faced with the task of dealing with this form of guilt, with the problem of re-establishing trust in the human order, and with the continuing sense of encounter with death, the survivor of a nuclear disaster needs nothing less than a new identity in order to come to terms with his postdisaster world. And once more extending the principle beyond the victim's experience, it may not be too much to say that those who permit themselves to confront the consequences of such a disaster, past or future, are also significantly changed in the process. Since these consequences now inhabit our world, more effective approaches to the problem of human survival may well depend upon our ability to grasp the nature of the fundamental new relationship to existence which we all share.

Notes

1. Portions of this paper were presented at the Annual Meeting of the American Association for the Advancement of Science in Philadelphia,

December, 1962. The work it describes was done in Hiroshima from April to September of 1962, 17 years after the dropping of the atomic bomb. I am profoundly grateful to a large number of friends and colleagues from the various divisions of Hiroshima University (particularly the Research Institute for Nuclear Medicine and Biology), the Hiroshima City Office, and many other groups for their generous assistance in the extensive arrangements necessary for the work; to Mr. Kaoru Ogura and Miss Kyoko Komatsu for their dedicated and skillful research assistance during all of its phases; and to Dr. L. Takeo Doi for later stimulating suggestions concerning psychological formulations. Responsibility for conclusions is, of course, entirely my own.

2. Studies of the effects of ionizing radiation were instituted by Japanese medical and civilian teams within days after the bomb was dropped, with Dr. Masao Tsuzuki of Tokyo Imperial University playing a leading role, American medical groups began their work in early September 1945, and became consolidated in the Joint Commission for the Investigation of the Effects of the Atomic Bomb in Japan. Studies of longer-term effects of radiation have been conducted at the medical departments and research institutes of Hiroshima and Nagasaki Universities. The largest research program on delayed radiation effects is being carried out at the Atomic Bomb Casualty Commission, in both Hiroshima and Nagasaki, an affiliate of the United States National Academy of Sciences — National Research Council, under a grant from the U.S. Atomic Energy Commission, administered with the cooperation of the Japanese National Institute of Health of the Ministry of Health and Welfare. Much of the extensive literature on radiation effects has been summarized in the following: A. W. Oughterson and S. Warren, *Medical Effects of the Atomic Bomb in Japan* (New York: McGraw-Hill, 1956); J. W. Hollingsworth, "Delayed radiation effects in survivors of the atomic bombings," *New Engl. J. Med.*, 1960, *263*, 381–487; "Bibliography of publications concerning the effects of nuclear explosions," *J. Hiroshima Med. Assoc.*, 1961, *14* (10); and in the series of Technical Reports of the ABCC and the various issues of the *Proc. Res. Inst. Med. Biol.* of Hiroshima University, and of the *Hiroshima J. Med. Sci.*

3. There has, however, been some preliminary sociological and psychological research in these areas. See S. Nakano, "Genbaku Eikyo no Shakaigakuteki Chosa" [Sociological study of atomic bomb effects], *Daigakujinkai Kenkyuronshu I, Betsuzuri*, April 1954, and "Genbaku to Hiroshima" [The atomic bomb and Hiroshima], in *Shinshu Hiroshima Shi-shi [Newly revised history of Hiroshima City]*; Y. Kubo, "Data about the suffering and opinion of the A-bomb sufferers," *Psychologia*, 1961, *4*, 56–59 (in English), and "A study of A-bomb sufferers' behavior in Hiroshima: A socio-psychological research on A-bomb and A-energy," *Jap. J. Psychol.*, 1952, *22*, 103–110 [English abstract]; T. Misao, "Characteristics in abnormalities observed in atom-bombed survivors," *J. Radiation Res.*, 1961, *2*, 85–97, in which various psychosomatic factors are dealt with; I. L. Janis, *Air War and Emotional Stress* (New York: McGraw-Hill, 1951), particularly Chapters 1-3. Additional studies of social aspects of the atomic bomb problem, under the direction of K.

Shimizu, are now under way at the Hiroshima University Research Institute for Nuclear Medicine and Biology.

4. R. J. Lifton, "Youth and history: Individual change in postwar Japan," *Daedalus,* 1962, *91,* 172–197; and "Individual patterns in historical change: Imagery of Japanese youth," presented at the Annual Meeting of the Association for Research in Nervous and Mental Disease, New York, December 8, 1962.

5. R. J. Lifton, *Thought Reform and the Psychology of Totalism* (New York: W. W. Norton, 1961).

6. *Hibakusha* is a coined word which has no exact English equivalent but means: one (or those) who has (have) experienced, sustained, or undergone the (atomic) bomb. It conveys a little bit more than merely having encountered the bomb, and a little bit less than having experienced definite physical injury from it. *Higaisha,* another word frequently used, means "one who sustained injury" or simply "victim." But the words are frequently used more or less interchangeably, and both in translation are sometimes rendered as "victim(s)" or "sufferer(s)" from the atomic bomb. Thus, the English word "survivors" is in no sense an exact translation of either *hibakusha* or *higaisha,* but rather a means of designating in a single word persons who fit into the category of *hibakusha.* While *hibakusha* has come to convey many things in popular usage, it also is employed to represent the four groups of people covered by the official legislation on medical benefits for those exposed to the effects of the bomb: those who at the time of the bomb were within the city limits then existing for Hiroshima, an area extending from the bomb's hypocenter to a distance of 4000 (and in some places up to 5000) meters; those who were not in the city at the time, but who within 14 days entered a designated area extending to about 2000 meters from the hypocenter; those who were engaged in some form of aid to, or disposal of, bomb victims at various stations then set up; and those who were *in utero,* and whose mothers fit into any of the first three categories. (See "Genbaku Iryoho no Kaise Jishi ni tsuite" [Concerning the enforecment of the revision of the atomic bomb medical treatment law] [of August 1, 1960], published by the Hiroshima City Office). For studying physical aspects of delayed radiation effects, such factors as distance from the hypocenter and degree of protection from radiation (by buildings, clothing, etc.) are crucial, and from this standpoint a large number of those designated as *hibakusha* had little or no exposure to significant amounts of radiation. For psychological and social effects, these factors — and particularly that of distance from the hypocenter — are also of great importance, but one cannot make the same relatively sharp correlations regarding what is, or is not, significant exposure. I shall deal more with this problem in subsequent publications, and also with some of the special responses of the selected group of survivors; but in this paper I shall emphasize general psychological themes which apply, in greater or less degree, to virtually all *hibakusha.*

7. The one exception was an interview with a European priest who had been in Hiroshima at the time of the bomb, my only non-Japanese research subject.

8. It was, of course, inevitable that, after 17 years, elements of selectivity and distortion would enter into these recollections. But I was impressed with the vividness of recall, with the willingness of people, once a reasonable degree of rapport had been established, to express themselves quite freely about painful, and often humiliating, details; and with the over-all agreement contained in these descriptions, with each other and with various published accounts, concerning what took place generally and how people behaved. For corroborating published accounts, see, for instance: M. Hachiya (Warner Wells, Ed., Trans.), *Hiroshima Diary* (Chapel Hill: University of North Carolina Press, 1955); T. Nagai, *We of Nagasaki* (New York: Duell, Sloan and Pearce, 1951); H. Agawa, *Devil's Heritage* (Tokyo: Hokuseido Press, 1957); A Osada (Compiler), *Children of the A-Bomb* (New York: Putnam, 1963); Robert Yungk, *Children of the Ashes* (New York: Harcourt, Brace & World, 1961); John Hersey, *Hiroshima* (New York: Bantam Books, 1959); Robert Trumbull, *Nine Who Survived Hiroshima and Nagasaki* (Tokyo and Rutland, Vt.: Charles E. Tuttle, 1957); S. Imahori, *Gensuibaku Jidai* [The age of the A- and H-bomb] (Hiroshima, 1959); V. Matsuzaka (Ed.), *Hiroshima Genbaku Iryō-shi* [*History of the medical treatment of the Hiroshima A-bomb*] (Hiroshima, 1961); Y. Ota, *Shikabane no Machi* [Town of corpses] (Tokyo: Kawade Shobō, 1955); and the large number of back issues of the *Chugoku Shimbun*, Hiroshima's leading newspaper, which include accounts of personal A-bomb experiences.

9. American planes did drop leaflets warning Hiroshima inhabitants that the city was going to be demolished and urging them to evacuate from it. But these were apparently similar to leaflets dropped over all Japan's major cities, and there was no mention of the atomic bomb. Moreover very few people appeared to have seen the leaflets, and those who did tended to ignore them as enemy propaganda.

10. For estimates of damage, casualties, and mortality, see Oughterson and Warren, *op. cit.*, *Hiroshima Genbaku Iryō-shi, op cit.*, M. Ishida and I. Matsubayashi, "An Analysis of Early Mortality Rates Following the Atomic Bomb – Hiroshima," ABCC Technical Report 20-61, Hiroshima and Nagasaki (undated); S. Nagaoka, *Hiroshima Under Atomic Bomb Attack* (Hiroshima: Peace Memorial Museum, undated); and "Hiroshima: Official Brochure Produced by Hiroshima City Hall" (based largely upon previously mentioned sources). Concerning mortality, Oughterson and Warren estimate 64,000, believed to be accurate with ±10 per cent; K. Shimizu (in *Hiroshima Genbaku Iryō-shi*) estimates "more than 200,000," the figure which is accepted by the City of Hiroshima; Nagaoka estimates "more than 240,000"; the official estimate is usually given as 78,150; and one frequently sees estimates of "more than 100,000." Contributing to this great divergence in figures are such things as varying techniques of calculation, differing estimates of the number of people in Hiroshima at the moment the bomb fell, the manner in which military fatalities are included, how long afterward (and after which census count) the estimate was made, and undoubtedly other human factors outside the realm of statistical science. The obvious conclusion is

that no one really knows, nor, considering the degree of disorganization interfering with collection of accurate population data, is the problem ever likely to be fully solved.

11. These "fireballs" have no relationship to the fireball of the atomic bomb previously mentioned, and are here compared with ordinary fires caused by the bomb.

12. In such profound emotional experiences, feelings of shame and guilt become intermixed and virtually indistinguishable. In cases like this one, the guilty inner fantasy is likely to be, "I am responsible for their (his, her) death," or even, "I killed them." The shameful fantasy is likely to be, "I should have saved them, or at least done more for them." But these are closely related, and in mentioning either shame or guilt in the remainder of the paper, I assume that the other is present as well. See reference 28.

13. See Oughterson and Warren, as well as other sources mentioned in reference 2. Oughterson and Warren demonstrate statistically the relationship between incidence of radiation effects and distance from the hypocenter — the great majority of cases occurring within the 2000-meter radius — but these scientific distinctions were, of course, completely unknown at the time, and even after becoming known they have not eliminated survivors' fears of later effects.

14. See Hollingsworth, *op. cit.*, and other sources mentioned in reference 2 for discussions of delayed radiation effects and bibliographies of work done on the subject. Concerning the problem of leukemia, see also A. B. Brill, M. Tomonaga, and R. M. Heyssel, "Leukemia in man following exposure to ionizing radiation," *Ann. Intern. Med.* 1962, *56,* 590–609; and S. Watanabe, "On the incidence of leukemias in Hiroshima during the past fifteen years from 1946–1960," *J. Radiation Res.* 1961, *2,* 131-140 (in English).

15. The most extensive work on these genetic problems has been done by J. V. Neel and W. J. Schull. See their "Radiation and sex ratio in man: Sex ratio among children of atomic bombings suggests induced sex-linked lethal mutations," *Science,* 1958, *128,* 343–348; and *The Effect of Exposure to the Atomic Bomb on Pregnancy Termination in Hiroshima and Nagasaki* (National Academy of Sciences — National Research Council. Washington, D. C.: Government Printing Office, 1956). Belief in the possibility of an increase in various forms of congenital malformations in offspring of survivors has been stimulated by the work of I. Hayashi at Nagasaki University, reported in his paper: "Pathological Research on Influences of Atomic Bomb Exposure upon Fetal Development," In *Research in the Effects and Influences of the Nuclear Bomb Test Explosions* (in English, undated), though Dr. Hayashi, in summarizing his material, cautions that "one hesitates to give any concrete statement about the effect of the atomic bomb radiation [upon] the growth of fetal life, based on the data available in this paper."

16. These borderline complaints, as detected by the Cornell Medical Index (Misao, *op. cit.*) are consistently more frequent in *hibakusha* than in non-*hibakusha*. The cultural concern with bodily symptoms is no more than an intensifying influence, and generally similar psychosomatic anxieties

would undoubtedly be manifest in other cultures under similar conditions.

17. The following discussion of the question of medical benefits is based upon regulations published by the Hiroshima City Office (especially "Genbaku Iryōhō no Kaise . . . ," *op. cit.*), as well as upon extensive discussions of the problems involved with officials responsible for administering the law and physicians who deal with its everyday medical and psychological ramifications. My concern here is to point up these problematic areas as reverberations of the atomic bomb experience, rather than to pass judgment on policies or programs.

18. Censorship on matters relating to the atomic bomb and its various effects was imposed almost immediately by the American Occupation; fears of retaliation were undoubtedly an important factor, though it is likely that over the years other concerns and influences affected this policy. Reviewing Japanese perceptions of the censorship (see the later, October 6 to December 7, 1959, series of articles in the *Chugoku Shimbun* on the history of postwar Hiroshima literature; Imahori, *op. cit.;* and Jungk, *op. cit.*) one gains the impression that its implementation was often inconsistent but sufficient to be felt keenly by writers, and even to interfere with adequate dissemination of much-needed medical knowledge about the A-bomb; that descriptions of the A-bomb experience — reportorial, literary, and ideological — nonetheless made their appearance during the early postwar years; that restrictions diminished sufficiently during the last two years of the Occupation for writers to deal freely with the subject; but that the full revelation of the horrors associated with the atomic bomb did not occur for the majority of Japanese until the end of the Occupation in 1952 with the circulation of a now famous issue of the Asahi Graphic (a weekly pictorial of Japan's leading newspaper) in which these horrors were vividly depicted.

19. Leukemia, despite its disturbing increase in incidence, remains an infrequent cause of death. Hollingsworth, quoting Heyssel, reports that, up to 1960, 122 cases of leukemia had been discovered in Hiroshima residents. And where death is caused by other conditions it is extremely difficult to assess the influence of radiation effects. But the individual survivor will often automatically associate the A-bomb Hospital with radiation effects, and the situation is further complicated by the medical and legal complexities already mentioned, and by the generally sensitive psychological atmosphere of Hiroshima.

20. Nakano, *op. cit.*, gives evidence for the lower socioeconomic position of *hibakusha,* and discusses other social and psychological problems they face. See also Imahori, *op. cit.*, and Jungk, *op. cit.*

21. Survivors often marry each other, and frequently feel that by doing so they are likely to be best understood. But some express a strong preference to marry a non-*hibakusha,* and claim that by marrying one another they increase their possibilities for giving birth to abnormal children; they also here reflect an urge to transcend through marriage, rather than intensify, the *hibakusha* identity.

22. I have in this section barely suggested the Japanese cultural influences — particularly the tendency toward a sense of continuity with the dead — which affect survivors' reactions. These cultural influences are

important, and I shall attempt to say more about them in later publications. But I believe that the close identification with the dead which I have described, like the psychosomatic patterns discussed in the previous section, should not be thought of as exclusively "Japanese"; rather I would claim that it is also related to the nature of the disaster, although expressed in a particular (Japanese) cultural style. For Japanese attitudes about purity, see Lifton, *Daedalus, op. cit.*, and for relationship of attitudes toward death and purity, see R. N. Bellah, *Tokugawa Religion* (Glencoe, Ill.: Free Press, 1957).

23. These attitudes are related to Japanese cultural tendencies to stress human considerations, including apologetic sympathy where this is felt indicated, rather than more abstract determinations of right and wrong or matters of individual conscience. But again it is by no means certain that in similar circumstances, even in cultures with a reverse emphasis, similar hostilities might not occur.

24. Compilations of the general literature on disaster are to be found in: G. W. Baker and D. W. Chapman, *Man and Society in Disaster* (New York: Basic Books, 1962); Martha Wolfenstein, *Disaster* (Glencoe, Ill.: Free Press, 1957); "Human behavior in disaster: A new field of social research," *J. Soc. Issues*, 1954, *10* (3) (entire issue); *Field Studies of Disaster Behavior, An Inventory* (Washington, D. C.: National Academy of Sciences — National Research Council, Disaster Research Group, 1961); and F. L. Bates, C. W. Fogleman, and others, *The Social and Psychological Consequences of a National Disaster: A Longitudinal Study of Hurricane Audrey* (Washington, D. C.: National Academy of Sciences — National Research Council, 1963).

25. It is to those who were several thousand meters from the hypocenter, including many beyond the outskirts of the city, that the term "illusion of centrality" and its psychological mechanisms (as described in the literature on disaster) apply. Those who were closer, in terms of effects experienced, were sufficiently central to the disaster for the term "illusion" to be inappropriate.

26. As in other recent disaster studies (see, for instance, Bates et al., *op. cit.*) I did not (from discussions with medical, psychiatric, and other authorities) have the impression of a large increase of severe mental illness, such as psychosis, at the time of the disaster or immediately afterwards; in view of the limited available statistical data it would be extremely difficult to study this problem and I did not attempt to do so. My findings differ, however, from those of other disaster studies in the extent of the psychosocial consequences I encountered which, although emotionally profound, are not of a variety classifiable as "mental illness." This important difference stems mainly, I believe, from special features of the atomic bomb experience, but may also be related to variations in approach and method.

27. I have in this paper dealt only with Hiroshima as it was there that I conducted the research, although I did have the opportunity to make briefer observations in Nagasaki as well. In both cities there is a widely held impression that general reactions to the atomic bomb — mass media dissemination of its effects, peace movements, and even fears and

concerns of *hibakusha* — are considerably more intense in Hiroshima than in Nagasaki. I believe this to be true, but only in degree, and not in the more-or-less absolute sense in which it is sometimes depicted. There are a number of factors which have contributed to this difference in intensity, and to Hiroshima's assuming more of a symbolic role for both *hibakusha* and outsiders: Hiroshima was the first to be struck by the new weapon, and the bomb fell in the center of Hiroshima, a flat city made up almost entirely of flimsy structures, so that the entire city was virtually devastated. In Nagasaki the bomb fell at some distance from the center and destruction was limited by the hilly terrain, so that the greater part of the city (including a somewhat larger number of concrete structures) was left standing, and casualties and general effects were not as great despite the fact that the Nagasaki bomb was of greater explosive power; Nagasaki could therefore more readily resume some of its previous identity as a city — which included a unique history of having served for several centuries as Japan's main contact with the Western world — whereas Hiroshima had to recreate itself almost entirely, and without the benefit of a comparable tradition; and Hiroshima is closer to Tokyo and more sensitive to intellectual and ideological currents stemming from Japan's dominant city.

28. The psychiatric and psychological literature leaves much to be desired in its treatment of the subject of death, but recent studies which have made significant contributions to this most difficult of areas include: H. Feifel, *The Meaning of Death* (New York: McGraw-Hill, 1959); K. R. Eissler, *The Psychiatrist and the Dying Patient* (New York: International Universities Press, 1955); and N. O. Brown, *Life Against Death* (Middletown, Conn.: Wesleyan University Press, 1959). Two interesting reports are: T. P. Hackett and A. D. Weisman, "Reactions to the imminence of death" and C. B. Bahnson, "Emotional reactions to internally and externally derived threat of annihilation" (in this volume). There has also been an expanding literature on the psychological barriers, mostly concerned with death, which impair approaches to nuclear problems. See, for instance: "Socio-Psychiatric Aspects of the Prevention of Nuclear War," forthcoming report of the Committee on Social Issues of the Group for the Advancement of Psychiatry; J. D. Frank, "Breaking the thought barrier: Psychological challenges of the nuclear age," *Psychiatry*, 1960, *23*, 245–266; and Grinspoon, "Fallout Shelters and the Unacceptability of Disquieting Facts" (in this volume).

29. For discussions of symbolization of the self, see R. E. Nixon, "An approach to the dynamics of growth in adolescence," *Psychiatry*, 1961, *24*, 18–31; and Susanne Langer, *Philosophy in a New Key* (New York: Mentor Books, 1948), p. 111. For the relevance of shame to this kind of process, see Helen M. Lynd, *On Shame and the Search for Identity* (New York: Harcourt, Brace, 1958).

30. "Guilt and guilt feelings," *Psychiatry*, 1957, *20*, 114–129, p. 120. In attributing guilt feelings to Japanese, here and elsewhere in this article, I am following recent critiques of the concept of "shame cultures" and "guilt cultures": G. Piers and M. B. Singer, *Shame and Guilt* (Springfield, Ill.: Charles C. Thomas, 1953); and more specifically in

relationship to Japan, G. DeVos, "The relation of guilt toward parents to achievement and arranged marriage among Japanese," *Psychiatry*, 1960, *23*, 287–301. See also E. H. Erikson, *Childhood and Society* (New York: W. W. Norton, 1950), pp. 222–226. Feelings of shame and guilt, at their most profound level — their psychological meeting ground — as I suggest below (following Buber, Lynd, Erikson, and my own previous work) can be overcome only through a change in one's relationship to the world, and can under certain conditions be creatively utilized on behalf of achieving such a change. But my impression regarding the atomic bomb experience was that this constructive utilization was the exception rather than the rule, since there was so much that tended to block it and to cause feelings of shame and guilt to be retained in their negative, unresolved form.

PART FIVE

THE MERCURY ASTRONAUTS: PERSONALITY AND ADAPTATION POTENTIAL

SHELDON J. KORCHIN AND GEORGE E. RUFF*

PERSONALITY CHARACTERISTICS
OF THE MERCURY ASTRONAUTS

IT HAS BECOME commonplace to note that our knowledge of psychodynamics is still largely derived from the study of patients. When we do concern ourselves with the "normal," our studies most often involve people in roles and settings similar to our own. Much personality research has used students, hospital workers, and others readily at hand, and it is often based on brief contact; thus we welcomed the opportunity to work with the astronauts during their training and flights. Here was a chance to study psychologically mature and competent men while they were coping with new social and physical demands. Not only are the astronauts mentally healthy in any clinical sense, but also, because of prior history and selection, they might be expected to have particularly effective modes of stress adaptation. This has been an opportunity to study real men under real stress, of a sort which could hardly be simulated in the laboratory. Moreover, they could be studied over a period of years, during a crucial period in their lives when occupational role and personal and social behavior were in change. In this regard, our work has involved a longitudinal study of personality development —

* We are grateful to the National Aeronautics and Space Administration and to the National Institute of Mental Health for making this study possible. However, the opinions and conclusions expressed in this article are those of the authors and do not necessarily represent the views of the National Aeronautics and Space Administration or any other governmental agency.

197

but of competent men during maturity. As such, it may contribute to the conceptually neglected area of "adult socialization."

Early in 1960, at the request of the National Aeronautics and Space Administration's Space Task Group, a study was undertaken to evaluate reactions to Project Mercury flights, with particular emphasis on the mechanisms for maintaining adaptive behavior under flight conditions. In order to discover characteristic patterns of response, against which behavior in flight could be evaluated, more specific research objectives included the study of personality mechanisms possibly associated with effective functioning, and repeated measurement, over two or three years, of coordinate changes in psychological state, performance, and physiological functioning.

Here we will discuss two related parts of this study: first we shall consider those personality qualities which characterize the astronauts as a group; then we shall deal more specifically with their behavior in response to training and flight situations. Since much of the psychological and physiological data is still being analyzed, these reports are necessarily tentative and summary in nature. Moreover, we shall limit ourselves to those personality qualities and response patterns that characterize the men as a group, perhaps indicating something of the range of variation. We shall avoid discussion of the men as individuals.

The study has involved three phases. The first phase, during the summer of 1960, was an assessment period during which the men were interviewed and tested to gain some understanding of the personality mechanisms relevant to later stress response. This included about four hours with each man in which we explored such matters as the astronaut's history from selection to that time; the ways, if any, in which he felt he had changed; attitudes toward the project and toward the other men; his concept of the astronaut's role and his self-concept. To gain as full a picture as possible of affect arousal and control, we inquired into behavior under conditions of physical danger and psychological threat, and attempted to assess the liability, intensity, and control of such emotions as anxiety, anger, and depression. Energy level, fatigue threshold, capacity for positive affects, and conditions of effectance motivation in general were similarly explored. Defenses and modes of coping that had been available in the past were described. On the whole, the purpose of this phase was to discover what kinds of men these were, what kinds of self and affect organization they had, how these might have changed in fitting the evolving astronaut role, and in a general way, the sources of their competence in dealing with stress. Our concern was less with the history of the men than with an assessment of their present functioning and the changes that might have taken place during the project.

The second phase involved the application of a small battery of psychological and physiological measures on repeated occasions throughout training, whenever possible, bracketing such events as centrifuge runs, practice insertions, environmental chamber tests, in addition to control occasions, in order to develop a running baseline against which measurements made at the time of flight might be evaluated.

The third phase consisted of more intensive evaluations of behavior at the time of suborbital and orbital flights. The same tests were readministered, immediately before and after flight, and, in the same sessions, the pilots were interviewed briefly to explore the experience in prospect and in retrospect. A day or so before and after the flight, they were interviewed more extensively.

In addition to the material of our own study, we are fortunate in having available the extensive data collected about three and a half years ago when Dr. Ruff and his co-workers, then at the Wright Air Development Center, conducted an assessment program involving some 30 hours of interviews and tests with the initial candidates for the Mercury program (Ruff and Levy, 1959.)

A secondary purpose of the present research has been to

re-evaluate the initial selection criteria in terms of subsequent behavior, another opportunity not readily available in studies of assessment or clinical prediction. It might be noted, parenthetically, that this re-evaluation may not turn up much of value for future selection, partly because of the success of the original selection. The apparent success is probably due to the fact that men were taken from an already highly selected and well-qualified group — military test pilots — who, having demonstrated success in that role, were prepared for the new one, with the initial assessment program having screened out the less fitted. Since no clearly poor candidates were taken into training, and since the range of initial intellectual, aptitude, and personality qualities was small, possible relationships between early measures and later performance are obscured. Moreover, the three years between selection and flight, during which the specific skills necessary for flight were carefully developed, makes the initially small differences even less important. In retrospect, it seems that perhaps physiological stress resistance was overemphasized, and perhaps not sufficient importance was given to the need for adaptability to complex and demanding social situations. But, as every television viewer knows, not only have the men performed well as pilots, but they have also risen beautifully to the demands of being public figures.

What kind of men are the astronauts? What are the sources of their personality competence? The seven men were selected from 69 candidates, all experienced jet test pilots from the military services. At the time of selection, they were between 32 and 37 years old. All were married, and most of them while relatively young. All have children; five of the families had two, one had four, and one had one. The families of origin were from middle-middle to middle-upper class, and, although there may have been periods of deprivation, they were relatively well off during most of the astronaut's childhood. All came from small towns or farms. All the astronauts are affiliated with Protestant denominations, though they vary from occasional to dedicated church members. They and their families enjoy outdoor living and sports. All were educated in public schools and went through university training, generally in state universities or in the military academies. All majored in engineering. In many important respects, these men, as well as the larger population from which they were selected, are what Lois Murphy has recently termed "core American" in describing the families of her Kansas children.

Volunteering for Project Mercury represented a next logical step in the astronauts' careers and included an admixture of practical, professional, and more romantic motives. The men were eager to be a part of a national endeavor which would contribute to the country's status in international affairs. As heirs to the tradition of the Wright brothers, Lindbergh, and Doolittle, they wanted their place on the new frontier of aviation. To pioneer in manned space flight, and to be the first Americans to orbit the earth, was an important incentive. But besides the adventure and the contribution of being in at the beginning of manned space exploration, the men also saw the project as a career gain. Inevitably, the relative importance of jet aircraft will be reduced as rocketed vehicles are developed in military aviation; hence, moving from the role of test pilot of conventional aircraft to piloting manned spacecraft opened new career possibilities. As such, neither public acclaim nor possible material gain, which they came to realize might be by-products of the role, were primary motives, though they may not have been unwelcome secondary gains. The danger involved in the project was recognized and evaluated, but the astronauts conceived it to be similar in type and not necessarily greater in amount than in test flying. Mainly, they volunteered because the new role gave greater opportunity for achievement and greater scope for the practice of their craft, while serving the nation's interest.

At present, the astronauts still feel the challenge of their work and enjoy the opportunity to use their capacities fully. They are satisfied to be participating in something they consider important, and all have the conviction that they are making a social contribution, one that is more important for being in the national interest. These feelings are reflected in their answer to hypothetical questions about future plans. Even if they were unable to fly, and were financially independent, most of them would prefer to continue in the space program.

Most of the men have no special wish to face danger, although they are willing to accept the risks demanded by their work. Some may enjoy certain types of risks, but this had little to do with their volunteering, and it enters even less into their work in the project. Aside from all else, their professionalism and feeling of craftsmanship would block any unnecessary risk-taking, if it were likely to jeopardize the success of a mission.

From the outset, the men have differed in their feeling of obligation to serve·as a public symbol of national achievement. Even early in the project, some of the men were quicker than others to realize that the astronaut's role carried a social responsibility and to feel obliged to live up to the ideals of such a role. Like Caesar's wife, they felt they had to be above reproach. For others of them the astronaut's role was more narrowly defined, anchored in the piloting job. These men saw themselves as craftsmen who had to do an important job as well as possible, but what they were or did beyond that was only their own concern.

Although there is a feeling of group identity as astronauts, group and personal loyalties do not provide major incentives. There is the common and sincere belief that this is a "team effort," along with the awareness of the many individual contributions necessary for its success. But it is as if each one were working for similar objectives, rather than their all working for the team as such. In general, these are men with strong feelings of individuality and reluctance to lose identity in a team, a personality quality we feel is important in understanding their behavior and which we will discuss later. It is interesting to note that the men favor sports in which individual skill is pitted against nature, i.e., waterskiing, fishing, and hunting, rather than man-against-man or team-competition sports.

These are men of superior intelligence. In terms of the Wechsler Adult Intelligence Scale, their IQ's range from 130 to 141 with a mean of 135. But they are less concerned with abstractions and ideas as such than with the application of thought to problems solvable in terms of technical knowledge and professional experience. They are concerned with problem-solving and can focus effectively on the essentials of the problems confronting them. Their thoughts are quickly organized and effectively communicated. They prefer the more concrete to the more abstract or speculative. Facts, rather than theories, are emphasized and valued. The uncertain or unknown is avoided, or efforts are made to make it known. There is the faith that knowledge is attainable, and with knowledge problems are solvable. Issues irrelevant to their areas of concern are largely avoided.

They are not introspective men and tend to have little fantasy life; yet, though they seldom dwell on their own inner processes, they are sensitive and can describe them quite fully when asked to direct attention inward. Normally, however, their regard is outward and directed toward reality rather than inward. They are oriented toward action rather than thought. They prefer action to inaction and dislike assuming a passive role. At the same time, they are not overly impulsive and can refrain from action when it is not appropriate.

Although most of the astronauts tend not to be highly involved in relation with other people, their techniques for dealing with people are effective. They can be sensitive to the feelings of others and can usually avoid interpersonal difficulties in getting a job done. While they prefer independent action whenever possible, all are comfortable when dependence on others is required. One of the paradoxes of the project lies in the opposition of independence and dependence, of faith in one's own skill and competence versus the need to depend on the technical skill and attentiveness of others. These are strongly independent men with deep needs to master their own fate and with faith in their ability to do so. But in the nature of the project, they are dependent on the work of many others for the success of their mission. Their capacity to maintain *trust,* in what might seem conditions for *distrust,* seems to depend largely on their sharing common standards of professional and technical competence with co-workers. It is faith in the *expertness* of the man, rather than dependence on the *man* himself, that allows them to accept interdependence without suspicion.

There are few deep attachments within the astronaut group itself. They share a common purpose and realize that the actions of each one affect the others; yet their independence of each other is more striking than their existence as a team. They show, for example, little of the interrelatedness of an infantry squad in combat. On the other hand, they respect one another and have usually been able to keep their competitive feelings from interfering with their joint work. In fact, except for the issue of who is best qualified for a flight, evaluations of each member of the group are almost identical. They may not share the same standards of personal behavior, but they have common professional values which center about respect for technical competence. This gives a common metric to interpersonal evaluations and relations.

Central in their personalities are strong needs for achievement and mastery. These are men who must do, and do well, and this quality is obvious early in their histories. In some cases, the heightened drive for mastery once served to reduce self-doubts. But in most cases the need is now functionally autonomous of its origins and remains a salient quality of the man. As independent, autonomous men with strong needs to achieve on their own resources, it is not surprising that there is deep pleasure in accomplishment. Indeed, in one flight, the failure of automatic instruments intensified the feelings of personal contribution and success in the mission.

By the same token, their potential for disappointment is

high. With strong needs for achievement, and strong feelings of individual responsibility, failure can be disturbing, for it cannot readily be minimized or rationalized. Nevertheless, they display striking resilience in the face of frustration. In large measure, this is because of their faith in the eventual outcome, and in their ability eventually to reach desired goals. Thus, they look beyond the immediate obstacle and toward the means for future resolution. Where there is a possible course of action, they embark on it as quickly as possible.

As committed men, disappointments are keenly felt; as ego-strong men, hope is sustained and disappointment leads to renewed effort. Similarly, affects are readily aroused and strongly felt, but there is good control of potentially disabling effects on behavior. It is an easy, and perhaps popular, misconception to suppose that these are men who "know no fear," that they have very high thresholds for arousal, are relatively insensitive to feelings, and hence are capable of functioning under great stress — phrased one way, this is heroism; phrased another, psychopathy. The fact is that emotions, both negative and positive, are strongly experienced; however, control is good. Each of them has faced situations in which fear was appropriate and found that he was able to function despite its effects. They have confidence that they have the skills and knowledge necessary to overcome realistic threats, and they are not given to dwelling on unrealistic ones. In describing their reactions to combat, they readily admitted fear but pointed out, in one or another way, that they knew they were good pilots and had the resources for coping effectively with danger.

This study was undertaken on the assumption that the astronauts were men of more than average personality competence, and knowledge might be contributed to the understanding of effective functioning in psychologically healthy persons in general. Certainly, the material discussed here would seem to bear out the initial assumption: there is little question that the astronauts as a group are not only mentally healthy but are also, indeed, men of particular psychological competence.

In some respects they are like the "homoclites" recently described by Roy Grinker (1962). In his usage, the term describes psychologically healthy men who are realistically oriented to their world, without unattainable ambitions and consequent neurotic concerns, who are adequate to the demands on them and able to function well without emotional distress. In important respects, however, the astronauts are different from, and more than, the homoclite. If, as Grinker suggests, the homoclite students he studied "form a solid, steady core of stability" in society, our subjects are at least "uncommon common men." On the whole, they are more ambitious, more committed to career advancement, more concerned with success and more sensitive to failure, in addition to having a higher order of ability and intelligence. They share being free of consuming self-doubt. In general, they are strong egos, capable of dealing with psychological events without undue disturbance, with good reality testing and control of inner processes, persevering toward long-term goals.

Here are some speculations, based admittedly on incompletely analyzed and insufficient material.

In the main, these are men with firm identities. They know who they are and where they are going. This, in turn, has derived from development in a well-organized family with considerable solidarity. They grew up in stable communities, usually smaller ones, where the family's position was socially secure if not very influential. Within the family, there was usually strong identification with a competent father or surrogate. It is noteworthy that four of the seven men are "junior." A common theme in many of the interviews is the happy memory of outdoor activities shared with the father — hiking, fishing, or hunting.

From childhood on, their lives flowed in relatively smooth progressions. There were relatively few crises or turning points, as each phase led naturally into the next. Rarely were there overwhelming numbers of competing alternate possibilities to choose among, but rather one predominant choice. Development seemed to flow from stage to stage, rather than to involve successive crises and the mastery of these crises before progression could continue. Where there were obstacles, and a man may have been inadequate to the demands of a realistically difficult situation, compensatory mechanisms were called into play. Although these may have been of neurotic origin, they became integrated syntonically into the larger organization of a healthy personality. Subsequently, such behaviors became functionally autonomous and, dynamically freed of neurotic functions, remained as sources of personal gratification and social utility.

The high order of innate intellectual and physical abilities of these men should not be overlooked. They started with considerable ability and have been exposed to situations which could be mastered within the repertory of their capacities. This has led to success, and from success to heightened self-esteem. One might picture life histories that start with fine abilities and a favoring childhood environment, providing basic emotional security and firm identification. Thereafter follow recycling progressions, consisting of appropriate aspiration, success, increasing self-esteem, increased aspiration, and so forth. Examination of their professional careers indicates smooth progressions without major setbacks. Their development, conceived in this way, seems congruent with the astronauts' present personal competence and stress resistance.

References

GRINKER, R. R., SR., with the collaboration of R. R. GRINKER, JR., and J. TIMBERLAKE. "Mentally healthy" young males (homoclites). *Arch. Gen. Psychiat.*, 1962, *6*, 405–453.

RUFF, G. E., and LEVY, E. Z. Psychiatric evaluation of candidates for space flight. *Amer. J. Psychiat.*, 1959, *116*, 385–391.

GEORGE E. RUFF AND SHELDON J. KORCHIN

PSYCHOLOGICAL RESPONSES
OF THE MERCURY ASTRONAUTS
TO STRESS*

AS WE NOTED in the preceding paper,† our study of
the Project Mercury astronauts includes three major phases:
a period of assessment, repeated measurements during training, and studies of flight behavior. In the first report, we have
tried to characterize the personalities of the astronauts, drawing largely upon the assessment findings. In this paper, we
will consider their psychological functioning during training
and flight activities. These comments are in the nature of a
progress report and are necessarily tentative.

Procedures

Before and after each major event, an attempt was made
to evaluate performance, affect, and other aspects of behavior.
Measures were chosen which could be administered repeatedly
in the field, within the small amount of time available. Tight
scheduling of the astronauts at these critical periods made it

* We are grateful to the National Aeronautics and Space Administration
and to the National Institute of Mental Health for making this study
possible.

The opinions and conclusions expressed in this article are those of
the authors and do not necessarily represent the views of the National
Aeronautics and Space Administration or any other governmental agency.

† "Personality Characteristics of the Mercury Astronauts" by Sheldon
J. Korchin and George E. Ruff.

necessary to focus on what we considered the barest essentials.

In order to assess possible alterations in psychomotor and intellectual functioning, three measures developed for repetitive testing by Moran and Mefferd (1959) were used. These had previously been given all Mercury candidates during the selection program in 1959. The subtests used in the present study were: (1) aiming, which requires that a subject dot the center of a series of circles; (2) number facility, a test of addition; and (3) perceptual speed, a number-cancellation procedure. Twenty alternate forms of matched difficulty are available for each subtest. All tasks are timed measures of familiar overlearned functions which were expected to be stable in repeated testing. It was thought that they would reflect gross changes resulting from stress or other temporary states of disorganization.

The affective state on different occasions was described by the Clyde Mood Scale (Clyde, 1959, 1960). This requires a subject to indicate, on a four-point scale, the degree to which each adjective describes his mood at the moment. It was supplemented by a brief questionnaire which asked the astronaut about his perception of the adequacy of his performance and about any special circumstances that might have influenced his behavior.

Changes in personality variables were assessed by considering all the data collected, with emphasis on analysis of interviews. Brief interviews were done immediately before and after major events, supplemented by longer sessions two days before and two days after. They enabled us to review the astronaut's experience since our last contact with him, to explore his feelings and anticipations concerning the coming event, to determine his immediate response to the event, and then to review it in some detail. Where possible, both investigators interviewed the man together. All interviews were tape recorded so that the transcripts could be studied later in more systematic fashion. Behavioral ratings were made for a series of performance, affective, and personality variables.

Changes in Performance

It is interesting to look back at the performance scores obtained during the original psychological evaluation. At that time, all six subtests of the Moran battery were administered to the astronauts and to 24 other candidates before and after a series of stressful experiences. The stress situations included a 3-hour period of isolation, without light or sound; a "complex behavior simulator," which confronted the subject with a frustrating information overload problem; a simulated altitude chamber test of 65,000 feet, during which the subject was in a poorly functioning pressure suit; and a 2-hour period in a heat chamber at 140°F. Since the Moran tests require concentration and focusing of attention, it might be expected that disruptive stress would lead to a deficit in performance. It is thus striking that poststress scores tended to be higher than prestress scores, although the differences were small. This suggests that all candidates were men who respond to stress with increased effort and improved performance.

Beginning in September 1960, at the Naval Aeromedical Acceleration Laboratory, the stress battery was administered before and after three separate simulations of suborbital and orbital flights on the human centrifuge. Data were also obtained before and after a simulated flight in an environmental chamber at the Naval Air Crew Equipment Laboratory. The tests were then given during various nonstress events to provide control values and to maintain performance at practiced levels. Prior to each suborbital and orbital flight, the battery was administered before and after various prelaunch activities, such as trainer runs and mission simulations. Finally, it was given two days before the flight itself, again on launch morning, following recovery, and two days after flight. The purpose of repeated testing during training was to establish a baseline against which results before and after flight could be evaluated.

The performance data are summarized in Figures 1, 2, and 3. The height of each column indicates total responses. The cross-hatched portion indicates correct responses. It can be seen that the aiming test shows the clearest evidence of change. For all the men, there was some improvement in functioning after such training situations as centrifuge and simu-

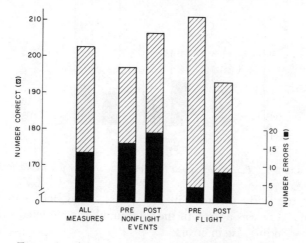

FIGURE 1.   *Aiming test: mean scores for five astronauts.*

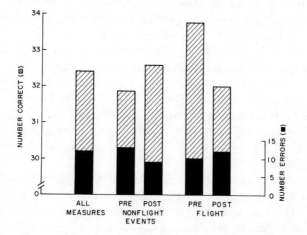

FIGURE 2.   *Number facility test: mean scores for five astronauts.*

George E. Ruff and Sheldon J. Korchin

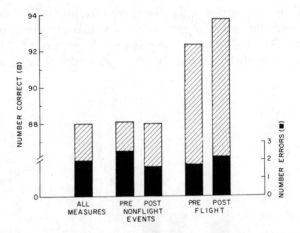

FIGURE 3. *Perceptual speed test: mean scores for five astronauts.*

lator trials. By contrast, in every case, from before to after
flight, there was a drop in the total number completed, with a
corresponding rise in errors.

The findings on the other two tests are less clear. The mean
scores of all five astronauts for the number facility test are
generally parallel to those for aiming — improvement following training events and deficit following flight — although
to a smaller extent. The perceptual speed test showed the
greatest range of individual differences in over-all performance and the least systematic response to flight. The men
tended to show the same type of response to the flight as
they did to the training. Thus, a man whose performance improved after training events improved after flight, whereas
another showed decrements after both training and flight
activities. However, in all cases, the pre-to-post differences
were small.

It is worth noting that scores taken immediately before the
flight for all tests were above the general level of performance. The reverse might have been expected, since these measures were made at a time when anticipatory anxiety might
have been highest, and since they measure performance in the

early morning hours when efficiency is often low. That performance was so good at this hour, during the preflight excitement, suggests a state of facilitatory activation. Whatever anticipatory anxiety was present not only did not lessen, but seemed to improve, psychological functioning in the immediate preflight hours.

Changes in Mood

As part of the same test battery, along with the psychometric procedures, the mood scale was administered on each occasion described above. By factor analysis, Clyde has extracted six factor variables from the 53 adjectives on his list: (1) friendly, (2) energetic, (3) clear-thinking, (4) aggressive, (5) jittery, and (6) depressed. The scores for each of these variables are the sum of ratings for the adjectives found loaded on that factor. To facilitate consideration of these data, two combinations of variables are used. On logical analysis, the scores for energetic and clear-thinking are combined and contrasted with those for jittery and depressed. The first of these pairs is named "effectance," the second "disturbance." It is expected that the well-functioning person would normally be higher on effectance and lower on disturbance, whereas emotionally stressful states should elevate the disturbance rating and lower the effectance. The residual two variables, friendly and aggressive, again suggest a polarity. Both are concerned with relations with other persons. Figure 4 presents the effectance versus disturbance analysis, and Figure 5 contrasts friendly and aggressive.

It is clear that on all occasions the men described themselves more in terms of the positive than the negative emotional states. The highest ratings were obtained for friendly, energetic, and clear-thinking; and the lowest ratings for aggressive, jittery, and depressed. As in the case of the performance variables, the pre-to-post changes were rather small, although the flight-induced changes were greater than those produced by training events. Following flight, there was a

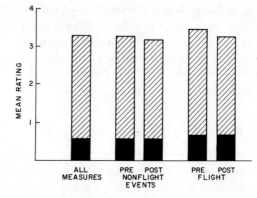

FIGURE 4.   *Effectance (hatched) versus disturbance (solid): mean ratings for five astronauts.*

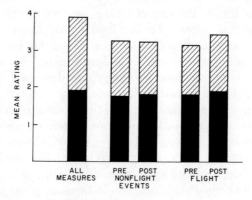

FIGURE 5.   *Friendly (hatched) versus aggressive (solid): mean ratings for five astronauts.*

general tendency for effectance to drop, and for greater anxiety to be expressed. There was a parallel increase in the friendly variable. Thus, compared to their state prior to the launching, after flight they tended to be less energetic and clear-thinking, more anxious, and more warmly related to people. It should be noted, however, that most of these changes in scores are small, and that both before and after flight the men describe themselves as alert and attentive and generally without fear or other disturbing affect. They felt vigorous, alert, and positively oriented toward others. Neither flight nor nonflight training situations significantly changed these mood states.

Behavioral Responses

Throughout this study, emphasis has been placed on determining each man's characteristic method of dealing with stressful events. This has been done on the basis of past histories, interview data, and observations during training and flight activities. Although the men differ in techniques for handling stress, certain features of the group as a whole can be summarized.

The situations to which they have had to adapt fall into several categories. First, as in any job situation, there have been day-to-day problems. Since the program has involved the development of complex equipment, the number of delays and frustrations has been large. Furthermore, responsibilities and procedures have often been unlike those in the military services where the astronauts have spent their professional lives. Both the different techniques and the social organizations were potential sources of difficulty.

In spite of these differences, few adverse reactions have been noted during the development and training phases of the program. The astronauts have taken a practical, realistic approach to their problems. They have assumed that problems are inevitable and have accepted what they cannot change.

None of the training activities, as such, have been emotionally stressful, except where performance fell below aspiration. Such "failures" have produced disappointments but have usually served to stimulate increased effort. The men differ in the extent to which self-esteem is bound up with achievement. Some set their levels of aspiration high and then struggle strenuously to attain them. Others accept a lower level of accomplishment. For them, performance at objectively lower levels, which may reflect less effort in training, is not always looked on as personal failure.

For most of the men the hardest problem to master was not being chosen for the first flight. The immediate disturbing implication was that those not selected were not doing as well as they had thought. They sought to learn in what ways their performance might be lacking, and eventually each was able to decide that his day would come. Once a man was assigned to a flight, further delays had little impact. From then on, the issue of "when?" was of secondary importance.

During the period between selection and flight, the major concern has been with achieving a sense of readiness. Until the men feel "on top" of things, a sensation of tension is sometimes evident. This has arisen from such matters as changes in the flight plan or insufficient simulator experience with particular procedures. Conscious thoughts of danger and possible death are of secondary importance.

The astronauts have achieved a sense of readiness at different intervals before the flight. Where everything has "fallen into place" well ahead of time, the final phase of the training period provides an opportunity to relax and polish details. But where readiness is achieved only during the final days before flight, more strain is evident.

During the immediate preflight period, all the men have felt ready to go. They are preoccupied with operational details and show little anticipatory anxiety. When anxiety appears, it is described as a feeling of tension or of being on edge. It is similar to sensations in combat or other stressful situations and, being familiar, is seldom disturbing. Anxiety often seems more related to intense concern that the flight will be successful than to fear of injury or death.

All the astronauts have considered the risks before their flights. They are convinced that, as a result of their past experience and intensive training, they are prepared to handle any emergency. Much of the ability to control anticipatory anxiety comes from their confidence in this preparation. Having considered each eventuality, and having done all they could, they feel there is little point in worrying further. When thoughts of danger have arisen, they have been put aside in favor of a review of the flight plan or other technical aspects of the flight.

During the period between entering the vehicle and the launching, the men report being on edge, which they view as a positive sign. If tension has begun to build up, their response has been to stop, take hold of themselves, and decide what to do in order to bring matters under control. No man has been unable to do this. Although we have noted evidence of activation, no instance of severe anxiety has been observed.

The same pattern has emerged during flight. Thoughts have centered on procedures to be carried out and on the experience of being in orbit. The successful launch and subsequent course of the flight often induced a feeling of exhilaration which may have been reinforced by the pleasant sensation of weightlessness. Anxiety levels have not been abnormally high. Even in the instances where a possibility of death has been confronted, emotional reactions have remained within normal limits.

Responses after the flight have universally involved some degree of elation, coupled with fatigue. Elation comes both from the sense of a difficult job well done, and a sense of relief that the long-anticipated flight is over. Concern with public-relations functions and other postflight activities is not great. The astronauts appropriately feel that they have mastered a major challenge, and little can bother them from now on.

Discussion

Taken together, our findings suggest a state of heightened energy and greater capacity for adaptive functioning during the focal stress of flight. It should be noted, of course, that the flights so far have been of relatively short duration. If the same order of performance were required over a longer period, we could not be certain that the same coping mechanisms would serve as effectively. More sustained stress, even of the same intensity, might call into play other mechanisms or even lead to some disorganization of behavior. In the present situation, however, it is clear that all the men have functioned effectively, and that none were taxed beyond their limits.

Even though our concern is principally with the focal stress — the flight itself — it is important to remember that it is actually the terminal event of a series that may be equally or even more stressful. The days and weeks preceding flight are a harried period for the astronaut, as competing demands are balanced and compromised. All this activity occurs in an atmosphere of heightened excitement and public attention. For certain men, the flight may come as an emotional release. In general, any particular stress imposed on a background of continued general stress, and the response evoked by the focal stress, is a function of how well it cumulates or contrasts with the background level.

One feature of the astronauts' response to stress deserves special emphasis. This is their apparent capacity for the conscious control of emotion arising from external danger. Although each man knows of the diverse possible malfunctions which might end his life, this knowledge fails to elicit disrupting affect. The capacity to control emotion seems to be gained through past experience in the mastery of stress, and through confidence in training and technical readiness. It requires a high order of ego strength and self-esteem. Perhaps the comments of the men themselves will illustrate what we mean.

One of them recognized some inner tension, but found his thoughts immersed in the flight plan. He said, "I know this flight is more dangerous, but the training has been more rigorous. If I get unnerved, I'll fall back and regroup, then focus my attention on what has to be done." Another said, "Of course I'll have some fear, but I've been afraid before and I know what it's like."

Still another commented, "In tight situations you have to stop, take stock, decide what you're going to do, and go ahead and do it. I've often told cadets that sometimes you've got to do something — even if it's wrong. The main thing is to get your mind busy thinking and not worrying. When you can't do anything, that's the worst time." He feels that the essential step in being able to do what he recommends is training that offers a rational selection of possible courses of action. Considering these courses ahead of time diminishes anxiety. As he said, "Whenever I think of what might go wrong, I think of a plan to take care of it. Other than that, there's nothing I can do about it, so I see no point in worrying about it. I know the worry is still there, but it doesn't bother me any more."

The effectiveness of this man's use of such a technique was indicated by a remark describing his feelings while sitting in the spacecraft waiting for lift-off. He said, "After all the training, it seemed as if I'd been sitting there all my life." When asked if he had any prayers, he said there were two: "That the shot would go," and that "I'd be given the strength and courage to do a good job."

Summary

At the time of selection, both the astronauts and the unselected candidates showed a high level of performance, with improvement following experimental stress. Training events produced mild changes in performance, often in the direction of improvement. Immediately prior to flight, performance was above baseline values. The flights themselves led to a small but consistent deficit in one test but had little effect on the others. The measures used suggest over-all stability of functioning, a state of heightened efficiency prior to flight, and a slight decline in performance after flight.

Varied emotional states were observed; however, no disabling responses were noted in the preflight and flight situations studied. The astronauts approached their flights with

George E. Ruff and Sheldon J. Korchin

confidence in their technical support and in their training and ability. By intensified concern with goal-directed activity, and by blocking negative feelings, they effectively coped with the potential psychological difficulties of space flight.

References

CLYDE, D. J. "Clyde Mood Scale." National Institute of Mental Health, 1959 and 1960. Mimeographed manuals.
MORAN, L. J., and MEFFERD, R. B., JR. Repetitive psychometric measures. *Psychol. Rep.*, 1959, 5, 269–275.

PART SIX

BEHAVIOR UNDER
ARBITRARY HUMAN CONTROL

ALBERT D. BIDERMAN

CAPTIVITY LORE AND
BEHAVIOR IN CAPTIVITY *

Introduction

Largely impressionistic observations from a number of
documentary and interview studies of the subject of captivity
suggest hypotheses concerning relationships between precapture exposure to cultural lore about captivity and behavior
as a captive. The present discussion focuses, as has the writer's
research, on the prisoner of war, particularly on studies of
survivors of captivity in Korea and China. The writer has
also drawn upon information concerning other captivity
statuses, however, including civilian internees and political
and concentration-camp prisoners.

Anticipations

Very few former prisoners of war report that they had
seriously considered the possibility that they might be captured prior to the event and had mentally rehearsed the prospect. This was true even of those 137 Air Force prisoners in
the Korean War (about 54 per cent of the 235 surviving Air
Force prisoners) who had received some special training regarding the event of capture. In most of these cases, the
training had been limited to "resisting enemy interrogation"

* The research reported in this paper was supported in part by the
Air Force Office of Scientific Research under Contract AF 49(638)727 and
by the Inter-University Seminar on Military Organization of the University of Chicago.

and "escape and evasion" (Biderman, 1956*b*). Anticipation of the event is more common among political and concentration-camp prisoners, but even more among these people, unrealistic denial of the prospect of imprisonment has been quite common, if not the rule (see Jacobson, 1949).

Air Force ex-prisoners of war who were interviewed intensively reported that, during combat in the Korean conflict, conscious anxieties about the possibility of being killed (with some mental rehearsal of fatal situations, planning to insure that one's "affairs were in order," and even banter about "buying the farm"*) were much more common than equivalents involving the prospect of being captured. Although casualty figures show that the risk of being killed or wounded in action was considerably greater than that of being captured, the latter was nonetheless a significant possibility. Even late in the war when prisoner-of-war matters, such as the extortion of "confessions" from captured airmen, were receiving intense publicity, few of the men flying combat missions behind enemy lines had conscious anxieties about their falling into a similar fate. This was true even among air crews who "flew cover" over their own comrades who were downed behind enemy lines while attempts were made to rescue them by helicopter, and of those who had close personal friends known or believed to have been taken prisoner.

In research interviews after repatriation, it was difficult to get ex-prisoners to state detailed or explicit recollections of information or beliefs they had held prior to capture about what being a prisoner of the Communist Chinese might be like. Typical responses were: "They once showed us a World War II training movie about interrogation"; "We used to joke about Siberia and the salt mines"; "A briefing officer told us that the Communists had ways of getting almost anything we knew out of us"; "I knew we were supposed to tell them nothing but our name, rank, and number."

* Euphemism for "getting killed."

Extensive attention to prisoner-of-war matters in the press and in armed-forces indoctrination presumably has made for far greater consciousness, and perhaps anxiety, about capture among combat personnel today than existed at any time during the Korean conflict.

Unpreparedness

The most frequent type of complaint of American prisoners captured during the Korean conflict was: "We were not told what to expect." The most frequent type of recommendation that repatriates made when asked what lessons the armed forces should learn from their experiences was that soldiers should be given some knowledge of what life in captivity might be like.

Postwar discussions by social scientists and military experts also cite the element of unpreparedness as a major explanation for the allegedly poor manner in which most American POW's coped with the problems of captivity (see U.S. Department of Defense, 1955; U.S. Senate, 1956). But some of these expert judgments point to the lack of preparedness of the Americans for harsh treatment; others to their lack of preparedness for good treatment, or for treatment that was at least only subtly bad.

In a way, there was also a contradictory element in the testimony of the typical repatriated prisoner. On the one hand, he would say that he had never seriously thought about what being captured by the Communists would be like, nor had he seriously entertained the thought that he might be captured; and further, that he had read or heard very little about the matter. On the other hand, he would constantly report his surprise at what he did indeed encounter. That he was continually encountering experiences that differed from his expectations indicated that he must have had expectations from which experience differed.

Albert D. Biderman

Bad Treatment, Expected and Experienced

In anonymous responses to a questionnaire mailed to Air Force repatriates after their return, more than two-thirds of the repatriates indicated on a multiple-choice scale that their treatment had differed markedly from what they had expected before they were captured, although one-third indicated that it had not been *as bad* as they had expected and an almost identical number checked that it had been *worse or much worse*. Only one out of five indicated that what they encountered was neither better nor worse than they had expected. (Another 10 per cent refused to check a general answer and wrote that it had sometimes or in some respects been better and at other times or in other respects been much worse.)

When asked to rate their treatment separately with respect to food, medical care, sanitation, shelter, and "humaneness and consideration" on a five-point scale ranging from usually good to usually bad, in none of these respects did so much as 1 per cent of the survivors check the rating "usually good," and for none of these items did as many as 4 per cent of the repatriates check ratings on the "good" side of the scale. By objective indicators as well, these men had been treated quite badly. This they had expected. But for some, their pre-existing image of "bad treatment" was somehow worse than the reality they had encountered; for others the reality had been worse than their imaginings.

This would be the case if the questionnaire items and responses could be taken as showing genuine contrasts of prior expectations and experiences. That the questionnaire items tapped something other than how bad their treatment had actually been is indicated by the very different distribution of the direct evaluations of their treatment in terms of good-ness and badness, and by the low correlation between the responses contrasting experience with expectation and other indexes of treatment received, such as date of capture and involvement in "confession"-extortion efforts. It is quite clear, however, that a number of different kinds of thought proc-•

esses were responsible for the different kinds of responses.

One factor at work among those who said that their treatment was better than they had expected (even though they said they were treated very badly) was their surprise at being shown any consideration at all by the enemy. Under the conditions that prevailed in North Korea during the conflict, even the simple preservation of the lives of an appreciable number of captives could be accomplished by the captor only by quite considerable and obvious effort (Biderman, 1963). It is well to remember in this context that the interviews were confined to a very biased sample of the prisoner population — namely, the 50 per cent (approximately) that survived.

A related consideration which apparently entered ex-prisoners' contrasts of their expectations and experiences was a precapture image of a nakedly malevolent captor — images of torture and sadistic atrocities that did not fit anything in the personal experience of the majority (but far from all) of the survivors.* Only rarely, moreover, was contact with the captor characterized exclusively by unalloyed oppression.

Some of those who checked answers indicating that they had expected the worst and found the reality even worse than expected may have been merely using this means of emphasizing their indignation at how badly they had been treated. Others may have been venting self-vindication — they emphasized how badly they had been treated to cancel out qualms about how badly they had behaved. A remark of one of the men who checked this alternative suggests that another consideration may have been influencing these replies. After checking the response, "[My treatment by the Communists] was much worse than I expected," this repatriate scrawled in explanation: "I expected to be killed!"

This ex-prisoner's comment may be merely a dramatic variant of an almost universal type of remark in memoirs of per-

---

* This was not true of the nonsurvivors, however. The Army estimates that over 5000 American soldiers were killed in atrocities (U.S. Department of the Army, 1953).

sons who have survived extremely oppressive captivity. There is scarcely a preface to a book relating such experiences that does not make a comment similar to: "No one who has not actually lived through it can appreciate what it was like."

Affliction and Endurance

Both classes of responses that have been mentioned reflect the surprise experienced by people who have encountered extreme hardship at discovering what men can endure. One of the types of responses emphasizes the failure of imaginings to encompass the magnitude of how terrible things can get — a new realization of what degrees of wretchedness, starvation, degradation, exhaustion, and torment are possible. The other type of response, at least sometimes, emphasizes surprise at the human capacity to endure these things — "I never believed I could live through such hardships."

Unfortunately, the analyses of Korean conflict data do not permit going much beyond this to say anything about the personalities or differences in the experiences of those survivors whose reflections after the event have the former or latter emphasis, or indeed, whether these are the kind of mutually exclusive sets that would usefully discriminate among survivors.

Popular Culture Themes

The same two themes run through a great deal of popular culture about extreme situations. It seems to be difficult for any member of the public to escape some exposure to both of them. On the whole, it appears that popular culture communicates more and better about the kinds and degrees of suffering that are inflicted on men than about the ability of the ordinary human being to remain more-or-less intact through the suffering. The reason for this is that the usual story about incredible captivity hardships that is conveyed in popular culture serves one of two purposes: either to portray the extraordinary evil and hatefulness of some enemy, as in wartime atrocity propaganda, or to portray the heroism of some individual or group. The former tends to dwell on the terrible effects on victims, as well as the terrible causes. The latter is implicitly premised on the extraordinariness of the capability or endurance of the glorified hero.

As a consequence, the ordinary American who has experienced oppressive captivity seems to have entered the situation with a general underestimation of his ability to "take it." (Again, the caveat is necessary that among those who greatly overestimate their abilities may be those who do not survive to be interviewed or to write memoirs. There is, however, the somewhat inconsistent proposition that underestimation of one's capacity to endure hardship may be, by itself, a fatally demoralizing expectation and that confidence in one's ability to endure is a prerequisite of survival.)

Modern-day "Softness"

The modern-day Westerner has also been bombarded by another type of minimization of his ability to endure adverse circumstances. The Korean prisoner-of-war case provided a springboard for a considerable amount of propaganda of this type. This is the view that the luxuries of modern, affluent, mechanized society are making men soft, both physically and mentally, and are leaving them progressively less adapted to enduring hardship. Popular writing on the Korean conflict POW's purported to describe how readily American prisoners succumbed to minor hardship (e.g., Kinkead, 1957). That a considerable proportion of Americans seem to suffer from some guilt about their "softness" may explain the great appeal and credibility of the many patently distorted writings in this vein that circulated after the conflict (see Biderman, 1963). If by some miracle of communication they could experience vicariously the day-by-day details of what each of these captives had lived through, readers who were very receptive to this theme of weakness would be amazed that so many of the prisoners survived at all.

It is, of course, foolish to deny the significance easy living has for both physical and mental inadequacies in coping with severe demands. There is excellent and growing scientific evidence on the importance of acclimatization; on the role of training in increasing the capabilities of the involuntary as well as the voluntary systems of the organism for meeting sudden demands, and so forth. It does not appear that our loss of physical capacity to cope with adversity, however, has proceeded nearly as rapidly as the dwindling of everyday familiarity with adversity. One reason for this is that, in recent years, there has been largely lost from our *visible* midst the terribly poor who heretofore served as models of the wretchedness and oppression that could be borne by man.

Underestimation of Human Tolerance

In a somewhat related vein are observations made in a review of historical literature on extreme situations conducted for the Defense Department (Biderman, Louria, and Bacchus, 1963). If the historical literature can be accepted as accurate, many currently accepted estimates of the limits of human tolerance for deprivation and environmental extremes are inaccurately conservative. The heat, crowding, water privation, and lack of ventilation and sanitation below decks in slave ships of the Middle Passage or in the British convict transportations to Australia were fantastically more extreme than the levels assumed, for example, in setting minimum standards for fallout shelter occupancy.

At the same time, we tend to underestimate the fact that what to us is routine may have been taxing or frightening for a person of former times. We have in our language the phrase "within inches of death," but we daily hurtle in automobiles separated only from others hurtling in the opposite direction by a few inches of yellow line on the pavement. Whether our risk in probability terms is greater or less than that of the pioneer facing the prospect of Indian raids on his wagon train is objectively unimportant. Consider the Manhattan office worker who packs himself twice each day, including those of the torrid month of August, into a subway car with some 260 other souls (allowing a space of perhaps less than 2 square feet per person*) for a 45-minute ride to Benson-hurst or Jackson Heights. I am not at all sure that he is not undergoing inuring and training as potentially valuable for many situations of harsh captivity as is the daily experience of the plowhand. The human engineer presumably would be hard put to explain how the rush-hour subway riders manage this trip without casualties and while reading their evening newspapers. Such illustrations can be compounded by the imaginative.

Captivity Lore

To return from the subway, let us consider more generally common lore about captivity that presumably shapes conceptions that a person carries with him into a captivity situation — conceptions of what is in store for him and how he should behave. Similar cultural elements also influence the definitions of captor personnel and thus enter into the interactions of captive and captor that fashion the role of the prisoner in the situation.†

Evolutionary Perspectives

It was not long ago that writers on the history of the prisoner of war could view the past as a record of progressive evolution of more enlightened and humane concepts of the status of the war prisoner. The scholar's view of prisoner-of-war problems, as reflected in encyclopedias until World War II, were of this kind until they were disturbed by the events of the Second World War. Spaight (1918) and Trimble (1937) are representative.

The humaneness of prisoner treatment is the central organ-

---

* The legal limit of loading provides about 2 square feet per person.
† A more extensive version of the following exposition of culture concerning the captive is given in Biderman (1961).

izing concept of Trimble's discussion. He traces a development from Roman times in which the prevalent practice changed successively from extermination to enslavement to ransom to exchange and parole. The final development of what three decades ago he could call the "modern view" is attributed to the influence of Montesquieu and Rousseau.

These views became increasingly incorporated and elaborated in legal theory and in agreements between nations, beginning in 1785 with a treaty between the United States and Prussia. A series of international conventions embodied developing versions of these doctrines. These were formulated by conferences at Brussels in 1874, The Hague in 1899 and 1907, Copenhagen in 1917, and Geneva in 1929 and 1949.

The major principles of these agreements were as follows:

1. The prisoner was defined as in the power of the government that held him, rather than of the individuals who were his immediate captor;

2. The captor government was responsible for the safety, humane treatment, food, quarters, clothing, etc., with the standards of well-being of the captor nation's own troops being the measure of adequacy of provisions;

3. The prisoners were to be insulated from participation in the war, by guarantees against their exploitation by the captor for war-related functions, and by the detention of prisoners or their parole under obligation not to reassume arms. The prisoners also were assigned certain duties to the captor, including providing true identification of themselves and their rank (age being added by the 1949 Convention) and to abide by laws and rules for their detention established by the captor power.

Some ambiguity remained in the area of the assumed patriotic duty and motivation of the captive. Two major areas of continuing conflict were recognized. The first was the prisoner's obligation to escape and rejoin his own forces if he could. This right was recognized, and the punishment for recaptured escapees was restricted by these agreements. The agreements also recognized that a similar game would be played in the area of interrogating prisoners for military information. It was regarded as unrealistic to attempt to prohibit the captor from questioning prisoners for intelligence purposes, but all forms of "mental and physical" duress to elicit intelligence information were forbidden (see Prugh, 1956).

In recounting the history of actual prisoner practices, the articles and books during the century which saw the development and acceptance of these legal doctrines were largely records of the deviation of practice from these theories. Public attitudes toward the enemy of the moment in almost all wars were not as benign as they were to the symbols of humanity that were considered in formulating these international doctrines. The urgencies, disorganization, shortages, and emotions of warfare made deviations the rule, rather than the exception, even when governments felt that both morality and self-interest urged abiding by the legal doctrines.

Sociological Types of War and Prisoner Treatment

Two types of factors account for the extent and nature of the deviations from humanitarian practice that characterized prisoner treatment in recent warfare. One of these is, essentially, the fortunes of war; the relatively unpredictable outcomes of the applications of strategies and resources in conflict that determined how many prisoners were taken by a particular power at a particular time and place. In most of the extreme situations that have occurred, the severities of climate, the lack of logistical preparation and resources, and the disorganization of supplies by highly mobile or destructive combat conditions have had a greater role than the malevolence of the capturing troops or government. More benevolent intents on the part of the captor might have tremendously ameliorated but would not have entirely precluded conditions such as occurred during the U.S. Civil War, or during World War II in southeast Asia or at Stalingrad.

This matter of intent is a vital factor, however. A possibly broader way of considering it is in terms of how the captor defines the prisoners he captures and the determinants of his conceptions of what activities toward his prisoners are appropriate. Although peculiar features of the national culture of the capturing country account for some of these conceptions, many of them follow from the particular sociological type of war that is taking place. Speier (1941) has presented a typology of social types of war in which he suggests that major varying features of warfare can be distinguished according to the social definition of the enemy:

The three pure types of war may be called absolute war, instrumental war, and agonistic fighting. . . . Absolute war may be characterized, negatively, by the absence of any restrictions and regulations imposed upon violence, treachery, and frightfulness. . . . The opponent is an existential enemy. Absolute war is waged in order to annihilate him. . . . The absolute enemy is not a subject of predatory interests but rather a symbol of strangeness, evil, and danger to the community as a whole.

Instrumental war is waged in order to gain access to values which the enemy controls. Thus it is defeat of the enemy — not necessarily his annihilation — which is desired in instrumental war. . . . Violence in war is restricted for expedient reasons because the defeated and captured enemy himself becomes an immediate source of gain.

The extreme opposite of absolute war is the fight waged under conditions of studied equality and under strict observance of rules. Measured in terms of destruction such a fight is highly inefficient and ludicrously ceremonious. However, the agonistic fight, as we know it from ancient Greece and also from other cultures, is not oriented toward the destruction of the enemy, although his death may, of course, ensue. Nor is it directed toward the acquisition of wealth or other useful ends. It is fought for a prize, *i.e.*, for a symbolic value attached to victory (glory). Victory . . . is a fateful, symbolic revelation of justice, provided that the sacred rules according to which justice has to be sought were meticulously respected. The regulations in agonistic fighting are not rooted in expediency as are the restrictions possibly imposed upon instrumental war. Rather they are the quality of norms.

Rarely has a war accorded with any degree of completeness

to one or another of the ideal types of Speier's typology. How close the nature of the social conflict and the objectives were to Speier's models, however, has been an important determinant of the conception of the enemy and the general orientation to prisoner treatment during that war.

Total War and the Prisoner

Contemporaneous with the growth of international law concerning prisoners was the accentuation of nonrational elements in international conflict. Both nationalistic and political ideologies became more dominant as issues relative to "instrumental" and "agonistic" components. With the present century, wars became more "absolute" or "total" with sharpened "out-group" images of the opponent.

These definitions reached singular intensity during World War II, particularly in the German-Soviet and American-Japanese conflict.

The emergent form of war was "total" in an additional sense — there was a pervasive rationalization of potential means in the service of nonrational nationalistic and political ideologies. The entire physical and social environment of both one's own and the enemy's society in rationalized total war becomes open to attempted manipulation or elimination in accordance with the doctrinaire objectives of the ideology.

Restrictions of a sacred, sentimental, legal, or traditional nature which previously immunized persons, institutions, or physical objects from the war, or made particular practices unthinkable, lost much of their force. These developments were epitomized by the totalitarian state.

The absolute concept of warfare also provided the basic operating and organizational principle of these societies even in time of peace — for both Nazi and Soviet doctrine embraced the concept of the nation as at permanent war against hostile elements at home and encircling, hostile powers abroad. A product of this last element of totalitarian doctrine was the concentration camp — in conception, much like

Albert D. Biderman

the extension of the prisoner-of-war concept to the permanent, civil, absolute war (cf. Abel, 1951; Adler, 1958).

The distinctive features of recent prisoner-of-war history have reflected both forms of "totalism" that have been discussed; the nonrational and the rationalistic. On the one hand, there has been the accentuation of the image of the foe in total conflict as an individual of another antagonistic world; a nonperson meriting extermination, retribution, or, at best, reformation. On the other hand, there has been the rationalistic view of prisoners as an exploitable resource toward the total objective and the consequent attempt at rational exploitation of prisoners toward all conceivable war objectives: economic, political, and military (cf. Cohen, 1953; Kogon, 1950).

Though epitomized by totalitarian, particularly Communist, practice, observers see the same influences as affecting prisoner doctrine of the democratic nations. The notion of progress that formerly organized historical accounts of captivity has been largely replaced in the post-World War II world by one that implicitly or explicitly chronicles an "Advance toward Barbarism" (Veale, 1953).

Atrocity Concepts

Few captives possess much detailed knowledge of the elaborate doctrine that has been discussed. Newly captured prisoners are not completely devoid of concepts regarding captivity in general, or their particular captivity status, however. As mentioned earlier, song and story in all cultures, if not the more formal media of information and entertainment, expose even the most unsophisticated persons to some of the lore concerning captives. The basic images developed by these general cultural productions is that of the suffering and heroism of the captive at the hands of an oppressive, inhumane enemy.

In the post-World War I period, there was a reaction against war propaganda in general and against atrocity propaganda in particular. A propaganda consciousness arose permeating most strata of Western countries that inclined people to discount tales of atrocities (Kris and Leites, 1949). Consequently, the organized barbarity on an unprecedented scale that characterized the Nazi concentration camps only slowly registered on public consciousness. Indeed, a realization of public distrust of atrocity propaganda led the Allied nations in World War II to adopt a deliberate policy of underplaying Nazi atrocities in order to insure credibility for their output. Allied propagandists recognized that:

Because people now expect war to be horrible, it is not so easy to shock their sensibilities. An incident must be more intense than ever to qualify as an effective "atrocity." On the other hand, in the face of widespread consciousness and of resistance to propaganda in particular, the task of establishing belief is much harder. Many of the requirements of credibility, furthermore, conflict with those of intensity, creating an added dilemma (Jacob, 1942).

As a consequence, only in the postwar world did the events of the Nazi era penetrate public consciousness and then only dimly.

Nonetheless, the Nazi concentration camps have left a lasting association of captivity with unspeakable horrors that has shaped the cultural concepts of captivity of the present day. In wartime Germany, there was also an overlapping of the prisoner-of-war and the concentration-camp systems, which particularly affected the fates of French, Russian, and Polish prisoners of war.

For Western peoples in the postwar world, Communism became defined as an even more inhumane and dangerous foe than Nazism had been. Although there were distinctive aspects to anti-Communist atrocity reports and to reactions among Westerners to Communism as an enemy, there was a generalized identification of the horrors which totalitarian regimes inflicted on captives.

Although these developments of public attitudes involved a hardening of public response to reports of atrocities against others, the effect on those who became captives was different.

Expectations involved to a greater extent the fear of being subjected to unspeakable horrors — the terrorization toward which at least some atrocities have been directed (Biderman, 1956 *a, b*). The repression that characterized typical responses to news of atrocities has been further suspected of intensifying the anxiety element in these anticipations. At the same time, the characteristic skepticism of atrocity propaganda left the new captive with some element of hope that his fears were the result of his having been tricked by his own propagandists into thinking the worst of an enemy who was actually much more benign than he had been portrayed. Horror was expected as characteristic of the enemy whom the prisoner had been fighting and hating, but there was also the unsettling hope that the enemy would prove to be humane. The prisoner's hopes for his future thus involved a denial of his immediate past.

The Heroic Concept

In mass media and folklore, second only in prominence to depictions of the barbarity of captors toward prisoners, is the theme of the heroism of the prisoner. With surprising frequency, the ordinary man feels under some obligation to play the hero's part in extreme captivity situations, but much rarer are opportunities for playing the heroic role with any degree of visible success. This is true, at least, in the retrospective examinations of the event by survivors. Controls imposed by the captor, and the limited control the prisoners can exert over their environments, restrict greatly the scope of possible actions according to heroic models. In addition, the demands of the situation frequently require almost total concentration of energy on meeting one's own bodily requirements for survival.

Nevertheless, former prisoners writing on their own behavior and the behavior of others feel that vindication is necessary where their behavior was other than a model of heroism. Writings by nonparticipants also implicitly involve normative expectations that persons in extreme situations will accept far greater risks and greater altruistic subordination of the self than in ordinary life situations. This is particularly true with respect to attitudes toward military prisoners.

The Escape Tradition

The most highly developed aspect of the heroic model of captivity behavior is the escape story. Escape is reported to be the most precious of captive dreams. In recent wars, including the Korean, it has been the primary objective for which prisoners of war organized secretly among themselves. Although the escape tradition is possibly not as highly developed in the United States as in England, where it rivals detective and spy stories as a category of popular literature, it is nonetheless a prominent theme in American heroic lore.

In many British escapees' tales from World Wars I and II, captivity is treated as a setting for the game of escape. It is written about as a sport. There have been captor personnel who have approached the prisoner-of-war situation with a somewhat similar sporting conception. Their role in the game was conceived as something like that of a goalkeeper — a much duller position than that of the escapee's but still an exciting one to be played according to the rules and with mutual respect among the antagonists (see Reid, 1952, 1953).

These attitudes are characteristic of agonistic conceptions of war that were discussed earlier. There have been extensions of the idea of the "escapees' club" to more total conflicts, however, where captors had less sporting notions of their role and that of the prisoner. In part, this stems from there having been considerable continuity through successive wars in the escape tradition, especially among professional military personnel, with successful escapees from one war being prisoners in the next and passing along much of the lore to their younger fellows.

The escape tradition, and the many stories of successful World War II escapes, provided the setting for some people to regard the record of American prisoners of war in Korea as shameful in that it was reported that none had escaped "from an organized POW camp."

Military forces foster escape activities among their members who become prisoners of an enemy for reasons beyond the obvious significance of the number of men who may effect a safe return to their own lines. Even when unsuccessful, it is frequently pointed out, escape attempts function to divert the attention and resources of the enemy from other war pursuits. More fundamentally, escape activity is regarded as the keystone upon which organization, discipline, and morale of prisoners have frequently been built (see Hall, 1954; U.S. Department of Defense, 1955). This has been the case even in situations where escape was possible at best for only a tiny fraction of the men confined.

This view of escape activities is similar in some respects to the concept of the "heroic myth" of Sorel (1950), which he analyzed with particular reference to the role he advocated for the general strike in a socialist revolution. While regarding the general strike itself as unrealizable, he saw in it a heroic objective with capabilities of evoking fervent shared images and an intense solidarity. He also saw it as constituting a basis for discipline and training that was directly tied to the immediate problems, grievances, and natural groupings among the classes that would compose the ranks of a revolution.

Escape has functioned as the "heroic myth" among many groups of prisoners.

Resistance to Interrogation

A second well-developed theme in the tradition of the heroic prisoner is resistance to the captor's efforts to wrest information from the captive. To the extent that armed forces have given recognition to a need for preparing troops for the event of capture, it has been in the area of indoctrinating personnel to divulge no information to an enemy beyond the minimum demanded by international law — name, rank, serial number, and date of birth. This was the only aspect of captivity regarding which any significant number of Americans captured during the Korean conflict had any official instruction.

Other Heroic Models

Beyond escape and resistance to interrogation, there appears to be little specific content in popular images of the heroic role appropriate to the prisoner.

Another fairly frequent theme in writings by survivors of the more extreme situation, however, is the heroic portrayal of the feat of survival itself, and survival with the maintenance of the integrity of one's personality.

Comment has already been made on the more recent conception of the obligation of the prisoner "to resist by every means available" — the extension of the battle to the prisoner camp. Various accounts have glorified acts of harassment and sabotage against captors, and vigilante activity against fellow prisoners who deviate from the patriotic, political, or social code of the dominant prisoner group. In Korea, anti-captor acts extended from petty, schoolboy-like anti-authoritarian acts, such as taunting guards or chalking patriotic slogans, to the murder of captor personnel (Biderman, 1963).

Moral Lore of Remote Events

Two aspects may be noted of the culture products discussed here that predefine captivity situations for those who come to experience them directly. First, they do not involve the kind of communication that takes place among common participants in some immediate situation, but rather communication that allows the assimilation of meanings of the events by people remote from them — i.e., "back-home" meanings. Second, and as a result of this function, this culture constitutes more a moral lore than one of situational adaptation and practicality (cf. Schein, 1959, 1960).

From a functional standpoint, such lore has qualities noted by students of myth, propaganda, and "human interest" news. It serves such functions as testing and elaborating the moral values of a society, defining the group by symbolic incorporations and ostracisms, reaffirmations of solidarity, and so forth (cf. Merz, 1942; Hughes, 1939). Only vaguely and remotely does it reflect those adaptational demands that are experienced most acutely in the immediate situation by captives.

In the immediate situation, pre-existing expectations and role definitions are usually experienced by participants as having a highly unreal quality. Though they are rapidly modified by experience, however, these early conceptions continue to influence definitions of the situation by the captive.

Distinctions between Moral Lore and Operative Prison Culture

The disjunction between the moral lore about captivity and the operative culture of the prison camp accounts for some of the difficulty that was discussed at the outset of this paper — the difficulty that ex-prisoners have in relating their experiences in interviews and in answering meaningfully questions that ask them to contrast their precapture expectations and their actual experiences. One illustration is the problem some former prisoners have in expressing in the back-home context the rather complicated tacit fictions that captor and captive came to share in their everyday relations. More frequently than not, interactions between captor and captive maintain some overt pretense that captor and captive are not in conflict in the matter at hand at any given moment, with both parties conscious of the pretense and both aware that the other party recognizes it as a pretense. A number of sociological reasons make such an "etiquette" the rule in situations such as this, in addition to factors, specific to prisoner-of-war situations, that make it to the interest of both parties to adhere to these fictions.

Some cloaking of the area of conflict is characteristic of the kind of situation which has sometimes been called "antagonistic cooperation." In antagonistic cooperation, conflict is the dominant aspect of the relationship, but some degree of mutual dependence is also present. Illustrations are the relationships which frequently hold between buyer and seller, militant union and management, executioner and victim, and so forth. The elements of conflict in the situation are particularly likely to be submerged or cloaked when the outcome is largely or completely predetermined with respect to the major values in conflict.

The typical prisoner's definition of most of the immediate situations he encountered during his captivity was more of this nature than it was in accord with the image one would be likely to have of parties at war with one another. It is also decidedly different from the picture which has frequently been painted of POW behavior in Korea as "collaboration."

Some degree of antagonistic cooperation was present in the behavior of all Air Force POW's, including those who did most to thwart and harass the Chinese, as well as those who went furthest in doing their captor's bidding. To take an illustration from the autobiography of a soldier captured in Korea:

... [By the second day of the march] we were carrying the Chinks' food and their ammo. A lot of the guys were even carrying their guards' weapons. ... I had nicknamed my guard Slim and I was carrying all of his equipment (Pate and Cutler, 1956).

The quotation is from the memoirs of one of the most celebrated Army "reactionaries." Although part of the accommodation of the prisoners and these guards included the prisoners' helping the guards carry their equipment, according to this soldier, it did not exclude their killing each other when the circumstances were favorable. This former prisoner claims to have pushed "two or three" of his guards to their deaths over cliffs during this march and claims that one of this party thus dispatched "about 20 of them" (Pate and Cutler, 1956).

The relationships of prisoners to their guards and others among their custodians raise some interesting problems both practical and moral. Only the most fanatical or pompous guards can continue strict adherence to the rules of nonfraternization and vigilance to which they are supposed to adhere in their relationships with prisoners. Over a time, a degree of unarticulated understanding tends to arise between the prisoners and their custodians. The latter relax some of the more irksome security restraints, are sociable, and render small favors. In exchange, the prisoners accept the tacit duty of not taking undue advantage of the lowered guard of the former and of protecting them against the detection of the security breach by superiors.*

Prisoners can and do cultivate this tendency on the part of guards and others with the hope of exploiting it for some major objective (e.g., escape) in the future as well as for the moderate ameliorations of the immediate situation it provides.

These almost inevitable working agreements between prisoners and their custodians may give rise to several kinds of problems. One of these is that the implicit moral accommodations may develop so fully that the POW's may come to regard all the possible ways of fulfilling various obligations to their country as involving a "breach of faith" or a "dirty trick," considering their relationship with their captors. Escape, sabotage, and other circumventions of the captor's controls may come to conflict with the relationship built up between POW's and guards.

Another eventuality that sometimes arises is that an individual prisoner or POW group may take advantage of the trusting attitude of the guards prematurely or for a relatively insignificant objective, thus precluding more important exploitation at some time in the future. Thus a relaxed and moderated attitude toward the POW's may be replaced with

---

* Parallels with the literature on social relationships in American civil prisons are apparent here (cf. Clemmer, 1940; Sykes, 1958; Korn and McCorkle, 1959).

one of hostility and vigilance to the detriment of the prisoners' welfare.

Considered from a purely moral aspect, the violation of "working understandings" deliberately developed by prisoners with individual guards may involve wrongs which the POW's will regret. An example of such a violation resulting from thoughtlessness is given by General Dean's (1954) account of seizing a submachine gun from a sleeping guard in an unsuccessful attempt to murder one of his hated interrogators and then to commit suicide. The trusting guard from whom he had seized the weapon had previously taken risks to ease General Dean through one of the most difficult periods of his captivity. As Dean concludes the story: "I can only presume that he, my friend, was shot for being asleep" (p. 161).

Requirements of a Viable Role

The normal human being may be incapable of undiluted, overtly hostile interpersonal interaction over long periods of time without seriously destructive emotional consequences and associated physical consequences, particularly if this hostility is on the part of the underdog in the situation. A possible reason for this is the automatic mobilization of the body that is attendant to hostile interpersonal activity. One would assume that these responses are particularly intense when anxiety and frustration are associated with acting in accordance with the hostile attitude. Even in relatively "low-key" interactions, exhaustion might occur if such behavior were to be sustained over a long period. The "extreme apathy" which was frequently characteristic of POW behavior in Korea (Strassman, Thaler and Schein, 1956; Segal, 1954), as well as in the period of adjustment of inmates of Nazi concentration camps (see Cohen, 1953) in some cases may have involved defense against sustained overmobilization. Another type of defense is the restriction of the areas and conspicuousness of conflict through a *modus vivendi* based upon an "etiquette" of antagonistic cooperation (cf. Cantine, 1950; Goffman, 1957; Biderman, 1960).

There is a simpler factor precluding behavior by POW's toward their captor in a manner completely consistent with our stereotyped image of people at war with one another. The "socialization process" has ingrained ways of reacting to various common types of acts of others. With a view to the larger context of the situation, the individual is capable of departing from his usual mode of response toward a given type of act and of improvising a more appropriate response; e.g., knocking a proffered cigarette from the hand of an interrogator, rather than nodding "No," or saying "No thanks." Such innovations require considerable effort, not only the mental effort required to continue inventing and improvising modes of response, but also the effort of doing this while at the same time repressing more automatic, overlearned responses.

Constant improvisation of each successive act is, of course, not the manner in which human behavior in any social situation can best be described. The idea of the individual's adopting and playing a more-or-less coherent pattern of roles — that differ from situation to situation but have considerable consistency within each situation — describes behavior far more accurately.

Unlike the situation encountered in the prisoner-of-war camp, there is a highly developed lore in the underworld regarding prisons and prisoners, with which many if not most offenders who enter prisons have had contact. Furthermore, there is a great continuity that extends back at least two centuries in the culture of the penitentiary and the underworld culture of which it is a part. For want of a coherent concept for structuring the unfamiliar situation, the better known model of the penitentiary is applied to the prisoner-of-war situation by both captives and captors. Traditional prison slang has frequently come to be used by prisoners of war, even among such unlikely groups as the highly gentlemanly Union officers imprisoned during the Civil War at Belle Island in Richmond who, for example, referred to new prisoners as "fresh fish" (di Cesnola, 1865).

The lack of cultural continuity among war prisoners, and the limited acquaintance new prisoners have with the elaborate culture that does exist concerning the war prisoner, are sources of basic problems in their existence: the demands for behaving in an incompletely defined situation. In most situations of ordinary life, familiar, well-rehearsed roles exist for the individual which guide him to appropriate and effective conduct in the situation. Much of the strain that individuals experience in captivity derives from the lack of such patterns and from the labor, anxieties, and errors involved in improvisations to meet this lack.

These demands on the prisoner are aggravated by the fact that captor personnel who are the immediate authorities in the situation are handicapped similarly — they too frequently possess no experience and no adequate cultural models for guiding their behavior vis-à-vis the captives (Biderman, 1961).

These problems are likely to be less severe in a prisoner-of-war system like that of the Soviet Union in World War II which was characterized by greater continuity both with the past and with other institutions of incarceration of the country. Except where great masses of prisoners were taken and had little contact with older groups, there was in Russia a developed, pre-existing culture and social system into which war and political prisoners were integrated and could integrate themselves (see Kropotkin, 1887; Ciliga, 1940; Gollwitzer, 1953).

Commitment to the Immediate Situation and Continuity of Role

Adaptation to a stressful captivity situation is usually dependent upon a high degree of commitment to the immediate situation. This involves sharp breaks with previous definitions, identifications, and motivations.

The need for change varies somewhat with the extent to which there is a role available for the individual within the camp society that has some continuity with precapture roles. This has contributed to an overemphasis of the functionality for prison-camp adjustment of self-maintenance as opposed to change. Certain survivors record in books and articles their descriptions of and prescriptions for captivity behavior. Among these individuals are likely to be those for whom unusually great opportunities existed for playing roles in imprisonment that had high congruity with their precapture roles, e.g., physicians, clergymen, politicians, and, to an extent, those who, like Bettelheim (1960), could view their experience at least partly as instructive participant observation.

Prescriptive Comments

A general synthesis of the recommendations that are given by survivors for "ideal adjustment" involves some balance between (1) personal change and involvement in the immediate situation, and (2) self-maintenance and continued identification with "the outside." Illustrations of adaptive failures that are given involve overemphasis on behavior in both these directions. On the one hand, a failure of the individual to change from precapture modes makes him prone to complicate the problems of the immediate situation and to fail to cope with them adequately, and, on the other, overimmersion in the immediate situation can eventuate in anomic crises, social disorganization, and psychological problems of guilt in and after the experience from violations of norms and expectations of the larger society.

References

ABEL, T. The sociology of concentration camps. *Social Forces*, 1951, *30*, 150–155.

ADLER, H. G. Ideas toward a sociology of the concentration camp. *Amer. J. Sociol.*, 1958, *63*, 513–522.

BETTELHEIM, B. *The Informed Heart. Autonomy in a Mass Age.* Glencoe, Ill.: Free Press, 1960.

BIDERMAN, A. D. "Communist Techniques of Coercive Interrogation." Lackland Air Force Base, Texas: Air Force Personnel and Training Research Center, December 1956a. *AFPTRC Developm. Rep.* TN-56-132.

BIDERMAN, A. D. "The Objectives of Training for the Event of Capture." Air Force Personnel and Training Research Center, Intelligence Methods Branch, Jan. 5, 1956b. Unpublished.

BIDERMAN, A. D. Social psychological needs and "involuntary" behavior as illustrated by compliance in interrogation. *Sociometry,* 1960, 23, 120–147.

BIDERMAN, A. D. "Cultural Models of Captivity Relationships." Washington, D.C.: Air Force Office of Scientific Research Report AFOSR-452, 1961.

BIDERMAN, A. D. *March to Calumny: The Story of American POWs in the Korean War.* New York: Macmillan, 1963.

BIDERMAN, A. D., LOURIA, MARGOT, and BACCHUS, JOAN. "Historical Incidents of Extreme Overcrowding." Washington, D. C.: Bureau of Social Science Research Report *BSSR* 354-5, 1963.

CANTINE, H. R. *Prison Etiquette,* Bearsville, N. Y.: Retort Press, 1950.

CESNOLA, L. P. di. *Ten Months in Libby Prison.* Philadelphia, 1865.

CILIGA, A. *The Russian Enigma.* London: Labour Book Service, 1940.

CLEMMER, D. *The Prison Community.* Boston: Christopher Publishing House, 1940.

COHEN, E. A. *Human Behavior in the Concentration Camp.* New York: W. W. Norton, 1953.

DEAN, W. F. *General Dean's Story.* New York: Viking, 1954.

GOFFMAN, E. Characteristics of total institutions. In *Symposium on Preventive and Social Psychiatry, 15-17 April 1957, Walter Reed Army Institute of Research.* Washington, D. C.: Government Printing Office, 1957.

GOLLWITZER, H. *Unwilling Journey.* Philadelphia: Muhlenberg, 1953.

HALL, D. O. W. "Escapes." Wellington, New Zealand: War History Branch, Department of International Affairs, 1954.

HUGHES, H. M. *News and the Human Interest Story.* Chicago: University of Chicago Press, 1939.

JACOB, P. E. Atrocity propaganda. In H. L. Childs and J. B. Whitton, *Propaganda by Short Wave.* Princeton, N. J.: Princeton University Press, 1942.

JACOBSON, EDITH. Observations on the psychological effects of imprisonment on female political prisoners. In K. R. Eissler (Ed.), *Searchlights on Delinquency.* New York: International Universities Press, 1949.

KINKEAD, E. A Reporter at Large: The study of something new in history. *The New Yorker,* October 26, 1957, pp. 102–153.

KOGON, E. *The Theory and Practice of Hell.* New York: Farrar, Straus, 1950.

KORN, R., and MCCORKLE, L. W. *Criminology and Penology.* New York: Holt-Dryden, 1959.

KRIS, E., and LEITES, N. Trends in 20th century propaganda. In G. Roheim (Ed.), *Psychoanalysis and the Social Sciences I.* New York: International Universities Press, 1949.

KROPOTKIN, P. A. *In Russian and French Prisons.* London: Ward & Downey, 1887.

MERZ, C. The editorial page. *Ann. Amer. Acad. Polit. Soc. Sci.,* 1942, *219,* 139–144.

PATE, L. W., and CUTLER, B. F. *Reactionary.* New York: Harper, 1956.

PRUGH, G. S., JR. Prisoners at war: The POW battleground. *Dickinson Law Rev.,* 1956, *60,* 123–128.

REID, P. R. *Escape from Colditz.* New York: Berkley, 1952.

REID, P. R. *The Colditz Story.* New York: Lippincott, 1953.

SCHEIN, E. H. Brainwashing and totalitarianism in modern society. *World Politics,* 1959, *11,* 430–442.

SCHEIN, E. H. Interpersonal communication, group solidarity, and social influence. *Sociometry,* 1960, *23,* 148–161.

SEGAL, H. A. Initial psychiatric findings of recently repatriated prisoners of war. *Amer. J. Psychiat.,* 1954, *3,* 358–363.

SOREL, G. *Reflections on Violence.* Glencoe, Ill.: Free Press, 1950.

SPAIGHT, J. M. *War Rights on Land.* London: Macmillan, 1918.

SPEIER, H. The social types of war. *Amer. J. Sociol.* 1941, *46,* 445–454.

STRASSMAN, H. D., THALER, MARGARET B., and SCHEIN, E. H. A prisoner of war syndrome: Apathy as a reaction to severe stress. *Amer. J. Psychiat.,* 1956, *112,* 998–1003.

SYKES, G. *The Society of Captives: A Study of Maximum Security Prison.* Princeton, N.J.: Princeton University Press, 1958.

TRIMBLE, E. G. Prisoners of war. In E. R. A. Seligman and A. Johnson (Eds.), *Encyclopedia of the Social Sciences,* Vol. 12. New York: Macmillan, 1937.

U.S. Congress, Senate. Committee on Government Operations. *Communist Interrogation, Indoctrination and Exploitation of American Military and Civilian Prisoners. Hearings before Permanent Subcommittee on Investigations.* 84th Congr., 2nd Sess., June 19, 20, 26, & 27, 1956. Washington, D. C.: Government Printing Office, 1956.

U.S. Department of the Army. *Handling Prisoners of War.* Washington, D. C.: Government Printing Office, 1952. *Dept. of Army Field Manual,* FM 19-40.

U.S. Department of the Army. "Extract of Interim Historical Report." War Crimes Division, Judge Advocate Section, Korean Communication Zone, June 1953.

U.S. Department of Defense. *POW: The Fight Continues After the Battle. The Report of the Secretary of Defense's Advisory Committee on Prisoners of War, Aug., 1955.* Washington, D. C.: Government Printing Office, 1955.

VEALE, F. J. P. *Advance to Barbarism.* Appleton, Wis.: C. C. Nelson, 1953.

CLAUS BAHNE BAHNSON

EMOTIONAL REACTIONS TO
INTERNALLY AND EXTERNALLY
DERIVED THREAT OF ANNIHILATION

THIS PAPER deals with two different types of threat of annihilation, one originating from within and the other from without the individual. A discussion of external threat comprises the major portion of the paper and it will be exemplified by psychologic threats and by the destruction of human lives during the Nazi occupation of Denmark during the Second World War. However, since these reactions appear in greater perspective when they are compared with reactions of patients suffering from life-threatening or terminal illnesses, material from such patients will also be introduced.

On the level of theory of apperception we will assume here that there is no fundamental difference between the "outer" and "inner" worlds as they appear to the individual, since they both depend on what might be called "ego recordings" or "ego registrations" of events cathected by the individual. Obviously, the body and its organs play a qualitatively different role for the individual within his field of experience than do environmental configurations. However, from the point of view of ego recordings of events in time and space. both internal and external phenomena can be placed on a continuum rather than being considered dichotomous variables.

The emotional impact of external threat and the way in which the individual proacts toward it depend on the dynamic isopomorphism between ontogenetically earlier internal threats and these later external threats confronting the

251

individual. As regards the infantile period we usually hypothesize that certain conditions which disturb the psychological homeostasis may evoke a disproportionate increase in tension that is not easily mastered by the young ego and so results in anxiety, panic, and regression (Freud, 1922, 1936). The sudden encounter with torture and death, or with destruction from within due to serious illness, may for the adult represent situations which do not differ significantly from the archetype of infantile threats against the psychobiological organization. However, the panic triggered off by internal threat is often met by displacing this threat from within to an apperceived threat from without. Vice versa, the individual sometimes deals with a threat from without by withdrawing cathexis almost completely from the environment, with the result that the threat is "transcribed" to an internal one that endeavors to overthrow ego-control and value systems and which therefore can be met with defenses already well established in the individual.

Although outer and inner spheres are thus frequently interchanged as battlegrounds for tragedy, an important qualitative difference does seem to exist between the two types of threat. External threat tends to make man "stand up to the occasion," whereas internal threat has a tendency to undermine man's self-image and resistance, causing it to crumble. He may then, unlike St. George, fail to fight the dragon, but may react as if the illness had rendered him defenseless by stealing away the very weapons with which he might have fought the battle.

The external threat is more ego alien and does not imply a symbolic gangrene of the first seat of self, the body. All of what laymen call "the best in man," that is, superego values and mores, can easily be mobilized to meet it. Aside from these implications which ensue for modal reactions to internal somatic threat, we may also hypothesize that the illness may be produced by the psychobiological organism itself, whereas external threat, such as war and natural catastrophe, is forced upon the individual by the environment.

Thus, the external threat, not being wrought in guilt and shame, can be met more easily as an ego-alien problem.

We shall deal here not only with the emotional reactions proper to the threat of annihilation, and with the proaction or adaptation to these threats, but also with the more specific apperceptual reactions which certainly may be understood as the effects of ego defenses, but which can best be described on the purely phenomenological level without immediate reference to their ego-defensive classification.

A part of the paper will draw from my own experiences during the Nazi occupation of Denmark and from the recorded experiences of a talented young freedom fighter, who was shot by the Germans after a long period of incomprehensible torture. The material collected from a large number of seriously ill patients is in the form of transcribed interviews and recorded responses to different kinds of projective procedures. In this paper, brief and condensed material is presented from only one cancer patient and from one young patient with very severe asthma.*

The first material to be presented consists of personal memories from the Nazi occupation of Denmark. I was 17 years old when the occupation took place and had advanced to my 21st year when it became necessary for me to seek refuge in Sweden. Since I was still quite young and not quite as prone to analytic scrutiny of self and others as I have since become, my impressions may have been rather untainted by theoretical deliberations. Three out of many memories have been selected to furnish material for this paper. Instances have deliberately been chosen which were relatively free of action since the more active episodes, as might be expected, were relatively free of emotion, whereas the inactive episodes, not allowing for discharge in overt behavior, were mainly emotional experiences.

The first episode took place when the German Army with-

---

* In the original paper, data from several patients were presented. For reasons of brevity, only two patients are included in this version of the paper.

out warning overran Denmark on April 9, 1940, and Hitler forced through a capitulation mainly by threatening to destroy Copenhagen as he had destroyed Warsaw — by means of bombs from the German Luftwaffe. Hundreds of German bombers were swarming in the air over Copenhagen at the time that King Christian decided to call a halt to the scattered fighting throughout the country.

I remember being awakened very early in the morning by the roar of German bombers. Running to the windows together with the rest of my family, I remember being spellbound with curiosity, staring at the incredible swarm of hostile grasshoppers. It was impossible not to keep looking at the bombers although, obviously, it would have been wiser to seek shelter. It was as if the situation had first to become better defined and as if, in doing so, one had to focus on the source of danger with intense curiosity and fascination, but apparently without any trace of conscious anxiety. Curiosity took over — a bit of behavior quite similar to that so frequently seen in small or helpless animals when suddenly confronted with one of their less friendly carnivorous neighbors (Shand, 1914).

My next memory is the peculiar reaction of the older members of the family around me. Subsequent to expressions of amazement, a complete denial of the seriousness of the situation became apparent. Although the war had been at our doorstep for many months, they stated that this could only be a realistic exercise of our own air force or that of a friendly neighbor, in spite of the fact that Denmark had very few airplanes and that England would certainly not send the Royal Air Force cruising over Copenhagen for no good reason. Other interpretations were that the airplanes were surely on their way to some other target despite their persistent circling over our heads, or that the pilots must have mistaken our city for another target, and so forth. This immediate denial of the threat, even with the airplanes in plain sight was a persistent reaction among most people in the house, on the street, and even downtown. Similar reactions to threat have been reported by Bettelheim, Blum, and others (Bettelheim, 1943; Blum and Klass, 1956; Cantril, 1940; Funkenstein, King and Drolette, 1957; Meerloo, 1958). This original "set" of denial of the occupation was very difficult to extinguish. It was for most people only modified in small steps and with incredulous disbelief. People persevered with their everyday tasks as if nothing were happening and were quite resistant to changing their routines. When German soldiers appeared in the streets, they were first described as "Danish soldiers in German uniforms on exercise"; then they became "friendly soldiers in transit," and only at the very last, after the accumulation of a full day's impressions, was the original set given up and the much more unpleasant and realistic one accepted — and then still with severe doubts. This reaction is similar to the well-known daze or shock reaction described by many students of natural catastrophe (Bakst et al., 1955; Form and Nosow, 1958; Janis, 1951; Kendrick, 1957; Marks et al., 1954; Wolfenstein, 1957) but with the important difference that in this case, where full-blown catastrophe had actually not taken place but existed only as a very realistic threat, disorganization and paralysis were less conspicuous and were replaced by disbelief and denial of the danger.

Constriction of the phenomenal field and preservation of predanger activities also were apparent in this classical threat situation and actually produced many tragicomical incidents. One humorous example of such rigid perseveration of the predanger set was the behavior of a commanding officer at a military air field just outside of Copenhagen. He was said to have been raving and shouting because some routine visual signals from different posts of the air field were not performed correctly and punctually, and he dispatched serious reprimands to the soldiers for not performing according to schedule. Although German soldiers were invading the field, he completely ignored the current situation and instead expressed dismay and anger because his precious routine was not correctly adhered to.

I remember many examples of the phenomenon which may

be called "shrinking of the field." In terms of dynamic theory, this phenomenon may be described as a redistribution of cathexis with withdrawal from peripheral objects and reinvestment in central or focal objects. In dangerous situations the field, both spatially and temporally, shrank to very limited proportions — the previous few minutes and, especially, the next and decisive few moments constituting the limits of awareness. Spatially the world then consisted only of the crucial immediate loci involved in the outcome of the problem situation.

This experience resembles the familiar regressive reaction of the somatically ill for whom the body itself and a few external relevant objects may constitute the total apperceived universe. In both cases only those spatial and temporal cues that have a direct bearing on overcoming the immediate danger are apperceived, or, as it may be described with more expressive color, the world shrinks. This does not necessarily imply that (à la Stanislawski) a smaller convex circle of experience is substituted for a larger one, but rather that a total rearrangement of a much smaller number of items or cues, either more distant or closer to the center of the field, takes place, thus constituting the new "essential field." The crucial characteristic of this new field is that only a few significant items are included, and that every one of these items is directly relevant to the danger situation. According to Kurt Lewin (1936) a continuous restructuring of the field always takes place, rearranging the environmental foci in clusters corresponding to the perceiver's needs, but here we have to do with a discontinuous change that causes not only a rearrangement of the field, but a sudden deletion of all intermediate and less significant structures, retaining only the crucial and "skeletal" parts of the field. To continue this metaphor, it is as if all "connective tissue" of the apperceived field is brushed away, leaving only the barren and essential keystones to define awareness.

An apperceived world of this type is quite characteristic of the deteriorated schizophrenic patient. This fact may lead to many speculations concerning the schizophrenic's experience of the world as an emergency situation. Certainly this "shrinking phenomenon" is repeatedly observed in the supposedly normal person under the stress of an emergency (Fraser, Leslie, and Phelps, 1943; Glover, 1940; Grinker and Spiegel, 1945; March, 1960).

The next episode I shall describe illustrates the shrinking phenomenon along with some other reactions to threat. I have chosen as my second example a situation that developed in the attic of an apartment house in Copenhagen where Jewish refugees were kept in hiding before they could be sailed to Sweden and to safety. This house was located in the middle of a street that was being raided by the Gestapo shortly after I entered the house with another refugee whom I escorted to this temporary hiding place. From the small windows under the roof we could observe the German patrol vehicles blocking off the street from both ends and could see the soldiers entering the different houses in their search for saboteurs and other illegal prey. This situation obviously trapped both me and the refugees and immediately changed my spatial field in a way that made the two ends of the street appear as the end of the world, each and every inch of the street enlarged to become a significant space separating the Gestapo from us. The soldiers' moves from house door to house door became major events, and otherwise insignificant aspects of their behavior, e.g., a minor gesticulation or turning around, were overinterpreted and became cues from which to predict the future. As the Gestapo came closer and closer, these changes in apperceived space and time became more marked, so that when they at last entered our staircase each of their steps lasted an eternity and each little noise became a major event. Fortunately for us, they did not find our hiding place.

When it was all over and the street was vacated by the soldiers, a peculiar phenomenon took place. It was as if our small world exploded into a larger one, as if the ropes that held together a tightly contracted universe were suddenly cut so that it enlarged strikingly, again making the street appear as a small and insignificant part of the total environment.

Many manifestations of anxiety were apparent in this situation. One refugee fainted and others crowded around the small windows in tense pallor. However, to me the most significant reaction was again the spellbound curiosity with which the trapped people observed the aggressors' approach. Apparently, isolation of affect took place, and enhanced ego activity was ushered in, which simultaneously reduced anxiety and produced a "set" of observant alertness that would prepare for immediate action on clearly differentiated cues. One important condition defining this and the next situation to be described was that mobility could not be introduced without increasing the danger, so that intensified perception was the only ego function that could be enhanced. This may explain the sharpness with which everything was suddenly perceived.

Another effect of the investment in ego processes was the affective change in the evaluation of the enemy. Prior to this event, all participants in the group unquestionably had strong hostile feelings toward the Gestapo, but, as the crucial phase began, this emotion was swept aside and replaced by an intent, nearly obsessive attentiveness and curiosity about the crucial development. There were no hostile exclamations, just intense observation. One might say that the emotions motivated the enhanced ego activities which then absorbed the energy generated by the emotions proper, with the result that felt emotion decreased.

The people with whom I shared these straining moments were relative strangers to me. At the time I arrived, personal contact was formal and group cohesiveness low. As a matter of fact, there was some suspiciousness, jealousy, and hostility among the refugees, probably related to the covert competition about being the first to escape. Everybody made himself "figure" and the rest "ground," to speak in Gestalt psychological terms. When the raid began, a marked change took place; the field apparently was restructured by most of the participants from being a competitive escape situation to being a joint defensive situation. Foe had become friend and the new *common* danger broke down formality, hostility, and restraint. Actually, this sudden change in group cohesiveness and the remarkable increase in intimacy among the group members might be understood as a subeffect of the general "shrinking of the field," investing each available and possibly significant human object with immense importance.

Another change in apperception, difficult to describe, characterized this and the following scene. I have called this the "reversed-zoom" effect, borrowing from photographic language. The environment seemed to zoom back into the distance to become small and far away. This apperceptive reaction of feeling objects at a distance at first seems incompatible with the increased definition and clarity of the "shrinking" effect. However, both occurred simultaneously, and this is exactly why I have chosen to call it reversed zoom. At the same time, as the apperceived field "shrinks" it moves rapidly into the distance and is seen now as a small, delicately engraved etching, somehow within the extrasensory framework of the main parameters of one's life.

This reversed-zoom effect has its parallel in Rorschach imagery, where the perception of three-dimensional space on the basis of shading cues is often interpreted as an effort by the perceiver to control anxiety, which is triggered off by shading in the cards, by placing the threatening stimulus in "perspective." Certainly, in the actual threat situations the reversed zoom served to reduce anxiety, simultaneously placing the event in its proper perspective should the crisis reach an unfavorable climax.

The third episode I shall describe was my escape to Sweden in a Danish police boat that had been seized by the resistance for this purpose.

The human cargo for the transport met secretly at a warehouse pier in the harbor after previous isolation at different "stations" in Copenhagen, and after having been moved to the point of departure by ingenious methods such as in ambulances and mail trucks. It was a dark, rainy night in late November 1943, and the desolate harbor district appeared as ominous as the river Styx. We were whisked one by one from the warehouse to the police boat in a quite secretive manner, following nearly magical rituals in the form of coded light signals and whistle calls, making the event appear as a dramatized smuggler scene from a thriller movie, was it not for the fact that our lives were at stake in the race. We were reminded of this by the German patrol boats that circled the harbor and, with repeated stabs of light from their projectors, ripped through the already narrowed life space which now included only the boat and the pier. The outstanding feature in my memory was the increasingly narrowed field of experience, at first including the town as a whole, then only the harbor, then the boat and its surroundings, and finally being limited to the narrow womb of the boat from which we had to watch passively the success or failure of the risky game.

On the purely emotional level, I remember a frantic, nearly stifling, acute anxiety, at first nonspecific and diffuse, but soon changing its character as it was directed toward the particular sources of danger. With this differentiation of the field, anxiety decreased and shifted partly to curiosity and to anticipation of possible reactions to moves by the enemy. This was a kind of if-then situation in which probable and anticipated events were silently rehearsed. This cognitive "acting on the anxiety" decidedly lessened the anxiety felt and allowed the tension to be minimized by its motivational momentum.

The planned escape tactic was now for our police boat to zigzag through the inner and outer harbors impersonating the legal patrol boats on their regular routes. With each successful avoidance of a German patrol boat, bringing the maneuver closer and closer to success, we felt greater and greater apprehension and an intensified focus on the next hurdle to come. It was as if a given amount of apprehension had fewer and fewer targets to which to become attached, making each remaining problem appear even more crucial. We deal here with what might be called a condensation of both affect and attention on a smaller and smaller number of items in a finite universe of anticipated events. This crescendo of intensity of experience is probably a general phenomenon when a crisis takes place under conditions that delimit its duration, thus facilitating the apperception of a finite field.

Again in this scene, neutralization of affect took place together with intensification of cognitive observation and prediction. This mechanism may correspond to that responsible for some of the differences between anxiety hysteria and phobia, on the one hand, and anxiety neurosis, on the other, in the sense that affect becomes attached to a specific target serving to absorb the emotional charge. It marks the transition between the more primitive free-floating anxiety and the more systematized phobia. This repeated experience, reported on the phenomenological level, supports the general hypothesis that the establishment of a specific object for fear tends to reduce the anxiety felt, a sequence well known from the study of phobias, but that apparently also holds in situations where fear has a realistic external source.

Further support for this hypothesis is given by the fact that both my compatriots and I became quite anxious *after* the immediate dangers were overcome — after we had arrived safely in Sweden. This "hangover" of free-floating anxiety was marked, and for days it was difficult to settle down and concentrate on any task. Of course, the emotion was complicated by the admixture of excitement and exhilaration to the remnants of anxiety, but it still stands out in my mind that primary anxiety was first experienced when the immediate external source of threat had been definitely removed.

Concerning this free-floating anxiety, students of natural catastrophe (Marks et al., 1954; Wolfenstein, 1957) have described some frequent human responses such as daze, shock, or confusion. I think that it is more to the point here to emphasize experienced anxiety rather than cognitive disorganization, which, after all, should be understood as a result of the emotion, not as an independent phenomenon. The main theoretical point is that, in acute danger, ego processes may be motivated by anxiety, but the emotion anxiety as such is not apperceived. Rather, the energy released by the emotion is invested in increased precision of reality testing, and in an intensification and reduction of the field. Therefore, the several apperceptive changes delineated here may all be understood as results of alertness and intensification of ego functions, motivated by the emotion anxiety. One exception may be the reversed-zoom effect, which might be understood as an ego-defensive maneuver coping with that part of anxiety that has not been successfully converted into energy potentials available for the ego's emergency tasks.

Obviously, in people who break down under stress, the ego apparatus is unable to handle and "bind" the emotional potential within the process of an adaptive "boost" in the precision and intensification of reality testing. For these people the energy generated within the individual by the apperceived threat situation is released directly in the form of experienced anxiety which interferes with cognitive processes and leads to a disorganized state of panic.

Another source of material from the Danish occupation consists of some excerpts from the letters of Kim Malthe-Bruun, an aspiring young poet who wrote significant and remarkable letters to a few people close to him during his stay in a German prison, where he was tortured and finally shot for his participation in the resistance. These letters have since been published by his mother, and to me they constitute one of the finest sources of human reaction to Nazi torture and to death (Malthe-Bruun, 1961).

He was imprisoned for months, and during this extended period he lived under continuous threat, frequently undergoing severe torture that culminated with his execution. His reactions were not to the *possibility* of torture and extinction, but to the certainty and permanency of these conditions.

His immediate reaction to arrest by Gestapo was denial of the seriousness of the situation. He wrote in a letter to his mother that he felt "calm and trustful" and that he would "soon be home again." He emphasized in a letter to his girl friend the "interesting surroundings" and the opportunity to "study prisoners and all their reactions" on the spot. Denial and intellectualization are clearcut in this verbatim statement:*

> I have had great gain and pleasure out of my stay, and seldom does a day come to an end without a feeling of surprise that it has already gone by.... I assure you, that I was considerably more tied down and restrained when I was a student. Now I have all the time I could wish for to think as well as to read. [A little later in the same letter:] I have several times thought with astonishment that it is peculiar that I do not miss freedom.

Another example of denial is this passage from a letter written after two months of imprisonment:

> You all still think that all this is an experience of a particular caliber. That is not true. It is simply as if one had come from one room to another, where the furniture is different. Why deplore the situation because a man has gotten different furniture?

Kim was a complex person, and we see that he operates here on two levels. He denies the seriousness of the situation but also communicates awareness of this defensive denial. He is sitting back, evaluating himself, thus taking the initial steps toward the depersonalization that became so pronounced in his later letters.

In one of his next letters to his mother he wrote:

> Remember that there is plenty of adventurous blood in me, and that, even when I was first arrested, I at once felt excitement rather than anything else concerning what I was about to experience. The Gestapo, and anyone else I have been exposed to, did not frighten me in the least. They are simply primitive, and those who are not primitive are extremely interesting.

What Kim calls "excitement" is probably similar to what I described as curiosity above. Anxiety may not necessarily be spontaneously felt when real danger threatens. Denial, neutralization of affect, and the reversed-zoom effect seem to be expressed in this passage.

Describing his reactions to the first session of Gestapo torture, Kim writes:

* All translations are by the author of this paper.

It appeared to me, when I . . . stepped in to them for questioning, that this would be what an animal trainer would feel, when he stepped in to his animals. Such an animal trainer probably also feels a certain love for them, even if he can realize that some of them are scabby and must be got rid of.

This is a far cry from a direct and unmodified reaction to threat. Here Kim has reversed the situation so that he is the trainer and the Gestapo his puppets. Not only power control is reversed, but also affect. Kim states that he feels love for them rather than hate, thus introducing the masochistic strain in his personality fabric that also became so pronounced during his last days of tortured life.

Let it be said at this point that Kim did not live in a vacuum but in a culture that, although predominantly atheistic, had strongly incorporated the Christian ethic. Kim during his last days of life ruminated on both Jesus and Socrates, and after one of the worst sessions of torture, he wrote:

I can well understand the unlimited love he [Jesus] felt for all people and especially for all those who participated in driving the nails through his hands.

It is obvious that he had assimilated the masochistic aspects of the Christian ethic. We shall return to Kim's masochism below.

We have touched here upon the tendency for individuals to externalize internal events and to internalize external events, as if to bring about a balance on a continuum including the external world and self. This may be set within the theoretical frame of masochism, but here we shall emphasize the cognitive aspects of these adaptive processes that attempt to appease external threat by making it a part of internal fate.

Kim writes:

I have always lived with the feeling that everything that happens has its own meaning, and that this whole chain of events should lead me forward to something definite and prearranged. [And further:] . . . Our existence runs in some very definite tracks, and all that happens to us is always our greatest fortune.

Here Kim expresses contentment with and joy over his situation and ties this in to what he believes is a fate that eventually will turn everything to the best. He shows a suggestive "transcription" in the understanding of threatening events which makes them appear as predetermined meaningful sequences. Torture and hardship are understood as fixed successions of events arranged by fate, with the tacit understanding that all has a "meaning" and all will be for the best. This reaction is reminiscent of the use of the concept of fate in the old French satire by Denis Diderot (1797), who lets his hero Jacques exclaim after each misfortune or failure: "All is well and for the good, because it stands written in the heavens."

Threat is apparently disarmed when it can be apperceived as a predetermined event within a greater system that, by definition, must be benign. In this way the ultimate meaning of even catastrophic events can be denied, reversed, and interpreted in terms of their opposite. Thus Kim writes about his imprisonment:

It is a peculiar security that has descended on me by sitting here behind such infinitely solid walls. . . . It is wonderful to live; what it is to die is still completely unknown to me, but I feel as if it must be one of the most magnificent and grand events in one's whole life.

He certainly turned pain to pleasure.

After very severe torture just before Kim's death at age 21, he wrote:

I looked at my hands with surprise, they trembled. . . . It must then have a purely physiological effect on one. . . . I have since thought about the peculiar thing that has actually happened to me. Just afterwards [after torture] I felt an indescribable relief, a jubilant exuberance with victory, a happiness so unreasonable that I felt paralyzed. It was as if the soul had completely made itself free from the body, as if these two gamboled as free and independent beings, the one in a completely liberated unearthly intoxication, the other wallowing around in the most earthy and passionless convulsions. . . . When the soul again came back to the body, it was as if all exultation and rejoicing in the world was assembled, but it went as with so many sources of pleasure, when the exuberance was gone the reaction set in. I discovered that my hands trembled, there was something tense inside me, it was as if a battery at the roots of my heart were short-circuited and was now quickly discharging itself. I was like one addicted to pleasure, who wastes away of longing.

Kim's reaction to very severe torture apparently provoked both depersonalization and a masochistic euphoria, successfully protecting him from the unavoidable pain. Thus his reaction brings up the question whether a truly regressive, masochistic reaction pattern can serve as an adaptive maneuver by means of which the individual can tolerate inevitable pain forced upon him by the environment, or whether a presituational dynamic leaning toward masochism must be latent in the individual for him to be activated in such a situation. Obviously, if this distinction is pushed far enough, the question becomes meaningless in the sense that a masochistic reaction pattern is forced on every child at an early age as a temporary solution for his aggressive or sadistic impulses, so that these possibilities must exist as deeply buried channels of discharge in every adult individual. However, this comment would only force us to rephrase the original question at another level, and we would now have to ask: Can the old, buried masochistic release channels be reopened and reactivated in all individuals when necessity demands it, or must other conditions be met that serve to keep open this possibility of masochistic regression in some individuals? Whatever the answer, masochistic pleasure from even the worst torture was one of Kim's most outstanding reactions to overwhelming pain and mutilation.

We have now discussed a few examples of reactions, or proactions, to external threat of death and mutilation, and to the materialization of these threats. Let us now turn to a few illustrative examples of reactions to serious somatic illness that poses a threat from within, and see whether we may profit from the comparison. An extensive dynamic interpretation of the meaning of symptoms and of their general role within the personality structure of the patient is out of place here, and we shall therefore confine ourselves to three delimited tasks: (1) evaluation of the tendency to displace to the environment a threat from within, (2) scrutiny of other defensive mechanisms invoked to deal with internal threat, and (3) description of purely emotional reactions to somatic illness.

The first patient from whom I shall present material was a young man of about thirty, married and with children, who suffered from severe asthma. The material was collected during 1958, and the patient is now deceased.

Figure 1 depicts one of many drawings he made as a part of a repeatedly administered microbattery of projective tests which proved quite revealing of the way he perceived his own

FIGURE 1.   *Drawing by an asthmatic patient.*

respiratory difficulties.* He said about this drawing that "one snake is trying to swallow another, which in turn is swallowing a big rat." The snake to the right in the picture is "ready to pounce on himself, swallow himself," and perish in the

* A more extensive report on this material is presented in Knapp and Bahnson (1963).

act. We shall omit here the patient's lengthy associations concerning incorporation and death that were forthcoming on the basis of this drawing and state only the important fact that the inner respiratory problem was displaced by him to the environment. Instead of concern for the unreliable performance of his respiratory system, he expressed the fear that external objects would get caught in his throat, making him suffocate and perish. This type of externalization is also expressed in the next two drawings (Figs. 2 and 3) which

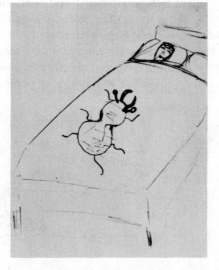

FIGURE 2.   *Drawing by an asthmatic patient.*

illustrate his fantasies about horrible, overgrown, monster bugs that would pursue and kill him. Like so many asthmatics, he had a pronounced fear of dirt and bugs, and bugs especially became the target for his fears. The bug monster in Fig. 3 became the main actor in an important fantasy in which in his imagination the patient had to encapsule the whole earth and to use many elaborate defensive devices to guard himself from being attacked by the monster. He expressed it this way:

FIGURE 3.   *Drawing by an asthmatic patient.*

It's a beast of my own making. It walks like an insect, it's got fins and wings like a fish and bird, it's got ears like a donkey and like a mouse, it's got whiskers like a cat, a mouth like a shark, eyes on stalks. It's a horrible creature. I try to kill it — all right I kill it — what happens — the black eye falls off and it grows an identical one like this — this whole thing. Then if you kill that, it falls off and grows into another one. I wonder how you could do it — what the hell could you do? If it were small enough and I were big enough I would squish on it. I would stomp on it, until it was no longer there. It would be a nothing, grind it with my foot into dust. I hate bugs — it is slimy, like a slug. Oh, horrible. Ooh — it gives you goose pimples.

Now the patient described how he would go about defending himself against the monster:

You can't kill it right out by shooting it because it'll make more. I don't know what you would do. Maybe the best thing would be to cut off its eyes. How about burning it? Fire? Maybe that's one way of getting rid of it. That might do it. But the smoke from the burning might be poisonous and kill everything. Well there are a lot of things you could do for that. First of all, you could build yourself a big, big, enormous roof over the whole world to be safe from that thing wherever that is. Completely enclose it. You build a glass dome around the whole earth except for one little place where that thing is, and there it is. Now you get all oxygen and methods of manufacturing and growing food and everything underneath here. Manufacture your own air — in other words, separate your atmosphere from this, plant your plants underneath the dome so that they will make oxygen for you. Let that stay out there. You could burn it. Close the doors real fast to this great big enormous chamber.

The externalization is clear: the fear of the inability to breathe was transformed into the fear of an external monster, in its origin relating to his respiratory problem, but developing into an independent external phobic object. This seems to be in sharp contrast to Kim's internalization of external threat.

In the next drawing (Fig. 4) the patient portrays himself as a death skull and a disintegrating body of a cow that

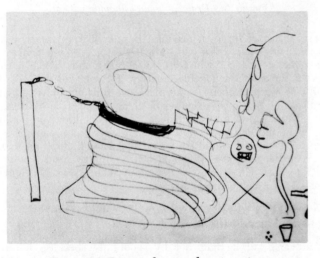

FIGURE 4.   *Drawing by an asthmatic patient.*

is dying because external supplies, in the form of medicine and food, are withheld. Contrast this horrible feeling of deprivation in a patient with an internal problem with the pleasure and bliss described by Kim when confronted with actual external deprivation and torture. It seems remarkable that, in both instances, in the mind of the sufferer the sources of threat were displaced away from their origin, from outer to inner, and vice versa.

In the next two drawings (Figs. 5 and 6) this patient again depicts death as pursuing him from without, rather than from within. In Fig. 5 he draws his analyst as death himself, ruling

FIGURE 5. *Drawing by an asthmatic patient.*

FIGURE 6. *Drawing by an asthmatic patient.*

over the patient in a casket. He verbalized about this drawing:

> I did not look at him [the analyst] when I left. Maybe if I look at him he is not there — a skeleton — a demon monster.

In Fig. 6 he is being peacefully "played into death" by another of his doctors. He said:

> This is me. See. That's a funny looking animal. It looks something like a dog's head, too. . . . He is putting me to sleep with his piano playing. . . . I am really a dog. Woof, woof, woof. . . .

In fantasy the patient acted upon this apperception of external threat, and, as is apparent from Fig. 7, he wished to kill the doctor rather than the disease.

The patient felt both strong anxiety and hostility toward his disease. He was always anxious lest he suffocate in an asthmatic paroxysm. He tried to safeguard himself as well as he could by carrying with him most of the time both medication and a nebulizer. An outstanding feature was that both anxiety and anger were usually directed toward external targets, such as the departure of his physicians or the possibility of lack of medical supplies. The general "irresponsibility" of his doctors could throw him into violent rages against them.

Comparing this patient's fear of and hostility toward his benevolent physicians with Kim's love and compassion for

FIGURE 7. *Drawing by an asthmatic patient.*

his torturers supports the hypothesis that personal strength and integrity can be mobilized against an external threat of annihilation with relative ease, whereas inner threat facilitates disintegration of the ego, dependency, suspiciousness, and anger.

The tendency to dramatize and externalize danger so prevalent in this patient is in sharp contrast to Kim's tendency to minimize, circumscribe, clearly define, and internalize danger. Obviously, there are factors that increase the probability that individuals with considerable ego strength and integrity become exposed to external threat, as did Kim, and that people with less ego strength revert to certain types of somatization. It would be incongruent and odd, not to say impossible, to think of Kim as getting asthma or of our asthmatic young man as a freedom fighter. However, even when this is kept in mind, it still seems striking how much easier it is to deal with external than with internal threat.

Comparing this patient's reaction to internal threat with the reaction to external threat discussed earlier suggests some similarities, although the differences are predominant. Both kinds of threat resulted in some form of depersonalization, or split of ego functions into the observer and the observed. Kim looked at himself as an observer and was aware of it; the asthmatic patient projected himself into different pursuer-victim situations, but he was not aware of this. Therefore, although the basic depersonalization process has a common denominator for the two types of threat situations, there are stark differences in the way it is handled. The ill patient renders ego-alien one or both parts of self, whereas the person under external threat is apparently able to bind both parts of self within the ego-syntonic sphere.

Reversal of affect and of the apperceived power field is characteristic of both types of threat. Kim and the asthmatic patient both reversed hate and love, although in opposite directions, and both had fantasies in which they were controllers rather than being victims of the threat. With respect to masochism, the asthmatic patient had traces of this reaction, but nothing comparable to Kim's intrapunitive bliss. More striking are the differences between the reactions to external and internal threat. Intensification of perception, and changes in higher-level ego functions reorganizing the field, are absent from the reactions of the somatic patient. Also, denial is much less prevalent and less effective in the asthmatic patient.

Denial, however, seems to intensify proportionally with the perceived seriousness of the illness, so that cancer patients make much more use of this defense than did, for example, the asthmatic patient just described. We shall now turn to a single example of patients suffering from terminal cancer and see how these people react to pending destruction.

The reaction to cancer, in the cases I have studied, resembles the reaction to external threat more closely than do the responses of the so-called psychosomatic patients, although their illnesses were certainly serious enough. The cancer patients, like Kim and other victims of external threat, deny and play down the seriousness of the situation and continue to operate with unimpaired reality orientation. However, they pay for this with a striking chronic impoverishment of existence that far supersedes the constriction and limitations observed in people under external threat. Kim, and others with him, continued to be a responsive, psychologically differentiated, and colorful personality, even if his perceptual field had "shrunk." However, the psychological picture presented by most advanced cancer patients is one of a barren, cold, disinterested, and impoverished realism. The dreams and visions that occur under external stress are absent here. Whereas, in the asthmatic, we see dramatization, involvement of fantasy, and projection to an external source of threat against life, the cancer patient presents a rather dull picture, basically void of both internal and external representations of the threat, and with a life pattern reduced to the maintenance of bare essentials.

Although cancer patients resemble people under external threat by exhibiting "shrinking of the field" and wiping away of unessentials, they are very different from those threatened externally in that they lack the concomitant increase in intensity of inner life and the use of fantasy material so characteristic of Kim and of others under external threat. Constriction of their field of apperception and interaction does not find a substitution in dream and philosophizing, as it does for the person under external stress. Thus cancer patients in many respects resemble patients with long-standing psychosis, who also are characterized by barrenness and parsimony of existence. In one respect, however, they are radically different: the cancer patients are experts in reality testing and never give an inch.

An example of the typical hopelessness, barrenness, and lack of both psychic differentiation and fantasy in cancer patients is presented by a young 32-year-old married woman with three children. She had advanced carcinoma of the colon. Her mother and older sister had both died of cancer, and the patient's life had been a long succession of losses and disappointments, leaving her despondent and empty-handed in spite of her efforts to carry through like a good mother and companion. She was unsuccessful in both respects and felt unloved, rejected, and lost. Her drawing of "herself" (Fig. 8)

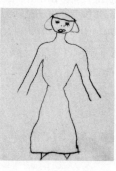

FIGURE 8. *Drawing by a patient with advanced carcinoma.*

shows a barren figure of tragic emptiness. The openness of the figure, which makes it appear as if the interior of the body had been "sucked out" of the person is characteristic for many of these cancer patients who feel depleted of internal strength and identity. Her picture of two persons (Fig. 9) appears even more depleted. The two figures, mother and daughter, are replicas, but have no faces. From other material it appeared that the patient repeated her relationship

FIGURE 9.   *Drawing by a patient with advanced carcinoma.*

with her own mother in her relationship with her daughter, so that this drawing may be understood as a double exposure of self. In the next drawing (Fig. 10) the patient gives us another expression of her self-image, this time in the form of a tragicomical elephant which she describes as a sad, nice, and tame animal, whose life consists of eating peanuts, doing

FIGURE 10.   *Drawing by a patient with advanced carcinoma.*

nothing, and sleeping, and who likes it this way. The bland and essential character of her life is eminently expressed in these drawings and in her description of this animal.

We see in this cancer patient the characteristic emptiness and lack of proaction to the threat of annihilation, and a marked willingness to "accept fate." However, although she, like Kim, accepts fate, she does not perceive fate as ultimately benign — she does not invest energy in the creation of a perspective allowing her to turn tragedy to bliss. Instead, her world becomes increasingly bleak and disappears into nothingness. The remaining few feeble emotions were directed toward an external object, her husband, whom she blamed for having provoked her illness by having actually given her a "kick in the back." Like the other somatic patients, she did not match Kim's love for his torturers and enemies. The only emotion left was a dissipating hatred towards a depleting and harsh environment.

Thus, in contrast to reactions to both external and psychosomatic threat, we see in most cancer patients a depleted barrenness and a lack of significant effort to meet the threat. We have seen that persons under external threat tend to internalize the problem and to deal with it in terms of an intrapersonal coming-to-terms with fate and with ethics. On the other hand, patients with a psychosomatic internal source of threat tend to externalize the threat and to deal with it in terms of felt loss of external supplies and in terms of paranoid fantasies of persecution and mistreatment. The cancer patients do neither. They flatly deny the seriousness of the situation, but do not substitute internal dialogue and excitement for the increasing threat. Unlike the asthmatic patients, who fight the windmills like a Don Quixote, they simply retreat further and further into their constriction until finally they exist only in terms of the most narrow day-to-day routine. Although, as mentioned earlier, the interactions between an illness and reactions to the illness are considerable and complicate the interpretation of these reactions, it seems apparent nevertheless that patients with advanced cancer show a marked lack of response and often an extreme denial of the threat to their lives.

We shall now summarize the conclusions. Denial of threat was clearly observable in both external and internal threat situations. It was most marked in individuals under external threat and in cancer patients. Denial of annihilation in these cases seemed to be a necessary prerequisite for continued coping with the immediate reality problems. This turning away from thoughts of extinction was in many cases combined with an apparently inappropriate perseveration of predanger routines, which in many cases attained significant defensive functions by, in turn, facilitating the maintenance of denial. This perseveration was most apparent in the cases of external threat and cancer.

A striking phenomenon is the tendency of sick patients to externalize the threat from within and, similarly, for people under external stress to internalize the problem with which they must deal. For the person threatened with death and destruction from without, the fight soon changes to one against his own weakness and urge to give in, and in this fight he can mobilize his usual ethical and moral defenses. For the sick patient, in contrast, the external world soon appears responsible for his sufferings, and the defensive efforts − if any − are mobilized against this external "straw man."

Masochism may be most pronounced as a solution in situations of externally derived pain. This is not incompatible with theory, since the two-person interaction between torturer and victim resembles the original parent-child situation quite closely. The question has been raised here whether, in situations in which unavoidable pain is forced upon the individual by the environment, masochism can be understood as an adaptive ego process, or whether this solution requires a personal predilection in the individual. Masochism was absent in the cancer patients studied, but a trend was observable in the psychosomatic patients.

Depersonalization and "splitting of the ego" were defenses

prevalent under the most severe strain in both externally and internally derived threat. It was most marked after severe strain. It went hand in hand with a groping for the conceptualization of a benign "fate" within the parameters of which the sufferings would become meaningful and profitable.

Finally, in acute danger situations, it was observed that perceptual ego functions were alerted and geared to the double functions of preparing for crucial action and defending against anxiety by setting the events in a "distant perspective." The concepts of "shrinking of the field" and "reversed-zoom" effect were introduced to describe the ensuing apperceptual phenomena. Whereas shrinking of the field was a temporary and functional process under external threat, in cancer it appeared to develop into a chronic apperceptual phenomenon, and it resulted in a barren and restricted outlook on life. The concept of shrinking of the field may thus be applied on different levels: under acute stress it refers to changes in apperception of the immediate reality situation; under chronic stress it refers to a gradual impoverishment of the perceived world, not only on the perceptual level, but also on the conceptual level.

References

BAKST, H. J., BERG, R. L., FOSTER, F. D., and RAKER, J. W. "The Worcester County Tornado — A Medical Study of the Disaster," Washington, D. C.: National Academy of Sciences — National Research Council, 1955.

BETTELHEIM, B. Individual and mass behavior in extreme situations. *J. Abnorm. Soc. Psychol.*, 1943, *38*, 417–452.

BLUM, R. H. and KLASS, B. "A Study of Public Response to Disaster Warnings." Menlo Park, Calif.: Stanford Research Institute, 1956.

CANTRIL, H. *The Invasion from Mars: A Study in the Psychology of Panic.* Princeton, N.J.: Princeton University Press, 1940.

DIDEROT, D. *Jacques le fataliste et son maître.* Paris: Bruisson, 1797.

FORM, W. H., and NOSOW, S. *Community in Disaster.* New York: Harper, 1958.

FRASER, R., LESLIE, I., and PHELPS, D. Psychiatric effects of severe personal experiences during bombing. *Proc. Roy. Soc. Med.*, 1943, *36*, 119–123.

FREUD, S. *The Problem of Anxiety.* New York: W. W. Norton, 1936.

Claus Bahne Bahnson

FREUD, S. *Beyond the Pleasure Principle.* London: International Psychoanalytic Press, 1922.

FUNKENSTEIN, D. H., KING, S. H., and DROLETTE, MARGARET E. *Mastery of Stress.* Cambridge, Mass.: Harvard University Press, 1957.

GLOVER, E. *The Psychology of Fear and Courage.* New York: Penguin, 1940.

GRINKER, R. R. and SPIEGEL, J. P. *Men under Stress.* New York: Blakiston, 1945.

JANIS, I. L. *Air War and Emotional Stress: Psychological Studies of Bombing and Civilian Defense.* New York: McGraw-Hill, 1951.

KENDRICK, T. D. *The Lisbon Earthquake.* Philadelphia: Lippincott, 1957.

KNAPP, P. H., and BAHNSON, C. B. The emotional field. *Psychosom. Med.,* 1963, *25,* 460–483.

LEWIN, K. *Principles of Topological Psychology.* New York: McGraw-Hill, 1936.

MALTHE-BRUUN, V. (Ed.). *Kim.* Copenhagen: Stjernebogerne, 1961.

MARCH, H. (Ed.). *Verfolgung und Angst, Dokumente.* Stuttgart: Klett, 1960.

MARKS, E. S., FRITZ, C. E., et al. "Human Reactions in Disaster Situations." Report No. 52, National Opinion Research Center, June 1954. Reproduced by the Armed Services Technical Information Agency.

MEERLOO, J. A. M. People's reaction to danger. In I. Galston (Ed.), *Panic and Morale.* New York: International Universities Press, 1958.

SHAND, A. F. *Foundations of Character.* London: Macmillan, 1914.

WOLFENSTEIN, MARTHA. *Disaster.* Glencoe, Ill.: Free Press, 1957.

PART SEVEN

THE THREAT OF DISEASE AND DEATH

JOHN P. SPIEGEL

CULTURAL VARIATIONS IN ATTITUDES TOWARD DEATH AND DISEASE*

THE PURPOSE of this paper is to describe some aspects of the way in which variations in the attitudes people form toward illness and death are systematically correlated with differences in cultural background. Although our topic is of general interest to any theory of behavior, its significance extends beyond the realm of theory. It is of the greatest importance to anyone responsible for the care of the sick and the dying that he understand the different ways in which people may respond to these events. It is an unfortunate correlate of our melting-pot culture with its overriding egalitarian ethos that, in order to think of people as being equal, we usually have to think of them as being the same. If we are forced to consider differences between people's behavior, we are apt to attribute the difference either to situational causes or to variations in the psychological mechanisms of the individual. To attribute such differences to variations in the cultural background of the group to which the person belongs makes us feel as if we were abandoning our democratic principles. For this reason we tend to overlook or even deny the differences due to social background, whether associated with class or with regional or ethnic affiliation.

* The investigation has been supported by a grant from the National Institute of Mental Health. It is sponsored by the Laboratory of Social Relations, Harvard University, and the Children's Medical Center, Boston.

My discussion of this topic will be based upon a study which I have been carrying on with Dr. Florence R. Kluckhohn and a number of colleagues of the interpersonal relations within families undergoing acculturation from an old world set of values to those of the urban United States. One half of our sample of families have had a mentally ill member, whereas the other half have been free of overt psychiatric disturbance. During the course of our study, many family members have had intercurrent physical illnesses and some have died, so that we have encountered a fair range of reactions to these events. Up to the present time, we have studied Italian-American, Irish-American, Greek-American and "old" American families — all at the working-class level. Because of space limitations, I will here present data only on the contrast between the Italian-American working-class culture and that of the urban, middle-class American. This will not give us an opportunity to examine the extent of the variations in a country with so many different subcultures, but I believe that it is more important to emphasize the principles involved than the differences themselves.

Two principles can be employed for this purpose and I now set them forth in a somewhat abstract fashion in order to show how they can be used for the analysis and comparison of concrete behavior. The first principle involves the use of the concept of social role for the description of behavior. A social role can be defined as a goal-directed configuration of acts, patterned in accordance with cultural value orientations for the position a person holds in a social group or situation. This definition takes account of the fact that roles are developed for some purpose or end of the social system, on the one hand, and of the individual, on the other. From the point of view of the social system, the role of the parent is to bring up children; of an educator, to educate; and of a sick person, to get well. From the standpoint of the individual, these goals may be pursued for a variety of reasons, not all of which are necessarily consonant with the aims of the social system. Whatever the personal motives may be, it is apparent that the pattern of acts assembled within the role structure varies greatly from one culture to another. English, Jewish, Arab, and Indian parents each behave differently toward their children and expect different behaviors from them.

By the same token, the behavior of doctors and patients and the expectations they hold toward each other varies for each culture. But before we go on to examine the specifically cultural basis for variation, we must discuss the place of the roles concerned with health and sickness in a general classification of roles. This is necessary because in any piece of concrete behavior a number of different roles may be simultaneously invoked, each having a different set of consequences. For example, the illness of a forty-year-old male may involve him in the role of patient toward his doctor, invalid toward his wife, wage earner toward his dependents, and absent employee toward his employer. Therefore, it is important to have available a set of categories generally descriptive of the kinds of expectations involved in various roles.

Role Categories

Social roles can be divided into three major categories: formal, informal, and fictive. Formal roles include the major activities which every society needs to regulate in order to survive. There are three subcategories of formal roles: biological, semibiological, and institutional. Biological roles, such as age and sex roles, concern straight biological functions and are universally ascribed to every member of the society; that is, not for one moment, except possibly in jest, can anyone safely step out of the pattern of behavior expected for his age and sex. Semibiological roles include domestic or family roles, ethnic, regional, and national roles — all ascribed on the basis of birth. The expectations for behavior are not as implacable as in the case of biological roles. For example, one can change, but only with considerable difficulty, the behavior associated with one's caste or class, ethnic or family background. Institutional roles, on the other hand, are more episodic. They include religious, occupational, educational, and recreational roles. One need not occupy any of them all of the time and one is free to change them under certain stipulated conditions. Still, everyone must occupy some of the institutional roles — such as the educational role — at some time in his life, and at such times the required behavior is just as strictly patterned and controlled by rewards for proper behavior and punishments for improper behavior as in the rest of the formal roles. Since the roles of doctor and patient are included in the formal category because they are occupational roles, we will be concerned with their formal characteristics in the course of this paper.

Informal roles are much more occasional and at the choice of the individual than are formal roles. They are also much less strictly patterned and thus are not so heavily involved in overt rewards and punishments for sanctioned behavior. There are two subcategories of informal roles. The first subcategory consists of the transitional roles. These are concerned with the matter of getting out of one situation and into another. It is in this subcategory that we place the roles concerned with the general aspects of health, illness, and death. Other roles in the transitional subcategory are those of visitors, guests, and travelers. The other subcategory of informal roles are the character roles. These include heroes and villains, liars and cheats, exhibitionists and voyeurs, sadists and masochists. Such behaviors are usually thought of as traits of character, but a moment's reflection reveals that the given behavior cannot take place without the reciprocal behavior of a role partner. Every hero must have his admirers, every exhibitionist must locate his voyeur, just as every masochist has to find his sadist in order to enjoy his role in life. But such roles are not required of anyone by the social system. They may be adopted by one person or assigned to another — as when we assign the role of fool to someone we do not like. Such adoptions and assignments are parts of the informal workings of social groups.

The third category, fictive roles, designates roles that are not pragmatically related to the ongoing work of any social system or group but serve the interests of imagination or play. For the most part, they are occupied quite deliberately on the basis of pretense or imagination, as when a girl plays the role of mother to her doll, or a boy plays cops and robbers. All fictive roles make room for fantasy behavior in everyday life and thus serve the purpose — for adults as well as for children — of relief from the stress and strain of reality. Every society sanctions such roles, provided they are accompanied by a communication that says: this is not serious; this is in jest or play. When fictive or fantasy roles are taken without this accompanying signal, that is, in earnest, then we say that the behavior of the person who shows it — and of a group that accepts it — is pathological. These distinctions are of importance in considering the roles of the dead in various cultures. Attitudes toward severe illness and the possibility of death are obviously correlated with the presence or absence of belief in survival after death. In our society, belief in an "afterlife" is disappearing so that the role of the dead — or what we shall call the "death role" — is undergoing a change from the category of informal roles to the fictive category.

Before going on to discuss the effect of cultural patterning on these role categories, I would like to review the different roles that must be considered in the area of health and illness. There are five of these roles that are important to keep in mind from the standpoint of their similarities and differences. They are the roles of the sick, the injured, the dying, the dead, and the patient. The distinctions are more than academic. Different cultures treat each one in different ways, and we shall touch upon some of the differences in a moment. Right now, however, I would like to add one more role to this list, the health role, which is not usually considered in discussions of this sort. Without entering into a technical discussion about how one decides that a role exists in one or another society, I would like simply to assert that in our society, at any rate, medical research, technological advances, and the public education based upon them have cre-

John P. Spiegel

ated a social role deserving this name. It is not only the role that one is expected to assume when one is pronounced cured of an illness, but it is also the role that one is expected to work at in order to stay healthy. To "keep fit" is a national preoccupation. It has become, like many of our informal roles, a matter of achievement and competence so that to become ill now has overtones of personal failure. Since this is merely an extension of the accent on achievement which has always been a central theme in our culture, it will serve as a good introduction to the systematic examination of cultural attitudes, which I would now like to discuss.

Value-Orientation Categories

Cultural attitudes are outgrowths of value orientations which vary systematically from one culture to another, as well as within cultures. The classification system which I will present is based upon the theory of variation in cultural value orientations which was developed by my colleague, Dr. Florence R. Kluckhohn (Kluckhohn and Strodtbeck, 1961). The theory states that value orientations are highly generalized solutions of common human problems. It further proposes that these solutions have (1) an evaluative component, which means that they serve as principles for making selections between alternative courses of action, (2) an existential component, which means that they help to define the nature of reality for those values that hold the given solution, and (3) an affective component, which means that people not only prefer and believe in their own values, but are also ready to bleed and die for them. For this reason, values, once formed, are changed only with the greatest difficulty.

There are five common human problems whose solutions form the classification scheme of the value orientations. There are three possible solutions for each of these problems, and the theory states that each of the three possible solutions exists in every culture — though with a different ranking in the order of preferences. Because of the shortness of time, I will present only the first, or dominantly preferred, solution for each of these categories. Occasionally, however, I will mention the influence of a second- or third-order choice since illness, by its intrinsic nature, frequently requires a shift away from the dominant values. I will illustrate the five value-orientation categories by a comparison of American middle-class patterns with those of the Italian-American working class. The value orientations to be described for the Italian-Americans are those characteristic of the native peasant cultures in southern Italy.

The first common human problem is concerned with the *time* dimension. This breaks down into the natural division of Past, Present, and Future. The American middle-class person much prefers the future for all sorts of choices and decisions. Prospective parents plan for their children's future before they are yet born, save for their old age, and are always watching the clock or inspecting their schedules and calendars to see what they should be doing next. They expect change and prefer anything new to anything old. The past is quite devalued, and accordingly Americans hate to be considered old-fashioned or out of date. There is a preference for novelty and an expectation of constant change in the circumstances of life and an awareness of the need to adjust to change when it comes. The Italian-Americans, on the other hand, prefer the present to the past or the future. They live in an extended present in which the future is scarcely differentiated from the past. They believe that things have always been the same and always will be. Accordingly, if change should come, it is usually for the worse. Time is demarcated for them not by the accusing clock or calendar, but by leisurely cycles of seasons, religious festivals, national holidays, anniversaries, and ceremonial occasions of all kinds.

The second value-orientation category is concerned with relationships within groups and is therefore called the *relational* category. The three possible solutions for this category are the Lineal, the Collateral, and the Individualistic. In the Lineal solution, relationships are ordered on a stratified, hierarchical, authoritarian basis, with the leader assuming great importance, and a chain of command down to the lowest echelons. The Collateral solution involves the group in a horizontal, teamlike, all-in-the-same-boat relation, and decisions are made, not by the authority at the top, but by group consensus. In the Individualistic solution, each person keeps his own rights to make a personal decision, and group decisions are made by a vote of the majority.

Americans much prefer the Individualistic solution. Parents train their children from an early age to make their own decisions, to control themselves, and to stand on their own two feet. Families live in small groups of parents and children and think nothing of pulling up roots and moving off to another part of the country at a moment's notice. For certain purposes, however, Americans can shift over to a Collateral solution. For example, in competitive sports, during a national or local crisis or disaster, or in severe illness, the Collateral solution is likely to be pushed to the fore and Individualism suppressed, for the time being. Such a shift is at best temporary, and the American can scarcely wait to get back to the assertion of his individual aims. Lineality is a devalued though often necessary solution. Hierarchical structures are necessary to any large organization such as a business or a hospital, but Americans are usually somewhat apologetic or resentful about their existence.

The Italian-Americans, in contrast, prefer the Collateral solution. They prefer to live in big families, in close proximity to relatives, and if anyone has to go away it is a tragedy for all concerned. Children are trained to be dependent upon their elders and upon each other. If anyone makes an independent decision, he is looked on as disloyal or uncaring. No one is expected to be able to get along by himself in strange surroundings — at least not without intense anxiety.

The third category is concerned with the preferred mode of *activity*. The solutions here are Doing, Being, and Being-in-Becoming. The Doing solution is preferred by Americans, who are always interested in each other's achievements. Parents train their children for success — in school, in sports, in social life, and in physical fitness — and they anxiously review their own records as parents, comparing themselves in this way, as in every other, with their friends and enemies. Italian-Americans prefer the Being solution. Success and achievements are not so important as expressing one's self, one's moods, feelings, and desires. Children are impatiently scolded or punished one minute and effusively given affection the next. What is always expected is spontaneity of feeling. To the Italian, accordingly, the self-control for the sake of achievement practiced by Americans looks hypocritical or exploitive. Thus, where illness is concerned, the American believes he should achieve health by cooperation as an equal partner in technical or medical procedures and that he should complain about his symptoms only for the sake of informing his physician about the nature of the disturbance. The Italian-American complains because it hurts or because he is miserable — that is, to express himself and to alert his collateral group that something should be done by someone to relieve the situation.

The fourth category involves the relationship between men and nature or supernature. The solutions are (1) Subjugated to Nature, (2) In Harmony with Nature, and (3) Mastery over Nature. The last is preferred by the American middle class. Man is expected to triumph in any contest with nature, in accordance with an optimistic confidence in the power of science and technology. Disease and outer space are rapidly yielding to research, weather control is just around the corner, and we may yet learn how to avoid war and other severe catastrophes. For any problem encountered by the individual, there is always an expert to be found in the Yellow Pages and, although we are always highly critical of our technical experts for any little failure they may exhibit, this only shows how much we expect of them. In contrast, the Italian-Americans prefer the Subjugated-to-Nature solution. This is in accordance with their religious belief, and it also fits in with the residue of primitive or pagan magical superstitions which their culture has retained. Man is considered weak and helpless, and his only hope lies in recognizing this situation. He is dependent upon the deity and the saints and is also the prey of malevolent powers such as the evil eye and magical curses, spells, and incantations. The most common reaction we heard when our Italian families were faced with a really severe problem was the fatalistic expression: "What can I do?" This means that it is better to recognize one's weakness than to have false pride or unrealistic hopes.

The last value category is concerned with the *basic nature of man* in terms of good and evil. The solutions in this category are (1) that man is born Evil but Perfectible, (2) that man is either Neutral or a Mixture of Good and Evil, and (3) that man is born Good but Corruptible. The Italian-Americans believe that man is innately a Mixture of Good and Evil. In a family of many children, one or two may turn out to be mainly good — and these will be expected to become nuns or priests — and one or two will turn out to be mainly evil, and these will be black sheep. The remainder will be real mixtures of both. Such children are expected to be little devils one minute and little angels the next, thus calling forth the quick spontaneous response of anger or love in the parent. Americans, on the contrary, believe that children are born neither good nor evil but rather are innately neutral. How they turn out depends on the nature of the child's relation with the parent. If the child misbehaves, the parents reason with him; and if the misbehavior becomes serious, the child is regarded as maladjusted, and the parents hold themselves responsible for the emotional problems of the child. Italian parents, on the other hand, regard such behavior as revealing the innately evil nature of the child, for which they could not possibly be held responsible.

This brief sketch of the two value-orientation profiles reveals the extent of the cultural gap that confronts Italian families when they arrive in this country and of the amount of change required of them as they move toward American middle-class values in the process of acculturation. However, it is necessary to remind ourselves to avoid cultural stereo-typing. Some Italians arrive in this country with values al-ready very similar to those of the American middle class, and some Americans have values similar to the Italians. In Italy itself there is much regional as well as rural-urban variation. Perhaps more important is the fact that many get stuck in the process of shifting from one to another set of values. For this reason, their behavior is apt to be inconsistent or conflicting as they orient now to one, now to another set of values. It would be interesting to discuss these cases of in-consistent value orientations as they affect behavior toward illness and death, but it would take too much space to enter into such complexities. I will therefore confine the discussion to the gross contrast between the effect of American middle-class values and Italian-American values on behavior during illness.

Values and Roles

Let us look first at the effect of the dominant American value orientations on the six roles which we have previously isolated for discussion. The health role, as we expected, fits neatly into these values. To keep fit and healthy, everyone is expected to stay abreast of the latest or newest medical dis-coveries, and our journalists and science writers, from *Time* magazine to the health columns of the daily press, are doing their best to inform us of what we need to know. Advertise-ments, too, advise us on how to pep up our tired blood, stim-ulate our flagging spirits, and calm down our excitements with various drugs, how to prevent our accidents with safety belts, avoid our sunburns with ointments, our infectious diseases with vaccines, and our chronic diseases through frequent check-ups and no smoking. If one took it all seriously, this future-oriented mastery of nature could easily become a full-time occupation. Then, if one has been so careless in one's planning as to undergo the disgrace of becoming ill, the dom-inant values clamp down all the harder on the sick role. Who-

293

ever becomes ill bears the individual responsibility for doing something effective about it as soon as possible, instead of waiting until matters get out of hand. He is certainly not expected to enjoy his illness, nor is anyone else to take pleasure in it. The illness is to be treated in an impersonal, technical fashion, complaints are to be kept to a minimum, and the doctor is to be notified over the phone so that he can decide whether his presence is called for. The doctor will put off making a personal appearance in the home for as long as possible since it is his technical knowledge, not his personality, that is called into play once the ill person becomes a patient. He is not particularly interested in giving comfort but rather in achieving a cure, or, failing that, the best possible result short of death.

So far, we have noticed only harmony between the American values and the patterning of the health, sick, and patient roles. The harmony changes to conflict, however, if the patient has to be hospitalized. Hospitals are large bureaucratic structures, which, for the most part, are based upon a Lineal organization of relationships. The doctors give orders, the nurses carry them out — more or less. House officers boss interns, and interns boss medical technicians. The patient takes orders from everyone, gives them to no one. He is occasionally allowed to put in a request for something, but he is likely to have his request ignored. The individualism that is honored in other roles is out of place in the hospital hierarchy. Nevertheless, even in the hospital, with respect to his actual illness — as opposed to his comfort — he is expected to pursue his individualism by making every effort on his own and in cooperation with staff to get well. Thus, while he is in the hospital, the sick role and the patient role are oriented to incompatible values and everyone concerned feels the strain of this conflict.

Among the Italian-Americans, the Present-time, Being, Collateral, Subjugated-to-Nature and Mixed-Good-and-Evil values create a different role pattern. Illness is a calamity which is to be endured or suffered or enjoyed, as the case may be. The health role does not exist, even though there is much folk-lore about the avoidance of certain foods and certain practices which may bring on illness. However, the assumption is that only fools, children, or ignorant people would be so imprudent as to need instruction about these obvious matters. For the rest, illness is something that just happens to people, it always has and always will, as a part of man's fate. On the other hand, it may happen more often and in a more severe form to some people, either because they are unlucky or as a punishment for their evil ways. These attitudes make the Italian look passive and somewhat irresponsible when viewed through American values.

The Being, Present-time, Collateral values of the Italian-Americans also are associated with an entirely different way of relating to the sick person. It is expected that he will need a great deal of comforting and company at all times of the day and night. If the sick person is in pain he will moan and groan, and if he is depressed he will cry. Therefore he must always be attended to. Since Italians like in any event to go visiting, an illness in the family is a signal for a continuous meeting of friends and relatives. Whereas the American believes that a sick person should have ample peace and privacy in order to concentrate on the job of getting well, the ill Italian-American is the center of constant social activity which may not be good for the patient but is enjoyed by everyone else.

When the sick Italian-American has to take the patient's role, nothing much is changed. The doctor's job is to give comfort, relieve pain and suffering, and, if everyone is lucky, help nature or supernature effect a cure. The doctor is merely one agent in a long list of agents who are appealed to for help. Prayers are directed to patron saints and other supernatural figures while magical charms and apotropaic ceremonies are invoked to drive away bad luck or to neutralize the effect of evildoers. If the patient then has to be hospitalized, his Collateral values produce a strain which is different from that experienced by the American. When the American says

295

he wants to go to a "good" hospital, he means one noted for the scientific and technical quality of patient care. He expects to find the conflict between Individualism and Lineality, already noted, and is prepared to endure it. When the Italian says he wants to go to a "good" hospital, he means "good to Italians." He has in mind a hospital that other Italian-Americans have used, so that the staff has become accustomed to their ways and has accepted them as a group. Acceptance means, among other things, tolerance for the practice of keeping up a constant stream of visitors to the patient. Strict visiting hours and other rules and regulations so important to the hospital bureaucracy are offensive to the Italian-Americans as a group. The hospital, in other words, represents to them an alien and hostile collateral group, unless proved otherwise. For this reason, admission to a strange or unknown hospital is likely to give rise to more than the usual amount of anxiety.

There is much more that could be said about the sick role and the patient's role in these two cultures but it is time to move on to a consideration of the roles of the injured, the dying, and the dead. Interestingly enough, the role of the injured tends to invoke similar values in both cultures. For the American, the person who is acutely injured tends to produce a shift from Individualistic to Collateral values, and from the orientation of Doing to Being. The person injured in an accident, for example, becomes the center of a group of curious, concerned people who want to help in any way they can. Since the situation usually makes it impossible for the injured person to help himself, passivity becomes permissible, comfort can be given, and technical aid is not judged by such severe standards as in the ordinary sick role. People who have never met before speak to each other like old acquaintances, drawn together by the emergency. To some extent this shift in values from the dominant configuration to the Present-time, Being, Collateral pattern accompanies any emergency or crisis in American life, and it is correlated with the peculiar and uncharacteristic expressive behavior of crowds seen during disasters. For the Italian, of course, these value patterns are representative of their dominant values, so that no shift is required. Once the American passes out of the injured role into the patient's role, however, and the crisis has turned, the moratorium on the dominant values is terminated and he is once again expected to be as independent as possible and to try to achieve a recovery.

When we come to the dying and the death roles, the differences again outweigh the similarities. In American culture the dying role is severely attenuated. The prospect of death does not fit well with the dominant values. Since there is little or no real belief in an afterlife, death represents the end of the line, the end of the story. In a culture that puts so much stress on the future, the prospect of not having any future at all becomes too dismal to face. That the dying role should turn out to be a transition to nothing, to extinction, robs it of some of its transitional properties. To make matters worse, the process of dying cannot even be treated as a tragedy since our Doing and Mastery-over-Nature values make it seem more like a technical failure. Tragedy, in our society, is something that should have been avoided rather than something to be appreciated. The implication is that someone slipped up or that research simply has not yet got around to solving this kind of thing. Thus dying is covered over with optimistic or reassuring statements and the dying person is scarcely given the opportunity to make the most of his position.

Just as the dying role has become vestigial in American culture, the death role, as we stated previously, is undergoing a shift from a formal role to a fictive role. Our dominant values leave no room for an empirical account of life — or, let us say, behavior — after death. Religion to the contrary, the dead exist only in our memories. This shift in the role of the dead has required an equivalent change in the role of the mourner. In the past, the mourner had to deal not only with his emotional reactions to his personal loss, but also with rites and ceremonies, prayers and graveside rituals which were somehow connected with the fate of the dead in the afterlife. The process being continuous and requiring activity, the mourner was in a better position to control his fantasies and to express his emotional reactions in socially approved efforts. With the conversion of the dead role to a fictive status, the ceremonial part of the mourner's role has only a token value, and the bereaved person is left alone with his fantasies and memories, which is a much more difficult process to work through.

For the Italian-American and his traditional values, the death role retains its formal status. Belief in the persistence of the soul means that the dying are actually in a valid transitional state which those close to him can help him with. The Subjugated-to-Nature orientation preserves the dying process as a tragic event which can be faced and participated in. No one has failed and no one has necessarily to be blamed. There is something enjoyable about it. The permanent black dress of the elderly Italian woman — which is assumed whether or not she is actually in mourning — is an honorable uniform. After all, there is always someone whom one *could* be mourning for. Thus anticipatory mourning starts before death occurs and the dying role is carried out in high style, sometimes to everyone's dismay when death fails to occur.

Just as there are cultural strains in the dying role, the death role, and the mourner's role in American culture, so do severe strains attach to these roles in Italian-American culture. For example, in the Italian-American culture, the ritual obligation placed upon the mourner to show grief in dramatic fashion can be a considerable strain when, in actual fact, the bereaved feels a sense of relief rather than grief at the occurrence of death. Similarly, the drama of the dying process can be a strain to all concerned when the process is enormously drawn out in time.

One view to take of such strains is that no set of cultural values can be perfectly integrated with the multifarious contingencies of life and death, of social necessity and of personality variability. But another view can be taken. We could, for example, use our knowledge of the nature of the strains in the American values to formulate new role patterns which would be more in accord with the values and with the biological and psychological facts. We could do this as social scientists and put forth our recommendations, based on research, with the same confidence that is involved in therapeutic recommendations based upon biological research. Such considerations lie in the area of social engineering and to discuss them in detail would take us beyond the scope of this paper. (Not, however, beyond the scope of this volume, even though it may be premature to take such prospects seriously at the present time.) We should put it on our agenda for a future discussion. For the merit of considering variations in cultural attitudes, as with scientific endeavor in general, lies in the increased possibility of dealing effectively with the timeless and universal problems of our world.

References

The following are some of the pertinent publications from the study:

BELL, N. W., and VOGEL, E. F. (Eds.). *A Modern Introduction to the Family*. Glencoe, Ill.: Free Press, 1960.

BELL, N. W., TREISCHMAN, A. and VOGEL, E. F. A sociocultural analysis of the resistances of working class fathers treated in a child psychiatry clinic. *Amer. J. Orthopsychiat.* 1961, *31*, 388–405.

BELL, N. W. Extended family relationships of disturbed and well families. *Family Process*, 1962, *1*, 175–193.

KLUCKHOHN, FLORENCE R. Family diagnosis: Variations in the basic values of family systems. *Social Casework*, 1958, *39*, 1–11.

KLUCKHOHN, FLORENCE R., and STRODTBECK, F. L. *Variations in Value Orientations*. Evanston, Ill.; Row, Peterson, 1961.

SPIEGEL, J. P. Interpersonal influences within the family. In B. Schaffner (Ed.), *Group Processes*. New York: Josiah Macy, Jr., Foundation, 1956.

SPIEGEL, J. P. The resolution of role conflict within the family. *Psychiatry*, 1957, *20* (1), 1–16.

SPIEGEL, J. P. Some cultural aspects of transference and countertransference. In J. H. Masserman (Ed.), *Individual and Family Dynamics*. New York: Basic Books, 1959.

SPIEGEL, J. P. and BELL, N. W. The family of the psychiatric patient. In S. Arieti (Ed.), *The Handbook of American Psychiatry*. New York: Basic Books, 1959.

VOGEL, E. F., and BELL, N. W. The emotionally disturbed child as a family scapegoat. *Psychoanal. Psychoanalyt. Rev.*, 1960, *41*, 21–42.

THOMAS P. HACKETT AND AVERY D. WEISMAN

REACTIONS TO THE
IMMINENCE OF DEATH

IN A LARGE general hospital, where numerous deaths occur in the course of a day, it is almost impossible to find a dying patient who is allowed to respond to the imminence of death in his own way. By the time he reaches his death-bed, the attitudes and fixed opinions of physicians and relatives have been thrust upon him. With the "best interest" of the patient at heart they encourage and offer hope even before the patient expresses a desire for such reassurance. The healthy human being assumes that the threat of death eclipses all other fears and does not realize that the dying patient may not share this point of view. Although the prospect of death is awesome and fearful to those about to die, it does not necessarily exclude other concerns.

This presentation deals with two groups of people: (1) terminal cancer patients who are facing certain death, and (2) patients with severe myocardial disease who have a chance of survival, but who are threatened with the possibility of imminent death. It will be shown that both groups react to the death threat by denying it in various ways, some effective and some not. The effectiveness of this denial (Freud, 1937; Lewin, 1950; Engel, 1962), we feel, depends to a large extent upon the way in which it is handled by those who care for the patient. We define denial as the repudiation of part or all of the available meaning of an event for the purpose of minimizing fear and anxiety.

Attitudes of Others

The importance of the attitudes of others and their influence on the way in which a patient reacts to the threat of his death became apparent to us a few years ago when we began to investigate the emotional responses of twenty-eight patients in the terminal stages of cancer (Weisman and Hackett, 1962; Hackett and Weisman, 1962). Each was seen approximately four times a week until he died. Relatives were interviewed when possible, and close communication existed between the psychiatrist and the surgeon or internist in charge of the case. All these patients had been told they had cancer, but none had been informed that he would die within a short time.

From our interviews with patients, families, nurses, and physicians we found two seemingly incongruous patterns. Relatives, nurses, and doctors substantiated what most of us believe to be true of the dying patient — that he is an expert at denying that he is dying. On the other hand, when the tape recordings of these interviews were examined in detail, we found quite obvious references to impending death. Threatening dreams, nightmares, slips of the tongue, references to loneliness and grief, and the tendency to recount stories of fatal illnesses they had witnessed in friends or relatives documented our suspicion that these patients were deeply concerned about the true nature of their disease. Hesitant and indirect questions about what could be expected of the future offered the investigators the opportunity to share the fears of their patients. Such inquiries were generally so unobtrusive that the physician could easily disregard them if he chose. Not all twenty-eight patients disclosed their fears to the same degree. Some directed their concern to continuing symptoms, especially to physical pain, rather than to death itself; but all revealed more about themselves as a result of having a receptive listener.

Because the attitude of the visitor so often determined the type of communication, it was possible for two people to come away from separate visits to a sickroom, each maintaining an opposite point of view. The first might say the patient was untroubled and confident, the other that the patient was deeply concerned about his immediate fate. More often than not, the visitor, intent on encouraging optimism, heard only what he wanted to hear. The fear of death was not openly expressed. Instead, the patient would complain of symptoms without inquiring about the reasons for their persistence. He would often speak tentatively about the distant future when he would be well. Such a remark offered an ideal chance for the optimist to join in the planning. If this were done, the patient appeared to be animated and pleased. Should the visitor refrain, the patient usually became silent and somber. All of the 28 patients were aware of false optimism. Yet, at the same time, they gave every appearance of being susceptible, grasping and clinging to the flimsiest of hopes. It was as though their ability to deal consistently with the reality of their illness was determined in large part by the attitude of their visitors.

It is difficult for most people to succeed in deceiving those who know them well. The husband of a patient in the terminal phase of carcinoma of the cervix said, "I couldn't tell her with a straight face she'd get better. She'd see right through me." With this man deception would impose a telltale strain. His wife might be heartened to receive good news, but would, at the same time, be aware of the way it was imparted. The doctor faces a similar scrutiny, even though he may be a stranger to the patient. Often, it is not what he says, but the manner in which he expresses it, that alerts the patient. Sixteen of the twenty-eight patients complained that their doctors told them too little and tended to generalize in the answers they did give. On the other hand, the patient's questions were usually asked in such a way that a generalization would supply a seemingly adequate reply. In only one instance did a patient ask her doctor whether she was going to die soon. The direct question is more often put to individuals who are not in a position to answer it, such as ward attendants and student nurses, whose discomfiture adds to the patient's sense of alarm.

Attitudes of the Patient

As a result of a change in the attitudes of those around him, a change based largely upon the desire to generate false hope, the patient comes to know that he is dying. It is a peculiar kind of knowledge because it seems to violate everything he most wants to believe or everything that people think he wants to believe. We have used the term "middle knowledge" (Weisman and Hackett, 1961, 1962; Hackett and Weisman, 1962) to describe the dying patient's awareness of his imminent death. He is between knowing that what his body tells him means death and what those around him deny is death. He yields to their encouragement because to do otherwise would risk the loss of human contact — a loss as genuinely threatening as death itself. His ability to reject selectively the significance of symptoms increases at times so that he can actually experience transient hope. But always underneath is the gnawing fear that a hoax is being perpetrated on him. He is truly in the middle of knowing and not knowing. Hinton (1963), in his study of 102 dying patients, observed that "at least three-quarters of the patients here studied became aware that they were probably dying." He goes on to say, "If a patient sincerely wanted to know his possible fate, and was met by prevarication or empty reassurance, he felt lonely and mistrustful."

The most agonizing and intolerable threat to the dying is loneliness — the feeling of being apart from the lives of others. This loneliness is compounded by a perceptible change which occurs in those who care for them. The living tend to draw away from the dying. Sometimes it is an obvious withdrawal, more often a subtle sense of growing estrangement. Anyone who has been through a deathwatch appreciates the difficulty of being a helpless observer when someone's life is dwindling away. Much of this hardship can be alleviated for the visitor if he encourages the patient to think about an eventual recovery and a return to health. This type of myth-making is largely for the benefit of the visitor. The patient soon comes to find that when he does hint at wanting to know more and when he is skeptical of what the doctors tell him, his inquiries are met with awkward silences, scoldings about losing faith, or broad blandishments of hope. He learns that to pursue his doubts by asking questions seldom yields more than uneasiness between himself and those upon whom he depends for companionship. Therefore he stops asking and becomes a player in the deathbed drama in which optimism is the theme. For the terminal patient the effectiveness of denial is sharply undercut by "middle knowledge," which is the product of both the patient's ability to assess the reality of the facts of his illness and his capacity for gauging the honesty of others.

Since the treatment of the terminal patient is not the major concern of this paper, the reader is referred to the principal contributors in this field (Eissler, 1955; Feifel, 1959; Worcester, 1940). The most controversial issue in therapy always revolves about the amount of information the patient should be given. Those who believe that the patient should be encouraged to deny focus their therapy on ways of judiciously supplementing the patient's use of denial. The others, who feel that many patients have less capacity to use denial than is commonly thought, direct their attention toward minimizing those factors, among which denial is a frequent offender, which augment the feeling of isolation and loneliness in the dying. They believe that being the victim of a silent conspiracy between doctors and relatives imposes as much pain upon the patient as the facts of his illness. If there is a way of preparing the dying for death, it will have as its foundation the affirmation of warmth and affection between the patient and those who are about to be bereft.

In contrast to the person dying of cancer, the patient who has sustained a myocardial infarction appears to derive more benefit from denial. Our work with the cardiac patient began with an investigation of 23 patients placed on the monitor cardiac pacemaker (Browne and Hackett). This group was chosen because it consisted of people facing a death threat in a setting which we felt might accentuate fear. As a rule, one of every two patients requiring pacemaker assistance succumbs. The appearance of the instrument was not designed to comfort the patient. It consists of an oscillograph which makes a continuous recording of the patient's EKG and an audible bleep which accompanies the pulse. The bleep, which sounds like the nagging peep of a newly hatched chick, alerts the nurse to cardiac irregularities. Should the heart stop, an alarm bell rings and an automatic shocking device sends jolts of electricity to stimulate the myocardium. This device is at the patient's bedside. We predicted that our patients would prefer having the apparatus out of their rooms, monitored at some central point where they could not hear the bleep or see the tracing. This was not the case — another reflection of how often the healthy fail in their attempts to empathize with the sick and dying.

Of the 23 patients, four were in semi-coma, five were delirious and fourteen were alert and responsive. Only one of the fourteen was frightened by the machine. The remaining thirteen patients regarded it as a friendly protector. This attitude was enhanced by the nurse who admitted them to the ward. She, with providential wisdom, introduced the pacemaker as a "mechanical guardian angel" without, of course, mentioning that its capacity for salvaging failing hearts was limited (Craffey, 1960). Even those patients who experienced the painful shocks did not mind having the pacemaker in the room. Instead of being apprehensive at having to listen to the bleep which accompanied every heartbeat, twelve patients interpreted the sound as a reassurance that everything was all right. One patient was annoyed by the sound but wanted the machine in his room despite it. The most common fantasy was that as long as they were attached to the machine their hearts could not stop. It was not unusual for these patients to experience anxiety when being weaned from the pacemaker. The majority chose to regard the machine as an ally and to reject the recognition that it also vividly presented evidence of their precarious condition.

Along with concentrating on the salutary aspects of the pacemaker, these thirteen patients consistently denied that their hearts were severely damaged and that they feared death. This type of denial can be separated into two groups which we may call major and partial denial. The group of major deniers consisted of seven males, all of whom denied having any fear or worry about their illness. Each believed that too much attention was being given his heart. Even though three of them had suffered from previous coronaries, and two others had been shocked by the pacemaker, they denied concern about the possibility of dying or even of being unable to return to their old manner of life and work. Their life histories were filled with situations in which the death stress was met with denial. For example, one who had been the victim of a bandit had charged the gunman, was wounded three times, and afterwards asserted that he had never considered the possibility of being killed before, during, or after this incident. Another had spent three weeks on a life raft in the Pacific, never doubting that he would be rescued. All had histories of anginal pain for which help was never sought. Characteristically, when the symptoms of the myocardial infarction began, these patients ignored them until others noticed their distress and insisted on their seeking hospital attention. Illness they considered a weakness and those who allowed themselves to acknowledge it, weaklings. They all shared what could best be described as an exaggerated Victorian concept of manly behavior. They believed that a true man did not feel fear or if he felt it, never admitted that he did.

The six patients in the category of partial deniers were similar to the major deniers, except that, upon closer questioning, they admitted having experienced fear as a reaction to their illness even while they tended to minimize it. Their pasts were not as florid with examples of stoicism in the face of adversity as were the others'. They tended to rationalize the symptoms of their heart attacks as "indigestion" or "muscle strain" rather than to attempt to ignore the symptoms altogether. One patient, a man in his late twenties with an extensive family history of coronary disease, experienced severe precordial pain following his participation in a wrestling match. He immediately thought that he was having a heart attack but felt that his age was against it. In order to decide the issue he determined to run up five flights of stairs to his apartment, thinking that if it was his heart he would die; if not, he would live. He made the effort, almost perishing on the way, and fell into bed gasping, but happy in the knowledge that his distress was not "coronary trouble." Even after he had been admitted to the hospital and diagnosed as having a massive myocardial infarction, he tended to doubt the diagnosis as the result of his experiment with the stairs. Nevertheless, he submitted to the restrictions placed upon him and behaved as though he fully believed what he had been told by his doctor. Like all other patients in the category of partial deniers, he spoke of the future as though it would in no way be altered by his illness.

Both the major and the partial deniers displayed emotions entirely consistent with what they said. Anxiety and depression were not in evidence. No patient required tranquillizers. However, as we analyzed the tape recorded interviews, there were inconsistencies, contradictions, and slips of the tongue which readily demonstrated the presence of "middle knowledge." It was not, however, as undermining or as minatory as the "middle knowledge" of the cancer patient. One reason for the difference, we feel, is that the cardiac patient's tendency to minimize or deny was honestly augmented by the attitude of those who attended him. There was no silent conspiracy between doctor and relatives because everyone was in agreement that hope was of paramount importance. The cardiac patient did not have to be deceived. The encouragement offered him stemmed from the knowledge that legitimate hope existed. He could indeed pull through this episode and live out a considerable span of years. Death, although a genuine possibility, was not an imminent certainty. Relatives, as well as hospital personnel, did not have to pretend or act out an optimism which had no basis in fact. Although the cardiac patient was more concerned about his heart and future than he would directly admit, he did not suffer the alien and lonely fear of being deceived. While it is true that he selectively denied many grim aspects of his illness and converted the pacemaker into an ally without recognizing its more sinister meaning, the cardiac patient's denial could honestly be bolstered by those who were responsible for his health.

Whereas the terminal cancer patient often has a legitimate basis for complaining that he has been deserted by his doctors and nurses, the critical cardiac patient was constantly looked after. None spoke of being lonely. On the contrary, their most frequent complaint was of receiving too much attention for what they considered a minor condition. Their denial was never challenged directly or inadvertently. The close attention they received was in marked contrast to the situation of the patient dying from a malignancy. When the latter is pronounced incurable, the physician often asks the chaplain to make regular visits and concomitantly withdraws his presence. At the same time that he substitutes the chaplain's visits for his own, the doctor frequently increases the amount of narcotics administered to the patient who has been declared terminal. This is especially obvious when the doctor has judiciously limited the narcotic intake over long periods against the patient's will. When this change is abrupt and unexplained, the patient invariably interprets it as a sign that nothing more can be done for him.

The tendency of the human being exposed to the threat of death to negate or alter the meaning of the threat along less stressful lines is further illustrated in another study of cardiac patients (Olin and Hackett). Thirty-two randomly selected cases of acute myocardial infarction were interviewed very shortly after admission to the hospital. None appeared anxious or overly concerned about his condition. Reassurance about prognosis and the future was not requested. All denied being frightened. The initial symptom in each case was chest pain, which was severe in twenty-seven cases. The average duration of the pain from its onset to the time active measures were taken to obtain medical help was 5.2 hours. This delay in seeking help is explained by the patient's attempts to rationalize the cause of his discomfort. Fifteen patients believed they had severe indigestion and sought relief through antacids and other self-administered medications. Four thought they were coming down with a lung condition such as pneumonia. Nine diagnosed themselves as possibly having heart trouble and the remaining four attributed the pain respectively to cancer, a cold, an ulcer, and fatigue. The nine who correctly diagnosed their condition as "coronary" delayed obtaining medical help an average of 10.3 hours (twice that of the others), indicating that suspecting a diagnosis does not always result in appropriate action. In fact, the longest period of delay in the group (60 hours) was endured by one of these nine. All thirty-two patients responded to the pain as though they were determined to avoid, at all costs, acknowledging its true significance. This came to light as the data revealed that twenty-four patients were familiar with coronary disease either through having had anginal attacks, a previous myocardial infarction, or through witnessing it in a relative or close friend. Thirteen of the twenty-four patients had histories of anginal attacks and of these, four had been hospitalized with previous myocardial infarctions. Obtaining a past history of symptoms suggesting coronary disease in either the patient or his relatives was not always a simple matter. Four patients in this series denied having had anginal attacks and six others gave a negative family history. Whereas subsequent interviews with relatives tended to substantiate the patient's account of his present illness, they also revealed alarming gaps in memory for significant past events. The wife of one man said that he had been troubled by severe attacks of precordial pain for a number of years before his present admission. Upon being confronted by this he minimized these spells as "acute indigestion." "They always went away when I burped or took sodium bicarb." When he was told that the "spells," as described by his wife, often occurred when he was working vigorously, he replied, "Yeah, that's why you sweat, to get the acid out. It builds up in your stomach and you get pain. My father had the same thing." It turned out that his father, who he said had died of a "shock" had complained for years of "indigestion" and then dropped dead suddenly. A check with the family doctor disclosed that the patient's father had been taking nitroglycerine tablets regularly, not antacids as the patient had remembered. In taking the history of the coronary patient, one must remember to verify the absence of symptoms with a relative.

For the groups of patients studied, denial was the common response to the stress of imminent death. The defense of denial is always accompanied by a "middle knowledge" which indicates underlying doubts antipathetic to the goal of denial. The power or extent of the "middle knowledge" depends in large part upon the patient's interpersonal relationships. Its effectiveness depends in large part on the way it is dealt with in an interpersonal setting. If the other party honestly endorses the optimism he offers the patient, which seems to be so with our cardiac cases, "middle knowledge" does not undermine the effectiveness of denial. When, however, the other party cannot genuinely reciprocate hopefulness and must rely upon myth-making to create an aura of optimism, the flaws of the deception do not escape the terminal cancer patient. "Middle knowledge" undercuts the usefulness of their denial whether it is experienced as open doubt or as vague uneasiness. In treating any critically ill patient one must always assume that he harbors many unspoken questions. The physician should not offer unsolicited answers for these questions but should develop a relationship in which the patient is free to raise whatever issues he chooses.

References

BROWNE, I., and HACKETT, T. Unpublished data.

CRAFFEY, REGINA. The cardiac pacemaker. *Mass. Gen. Hosp. Nurs. Alum. Quart.*, Fall 1960, *1*, 8–11.

EISSLER, K. *The Psychiatrist and the Dying Patient.* New York: International Universities Press, 1955.

ENGEL, G. L. *Psychological Development in Health and Disease.* Philadelphia: W. B. Saunders, 1962.

FEIFEL, H. (Ed.). *The Meaning of Death.* New York: McGraw-Hill, 1959.

FREUD, ANNA. *The Ego and the Mechanisms of Defense.* New York: International Universities Press, 1937.

HACKETT, T., and WEISMAN, A. The treatment of the dying. In *Current Psychiatric Therapies.* New York: Grune & Stratton, 1962, pp. 121–126.

HINTON, J. M. The physical and mental distress of dying. *Quart. J. Med.*, January 1963, New series 32 (125), 1–21.

LEWIN, B. *The Psychoanalysis of Elation.* New York: W. W. Norton, Inc., 1950.

OLIN, H., and HACKETT, T. Unpublished data.

WEISMAN, A., and HACKETT, T. Predilection to death: Death and dying as a psychiatric problem. *Psychosom. Med.* 1961, *23*, 232–256.

WEISMAN, A., and HACKETT, T. The dying patient. *Forest Hosp. Publ.* 1962, *1*, 16–20.

WORCESTER, A. *The Care of the Aged, the Dying and the Dead.* 2nd ed. Springfield, Ill.: C. C. Thomas, 1940.

PART EIGHT

PERSPECTIVES

GEORGE W. BAKER

COMMENTS ON THE PRESENT STATUS AND THE FUTURE DIRECTION OF DISASTER RESEARCH

THE AUSPICES which were provided by the American Association for the Advancement of Science for a disaster symposium in 1962 suggest the importance of this research for the scientific community. The professional identities of the various participants and the subjects they discussed amply illustrate the range of substantive and methodological interests that are evoked by an inquiry into disaster behavior.

During the past ten years, the largest single disaster research and coordination effort has been within the National Academy of Sciences — National Research Council. To provide a background and context for this paper, it will be useful to outline briefly the development of this program. It can provide useful insights both for the status of present knowledge and for the development of future research.

Background on Disaster Research

Although speculative and journalistic interest in disaster behavior is ancient, little research was done before the economic depression of the 1930's, and World War II presented strong challenges to control and manage behavior during extreme situations. One of the first efforts by a social scientist to observe this class of behavior was made by William James during the San Francisco earthquake. A few years later, Samuel Prince used the 1917 explosion in Halifax, Nova Scotia, as the basis for his doctoral dissertation in sociology on "Catastrophe and Social Change" (1920). The *American Soldier* series, evidencing significant growth in both theory and technique, was produced from World War II experience. With the advent of the atomic bomb, the need for systematic information in this area became much more apparent to a few planners in our armed forces. However, even at the time the National Academy of Sciences — National Research Council program was terminated, in January 1963, active interest in behavioral research was relatively small among the agencies with operational natural-disaster responsibilities. The established organizational mechanisms for assuring fruitful relationships between these agencies and the research community were almost nonexistent.*

From 1952 to 1957 the Academy-Research Council's disaster activities were guided by its Committee on Disaster Studies, which included distinguished representatives from both physical and social science. After 1957, this work was centered in a permanent staff known as the Disaster Research Group. This staff, after 1960, received policy guidance and research inspiration from an advisory committee of leading social and behavioral scientists, the NAS–NRC Committee on Behavioral Research (Advisory to OEP).

The research undertaken by the Committee and Disaster Research Group has yielded useful descriptive and analytic information. Based on these findings and the collective experience of the committees and their staffs, a fair amount of operationally oriented data has been provided to various agencies, especially civil defense. This evidence provides a

---

* This view was detailed in the last chapter in *Man and Society in Disaster* (Baker and Chapman, 1962). The situation has since been altered in at least one important respect. Mr. Robert Shea, vice president, The American National Red Cross, has initiated plans for the development of an operational manual for national, regional, and local Red Cross personnel, which will be based on all available disaster research findings. This plan was described in a letter to the author dated January 6, 1964.

basis for challenging some traditional beliefs about behavior during disastrous events. For example, we no longer anticipate panic except under specifiable circumstances, and we no longer expect the response to disaster warnings to be automatic and completely adaptive (see Janis et al., 1955; and Mack and Baker, 1961).

However, owing among other things to the stress of term-financing and the desire to get into the field while the event was still current, the research work was sometimes hurriedly undertaken, thus precluding the careful development of satisfactory research designs. Furthermore, the conceptualization and management of the work were generally somewhat limited with respect to disaster phenomena, e.g., types of disasters were not defined and subjected to systematic study with the objective of deriving a sample of behavior for a particular social unit. Nor was the completed work adequately focused on all relevant time phases for one type of disaster. In brief, we have not produced a carefully designed and executed program of basic research for one or more types of disaster, e.g., precipitate, such as tornadoes, or nonprecipitate, such as hurricanes.

In late 1959, the staff of the Disaster Research Group recognized a need and obligation to evaluate the completed work on the study of disaster behavior. This effort was designed to yield information which would ultimately permit a research staff to conceptualize the field more thoroughly, to integrate this work with theory and method in the broader scientific community, and to design a program for the systematic study of selected categories of disaster. The assessment project resulted in the production of two books. One of these, *Man and Society in Disaster* (edited by Baker and Chapman, 1962), contains contributions by seventeen authors on different aspects of disaster behavior and the methods and techniques for studying it. The second, Allen H. Barton's *Social Organization under Stress: A Sociological Review of Disaster Studies,* published as the seventeenth report in the Disaster Study Series, is an attempt to evaluate the field from one particular point of view: the community in disaster. Numerous research suggestions and hypotheses, both methodological and substantive, are presented in these two books.

Status of the Work

Given this background, it is understandable that the analysis and prediction of disaster behavior is still incomplete. From some points of view, the application of disaster findings by operational agencies is also unsatisfactory. One scholar, Stanley M. Newman (1963), has aptly characterized the research area as being " . . . politically controversial, empirically weak, and experimentally difficult . . ." In spite of this portrayal, I know that Mr. Newman and others would agree that progress has been made during the past ten years or so; however, before commenting on achievements, I would like to identify what I believe to be some of the major weaknesses in the past work.

1. No one subject, such as the family in disaster or the effects of disaster on mental health, has been systematically studied to the point where we have valid answers for a range of related questions on such subjects.

2. No one type of disaster agent, such as the hurricane, has been thoroughly studied with respect to individual and community reactions.

3. Most of the completed studies have not gathered and analyzed data before, during, and after the disastrous event.

4. Probably too much reliance has been placed on the *ex post facto* interview. This single technique is inadequate to deal with such areas as the effect on mental health of a disastrous event, nor does the interview provide all the answers needed to assess the impact of disaster on social change.

5. Not enough cross-cultural work has been accomplished, nor do we have a synthesis of studies completed in other cultures.

6. Large-scale disastrous events that threaten one or more major social institutions in a community or a region have not been thoroughly analyzed and reported. (An analysis of the effect of the March 1964 Alaskan earthquakes and tidal waves on the state's economy should yield most useful theoretical and practical data.)

7. A model for the extrapolation of findings from the study of natural disaster to man-made disasters has not been developed and adequately tested.

8. Finally, on the applied side, there is not an organizational mechanism for promoting direct and continuing contact between the several operational agencies having assigned disaster responsibilities (prevention, rescue, and relief) and the research community.

On the positive side, as the two recent books designed to assess the program have demonstrated, there have been useful accomplishments. If the disaster research has achieved no other purpose than the destruction of the panic myth, I believe that the work thus far completed has been worthwhile.*
Methodological growth within this research area was amply demonstrated during the course of the 1962 program on disaster at the American Association for the Advancement of Science meetings. The stimulating paper that Dr. Robert Lifton presented on his recent work with the Hiroshima survivors should challenge those who deny the usefulness of the *ex post facto* approach for the study of stressful behavior.† The

---

* The stereotype of panic and other antisocial behavior was suggested in Aleta Brownlee's review of disaster and disaster relief in the *Encyclopedia of the Social Sciences* (1937). Regrettably, the myth still appears in journalistic accounts of disaster behavior. A suggestion of the extent to which scholars have moved beyond the stereotype of panic was evident in a recent article by Robert E. Forman (1963).

† If more awareness of behavioral science competence and the cross-cultural sophistication of some of its practitioners had been evident at the outset of the National Academy of Sciences — National Research Council Atomic Bomb Casualty Study, we would be much better informed today on the psychological impact produced by this kind of man-made disaster. The research design for the ABC study offered an

completed work has also detailed numerous explicit hypotheses on a range of individual and community behaviors. These hypotheses are now ready for systematic testing in a variety of disaster situations.

A significant factor in the accomplishments of the National Academy of Sciences — National Research Council program was the support provided by the federal civil-defense agency. Without this interest, the activity probably would have been terminated in 1960, thus precluding the publication of several significant books; however, before its termination in January 1963, some features of the operational agency were found to be restrictive.*

An Outline for One Future Program

When the Disaster Research Group's major assessment effort was introduced in 1959, it was assumed by the director of the Group that one or more new and delimited research programs would be initiated as soon as the two surveys were completed. Before the Disaster Research Group was disbanded in 1963, basic decisions had been made by the Executive Council of the Group's Advisory Committee on the nature and direction of its future research, and the general design for one research program had been established. For a combination of reasons, the projected program was not initiated, and the staff of the group was disbanded. Within three to five years the new program would have yielded a fairly

* The role of federal civil defense in the support of disaster research and the general manner in which the agency should operate in a research context were ably reviewed by the NAS — NRC Committee on Behavioral Research (Advisory to OEP) and reported in its "Emergency Planning and Behavioral Research" (1962).

opportunity which is unusual in disaster research. Data could have been gathered from both an experimental and a control group. Keith Cannon reviewed this project in the *News Report* of the National Academy of Sciences — National Research Council (1962).

satisfactory body of information on human behavior in two of our major kinds of natural disasters.*

Clearly, the new program was designed to move ahead with the ultimate objective of disaster research: the prediction and control of human behavior in emergency situations. This implies the maximization of adaptive behavior in preparing for disasters, and the minimization of the effects when they occur. If such a program were productive, it would ultimately be refined and extended to all major classes of disaster in all societies. The discussion of methods and procedures which follows should be considered as illustrative of what could be done.

In the study of hurricanes and tornadoes, the community would be the primary sampling unit. Within this unit, special attention should be given to the family and to organizations having primary and secondary disaster responsibilities. Data should be gathered from each of these sources during three time periods: (1) at the time when there should be rational awareness on the part of families and organizations that a tornado or hurricane is likely to occur in their community; (2) during the disaster, or as soon as a research team can be moved into the disaster-struck community; and (3) at selected points during the recovery and rehabilitation process. Thus a study is anticipated which should eliminate the retrospective defects of some of the past work, and because of careful attention to sampling considerations and the gathering of follow-up data, should add new dimensions to existing information.

The following are the kinds of analytical categories and related questions which should be investigated in this program.

---

* In reviewing this projected research program for the study of natural disasters, I want to acknowledge the able and generous assistance I have received from Dr. Ira Cisin, as well as the numerous research suggestions that were earlier made explicit by several contributors to *Man and Society in Disaster* (Baker and Chapman, 1962).

The Community and Its Leaders

To what extent does an explicit mechanism exist for the coordination of federal, state, and local disaster services (e.g., rescue, medical care, relief, rehabilitation) in most disaster-prone communities? How well does it perform under crisis circumstances? How much does it have to be modified and supplemented? During the postdisaster period, what changes are introduced? What factors facilitate change? What factors impede it?

To what extent does the fact that primary disaster agencies need "social credit" in order to continue to receive public and private support create competition for social credit among these agencies? To what extent does such competition weaken the overall synthetic disaster organization for a community? Are there other ways of promoting social credit which have fewer disadvantages than the process of competition? Can these be devised and instituted prior to the next disaster?

During a severe community disaster, when institutional patterns of contract and authority must be redefined, how important is the willingness of leaders to accept and use authority that is "rational" but not "legal"? During the follow-up periods, to what extent have the community leaders changed their predisaster definitions of authority? How can this be facilitated for future community planning?

As an attribute of a community's performance in a disaster, how important is the willingness or unwillingness of a community to co-opt additional leaders as the synthetic disaster organization develops? Willingness or unwillingness to co-opt is associated with what features of a community?

What kinds of disaster training, for the general population as well as for the leaders of disaster-associated units, were conducted in the community prior to the hurricane or the tornado? What benefits did the training produce? What changes were later introduced? Did any aspects of the training focus on minimizing role conflict (members of primary disaster organizations torn between aiding their own family and performing their official disaster duties) or inoculating the community and its leaders against excessive worrying about disaster threats? (For an early discussion of this concept, see Janis' *Air War and Emotional Stress,* 1951.)

How was the informal mass assault (Allen Barton's term developed in *Man and Society in Disaster*) organized and integrated with existing community organizations? Did plans for this action exist prior to the disaster? What changes were made later in these processes?

Disaster Communications and Warnings

What kind of centralized communication system existed prior to the disaster? What existed during the disaster? How well did it function? What later changes were made in the system?

To what extent are emergency warnings for precipitate disasters (tornadoes) more likely to induce vigilant or adaptive reactions than emergency warnings for nonprecipitate disasters (hurricanes, economic depressions)? If significant differences do exist, how can these be reduced?

To what extent will vigilance tendencies aroused by a warning be dampened if the recipients have previously been exposed to one or more warnings of the same threat, provided that the warnings do not add any new information about increased vulnerability?

Which warning devices and procedures have the maximum effectiveness in tornadoes? in hurricanes?

The Family and Disaster

Are there great differences in action and processes in communities characterized by different family types?

Are kin-oriented communities less flexible, less well prepared, and less quickly adjusting during the postimpact period than individuated communities?

Are individuated communities less able than kin-oriented communities to aid individuals and families in long-term adjustment?

Is the family more highly adaptive and protective in all stages of disaster than other social groups? In what ways? Is the family with the authoritarian parent more or less adaptive and protective during disaster?

Disasters and Mental Health

The parallels between mental health and community disaster and their commonalties have been developed in detail by Robert Wilson in *Man and Society in Disaster*. Years of speculation notwithstanding, at this date we have little systematic information on the effects of a disastrous experience on mental health. Assuming that there is a negative association between a disaster experience and mental health, there are at least three major areas in need of investigation:

The pre-disaster state of personality functioning and community organization;

The immediate effect of the disaster experience as such on community mental health;

The enduring consequences of disaster for the interpersonal environment and the individual's perception of his social world.

Admittedly, the development of techniques for carefully studying these questions and for controlling other variables presents great difficulties, as well as challenges, to our art and science. Cooperation with health agencies and mental health specialists would be essential throughout this phase of the work. Whether sufficiently rigorous research techniques can be worked out to provide satisfactory results for this aspect remains to be seen. At any rate, a comprehensive effort should be made during the planning phase of such a program.

In order to arrive at answers to the foregoing research questions, both factual and attitudinal data should be collected from all respondents. Of special interest at the outset would be the collection of the respondents' definitions and descriptions of the kinds of events that constitute a disaster for themselves and for their community. These definitions should be reassessed during each follow-up period. After the existing community disaster plan has been examined, the respondents' evaluations should be obtained during each of the time periods.

Approved disaster roles for all relevant social units should be identified prior to a disaster, and the position of these roles in the power structure of the total community should be assessed. Role performance during disaster should be evaluated by the respondents, and role changes that occur after the event should be analyzed. Other role changes that may be desired in the community, but have not been achieved, should be examined.

In collaboration with community mental health authorities,

predisaster data should be collected on the state of mental health in the community. Special attention should be focused on the development of procedures for rapid stock-taking after crisis events. Among other things, the research should strive to establish whether such events generally influence what the specialists define as mental health; the kinds of effects produced by the stressful events, their direction and duration; the classes of individuals whose health is changed by disaster; the implications of these findings for future disaster planning.

Such demographic information as age, sex, educational attainment, and occupation should be collected. Theoretically relevant personality attributes, e.g., authoritarianism and religiosity, should be assessed and related to perceptions and performance. The identification of the respondents' previous experiences with natural disasters and other stressful events should also be established and related to other attributes and performance.

The primary research tool would be the interview, ranging from the structured and precoded instrument to the informal and unstructured one. From the numerous events studied in the past, considerable experience is available for the development of interview schedules.

It is highly desirable that trained research personnel observe behavior during the impact phase of the event. Systematic use of this technique generally has not been evident in past work. Some projective devices should also be examined for their relevance to the program's objectives. Familiarization with such pertinent documents as local news stories reflecting community evaluations and definitions of disasters, and community perceptions of appropriate role behavior, should be achieved.

In order to gather factual information, attitudes, and opinions in communities with high probability of disaster, interviews should be administered:

1. During the period when there should be an awareness that a tornado or hurricane could occur (approximately six

months before the season normally begins). This is the time when individual and group definitions of a disaster, and their plans for coping with it, can appreciably contribute to realistic and purposive behavior at a later date.

2. At the time of the disaster's impact or as soon thereafter as a research team can move into the area. During this phase, the "false alert" can be studied if it is feasible and appropriate. It should be deemed appropriate if there appears to be little likelihood that a real tornado or hurricane will actually occur. We have already learned from previous experience (see Mack and Baker, 1961) that the false alert presents fewer sampling problems than the actual disaster. If the population has been presented with an official warning by the Weather Bureau, the subsequent immediate behavior of the community can be assumed to be the same as it would have been as if the warning had been followed by the real event.

3. About six months after impact, the recovery and rehabilitation processes of the community should again be studied, and this procedure should be repeated a year or so later. Ultimately, a third follow-up, three to five years after the disaster, should survey selected events in the program. This phase is essential to an understanding of the effect of a disaster on social change.

The panel interviewed should be composed of formal community leaders, informal community leaders, official leaders in the primary and secondary disaster agencies, and a probability sample of families in the community. The principal family roles (father, mother, child) should be included. It is assumed that informal interviews would be administered with formal leaders, semiformal with the informal leaders, and structured interviews with the families.

Although tornadoes occur in all states, the tornado belt in the central part of the United States should be selected for this program. Within this belt, a few relatively small, self-contained communities should be studied. Essentially the same plan should be followed for the selection of hurricane-prone communities on the gulf and east coasts of the United States. In developing and executing the sampling plan, close coordination should be maintained with the Weather Bureau and the Disaster Services unit of the Red Cross.

In the event that none of the preselected communities actually experiences a disaster after a reasonable period of time, it may be possible to conduct the "after" study in a disaster-struck community that is comparable with one of those studied in the "before" phase. Thus, before-after comparisons of behavior could be made, though with much less confidence than if the same communities were studied both before and after.

Finally, it is conceivable that the anticipated disasters will not occur either in the selected communities or in comparable communities. In this case, the "before" studies should be analyzed as case studies of disaster preparation to answer such questions as: How do individuals and communities behave when they first sense the possibility of a disaster? How are decisions made on the probability of a disaster? What disruption is tolerable in the predisaster period to minimize the disruption during and after disaster?

Although it is appropriate to recognize the difficulties of a longitudinal study, it is generally agreed that the advantage to be gained through preventing a retrospective bias far outweighs the difficulties involved in execution. In the proposed study, a certain amount of attrition is anticipated among individuals and families. To the extent that this occurs, before-after comparisons will be weakened. However, if the evidence indicates that the threat of disaster was a reason for moving, this finding will be useful. Insofar as the proposed study is of community organization and community preparation, considerable turnover among individuals may be tolerable.

George W. Baker

Significance

The compelling need to learn and promote effective methods for managing society's response to large-scale disasters, evident in 1952 when the National Academy of Sciences — National Research Council initiated the disaster program, should be apparent to today's administrators and scholars. Annual deaths, injuries, and property damage produced by natural disasters can be expected to continue. Logically, the number of casualties may increase as a consequence of population growth and urban expansion. Although tremendous national resources have been allocated for the minimization of other types of disasters (e.g., epidemics and economic depressions), comparable widespread research and planning have not yet developed in the field of natural disaster.* As of now, representatives of several social sciences — anthropology, psychology, and sociology — as well as medicine have had a chance to contribute to the field. However, as this paper has tried to point out, their efforts have generally been limited in scope and duration, and the support provided by operational agencies has been term-oriented and circumscribed.

The work completed by NAS—NRC Disaster Research program provides the research-oriented person with encouraging evidence that useful applied information can be developed for the minimizing of human suffering, social disorganization, and deaths from natural disasters. The success reported in the evacuation of Hurricane Carla's victims in 1961 is a case in point.

The study of behavior in natural disasters contributes to

* Admittedly, the history of science records difficulties experienced in the development of sound and continuing support for such programs. One such experience is reviewed by Donald C. Swain (1962). One mature scientific observer, Dael Wolfle (1964), has recently taken the position that ample social science research funds are available and can be obtained on relatively short notice for the study of major unanticipated events. Some practicing researchers may not find Wolfle's position entirely consistent with their proposal rejection experience.

328

the larger field of behavior under stress. The value of stress studies for the understanding of personality adjustment, the family, and complex organizations, is demonstrated elsewhere by their frequency and range. If we imaginatively take advantage of the natural field experiment annually produced by such events as the hurricane and tornado, we can realistically expect to learn more about such diverse matters as the strengths and weaknesses of a community's mental health, the structure and functioning of its formal and informal leadership, the relative performance differences of various family types and family roles. It is to be hoped that this kind of basic work will not be impeded because of any existing confusion in such operational programs as civil defense, or because of the many heated discussions and issues that have devolved from that program.

The program presented here was not designed as another modest social science effort to yield a few more interesting answers and hypotheses, forming the basis for another fund-seeking proposal. The scope and purpose are consistent with the 1962 statement by the President's Science Advisory Committee on "Strengthening the Behavioral Sciences." This important document invited the social scientists to begin to think big, to design programs capable of making meaningful contributions to knowledge. If properly refined and carefully managed by a demonstrably senior research staff, encompassing such disciplines as anthropology, economics, psychology, political science, and sociology, this disaster program would contribute to these objectives. The cost would probably be at least half a million dollars, about half the amount already spent on the National Academy of Sciences — National Research Council disaster program that was terminated in January 1963.

References

BAKER, G. W., and CHAPMAN, D. W. (Eds.). *Man and Society in Disaster.* New York: Basic Books, 1962.

BARTON, A. H. *Social Organization under Stress: A Sociological Review of Disaster Studies.* Foreword by R. K. Merton. Disaster Study No. 17. Washington, D. C.: National Academy of Sciences — National Research Council, 1962.

BROWNLEE, ALETA. Disaster and disaster relief. *Encycl. Soc. Sci.,* 1937, *5,* 161–166.

CANNON, K. The atomic bomb casualty commission: The first 14 years. *News Report,* NAS — NRC, 1962, *12* (1), 1–7.

FORMAN, R. E. Resignation as a collective behavior response. *Amer. J. Sociol.,* 1963, *69,* 285–290.

JANIS, I. L. *Air War and Emotional Stress: Psychological Studies of Bombing and Civilian Defense.* New York: McGraw-Hill, 1951.

JANIS, I. L., CHAPMAN, D. W., GILLIN, J. P., and SPIEGEL, J. P. "The Problem of Panic." Washington, D. C.: Fed. Civil Defense Admin. Bull. TB-19-2, 1955.

MACK, R. W., and BAKER, G. W. *The Occasion Instant: The Structure of Social Responses to Unanticipated Air Raid Warnings.* Foreword by R. M. Williams, Jr. Disaster Study Number 15. Washington, D. C.: National Academy of Sciences — National Research Council, 1961.

NAS–NRC Committee on Behavioral Research (Advisory to OEP). *Emergency Planning and Behavioral Research.* Washington, D. C.: National Academy of Sciences–National Research Council, 1962.

NEWMAN, S. M. Review of *The Occasion Instant: The Structure of Social Response to Unanticipated Air Raid Warnings. Amer. Anthropologist,* 1963, *65,* 990–991.

PRINCE, S. H. *Catastrophe and Social Change.* New York: Columbia University, 1920.

STOUFFER, S. A., SUCHMAN, E. A., DE VINNEY, L. C., STAR, S. A., and WILLIAMS, R. M., JR. *The American Soldier: Adjustment During Army Life,* Vol. 1. Princeton, N.J.: Princeton University Press, 1949.

STOUFFER, S. A., LUMSDAINE, A. A., LUMSDAINE, M. H., WILLIAMS, R. M., JR., SMITH, M. B., JANIS, I. L., STAR, S. A., and COTTRELL, L. S., JR. *The American Soldier: Combat and its Aftermath.* Vol. 2. Princeton, N.J.: Princeton University Press, 1949.

Strengthening the behavioral sciences. *Science,* 1962, *136* (3512), 233–241.

SWAIN, D. C. The rise of a research empire: National Institutes of Health 1930-1950. *Science,* 1962, *138,* 1233–1237.

WOLFLE, D. Lost opportunities. *Science,* 1964, *143,* 999.

INDEX